There is no shortage of Western-centric critiques of Donald Trump from the vantage points of New York, Washington, London, Brussels and Paris. Nor is there any lack of Chinese analyses of what the 'great disruptor' means for them. Leading Indian scholar and pundit of international affairs Sreeram Chaulia takes a different approach. His barnstorming book looks at Trump from the perspective of Ankara, New Delhi, Brasilia and Abuja. The results will surprise you.

Brendan Simms, Professor in the History of International Relations, University of Cambridge, United Kingdom, and co-author of *Donald Trump: The Making of a World View*

The rise of Donald Trump and the return of emerging powers to the forefront of world politics are markers of our time. Until now, they have been treated separately. In this pioneering work, Sreeram Chaulia brings them together into a seamless whole, highlighting the many ways in which Trump's foreign policy opens new vistas for rising powers. Richly documented and brilliantly written, *Trumped* is a must-read for all those keen to understand the changing dynamics of today's world.

Jorge Heine, Wilson Center Global Fellow and former Ambassador of Chile to India, China and South Africa

This compelling book convincingly argues that, in our surreal Trumpian world, the US-led liberal international order is at a 'revolutionary' inflection point. Skilfully moving beyond standard Eurocentric scholarly and policy debates, Sreeram Chaulia brilliantly weaves together views from key emerging powers of the Global South to see how they understand, and, in time, with correct political choices may seize the opportunity to construct an alternative world order built on endogenous structures and collective action.

Karim Makdisi, Associate Professor of International Politics, The American University of Beirut, Lebanon

There is much scholarship in the West about the demise of the liberal international order, and many mourn its end. Indeed, there is still much in that order that should be preserved, but there is also much that needs to (and will) change. The rest of the world is rising, assuming responsibilities and displaying leadership. The analysis and the vision of this changing world needs to be told by scholars from those regions. Sreeram Chaulia's work on the rise of powers outside the conventional US–China duet does just that, providing much-needed nuance and illustrating that the crafting of a new global order is not the domain of the most powerful states alone.

Elizabeth Sidiropoulos, Chief Executive,
South African Institute of International Affairs, Johannesburg

Can the emerging powers step up their act in maintaining global stability and filling the void in global leadership as the US-led liberal international order crumbles? This book offers a timely corrective to the usual Western and China-centric perspectives on this question, and should be invaluable to academics, policymakers and the media.

Amitav Acharya, Professor of International Relations, American University, Washington DC, and author of *The End of American World Order*

Trumped

Trumped

Emerging Powers in a Post-American World

Sreeram Chaulia

BLOOMSBURY
NEW DELHI · LONDON · OXFORD · NEW YORK · SYDNEY

BLOOMSBURY INDIA
Bloomsbury Publishing India Pvt. Ltd
Second Floor, LSC Building No. 4, DDA Complex, Pocket C – 6 & 7,
Vasant Kunj New Delhi 110070

BLOOMSBURY, BLOOMSBURY INDIA and the Diana logo are trademarks of
Bloomsbury Publishing Plc

First published in India 2019
This edition published 2019
This export edition published 2019

Copyright © Sreeram Chaulia 2019
Illustration © Sreeram Chaulia 2019

Sreeram Chaulia has asserted his right under the Indian Copyright Act to be identified as the
Author of this work

All rights reserved. No part of this publication may be reproduced or transmitted in any form or by
any means, electronic or mechanical, including photocopying, recording or any information storage
or retrieval system, without the prior permission in writing from the publishers

Bloomsbury Publishing Plc does not have any control over, or responsibility for, any third-party
websites referred to or in this book. All internet addresses given in this book were correct at the time
of going to press. The author and publisher regret any inconvenience caused if addresses have
changed or sites have ceased to exist, but can accept no responsibility for any such changes

ISBN: HB: 978-93-89165-93-7; eBook: 978-93-89165-94-4

2 4 6 8 10 9 7 5 3 1
Typeset in Manipal Digital
Printed and bound in India by Thomson Press India Ltd.

Bloomsbury Publishing Plc makes every effort to ensure that the papers used in the manufacture of
our books are natural, recyclable products made from wood grown in well-managed forests. Our
manufacturing processes conform to the environmental regulations of the country of origin

To find out more about our authors and books visit www.bloomsbury.com and sign up for our
newsletters

*To emerging powers, which must heed the
call of destiny*

Contents

Foreword by Andrew F. Cooper   xi
Acknowledgements   xv

Introduction   1
I   India: Strategic Neglect to Strategic Assertion   59
II   Turkey: Spurned Ally to Potential Alternative   105
III   Brazil: Wary Rival to Willing Partner   147
IV   Nigeria: Counter-Hegemony to Pax Africana   187

Epilogue   225
Index   233
About the Author   239

Foreword

As Sreeram Chaulia highlights in his exhilarating book, US President Donald Trump deals with the world in a disruptive and unpredictable manner. But his casting of villains is clear. Through his prism, a soft and weak European Union is stigmatised as being over-regulated. And an assertive China is accused of being hyper-competitive.

But the main villain for Trump remains the liberal international order built up by an older US elite, along with the institutional architecture at its core: the United Nations, the International Financial Institutions and the World Trade Organization.

Some of this critique is based on a transactional view of the world. The US is being taken for a ride by allies and countries in which it has shared interdependence. Old arrangements, such as the North Atlantic Treaty Organization, fall into this category, as do newer potential regional deals, such as the Trans-Pacific Partnership.

In this sense, at least, Trump's emotions are no different—except in scale and intensity—than some earlier signs of pushback. What is different is the context of Trump as pivotal to a new era of populism. As Sreeram Chaulia carefully denotes, this shifts the challenge from an exclusively external locus to one that has an important internal dimension. For Trump, formal institutions, interpreted as a constraining force, are part of an entrenched repertoire of a self-serving and controlling establishment.

On top of all this, of course, is the serious threat to a contemporary diplomatic culture that Trump presents. In contradistinction to the twenty-first-century diplomatic culture symbolised by the Barack Obama administration, the Trump operational style is focused on personalism, the use of bilateral one-on-ones, constant surprises, and direct and highly targeted communication with 'his' domestic supporters. At its core is a 'winner-take-all' approach to any external engagement, in which asymmetrical structural advantages are translated into leverage. The goal is not to stabilise institutions or to enhance followership or goodwill among strategic allies or commercial partners but to extract material advantages on a self-help basis. The audience is exclusively domestic communities, with a great onus on publicising successful outcomes (or 'wins') with their interests in mind.

Sreeram Chaulia is well versed in the debates in the US and Europe about the implications of this challenge. However, this rich book is not preoccupied with going over these Western-centred critiques or, for that matter, what the Chinese state and academic commentators have to say about Trump as the great disruptor.

What Sreeram Chaulia is interested in, and does so well in his contribution, is to extend the debate beyond these well-rehearsed sites and themes, and take the interpretative debate about the challenge to other key countries beyond the West: India, Turkey, Brazil and Nigeria.

In some ways, Sreeram Chaulia's book, with its full title, *Trumped: Emerging Powers in a Post-American World*, serves as a natural progression from the bestselling book by Fareed Zakaria, on the 'post-American world'. The latter showcases the impressive albeit uneven rise of the 'Rest' in the early part of the 21st century, in the aftermath of 9/11 and first stages of the advance of the BRICS, and before the 2008 Global Financial Crisis. Sreeram Chaulia is, by contrast, interested in selected members of the 'Rest' with geopolitics framed both as an opportunity and as a constraint.

The countries that Sreeram Chaulia uses to illustrate his arguments share some common characteristics. None were well served in terms of status attribution in the establishment of the post-1945 order, being shut out either of the United Nations Security Council or the UN, in complete institutional terms due to the longevity of colonialism. As such, these countries, like others, have long felt frustrated by the inequitable makeup of the international institutional architecture.

None of these four countries shares a border or a continent with the US: so being 'Trumped' is a very different phenomenon than the one faced by Mexico or, for that matter, the vulnerable Central American countries. Although they have specific trade disputes with the US, none of them has the degree of complex interdependence faced by China. Moreover, while each has challenges of personalism of their own, all retain a level of democratic space with competitive electoral systems and to a greater or lesser extent, vibrant civil society and media presence.

As Sreeram Chaulia presents at the heart of his book, moreover, each of these countries has some regional space to offset the impact of an unpredictable and diminished global order. For all their differences, and internal controversies, India, Turkey, Brazil and Nigeria have a commonality in terms of an asymmetrical material advantage with respect to their neighbourhood.

To capitalise on these advantages, to be sure, will necessitate skill and Fortuna. With his deep and sophisticated knowledge of India's politics and geopolitical thinking, Sreeram Chaulia not only examines the disruption in bilateral relations with respect to transactional anxieties but Trump's neglect of Indian aspirations: referring in particular to the White House declining India's invitation to Trump to be the Chief Guest at its Republic Day parade in January 2019 by citing his domestic commitments.

Let down by the Trump administration, Indian Prime Minister Narendra Modi recalibrated Sino-Indian ties from the time Modi met President Xi in a crucial informal summit at Wuhan in April 2018. At the same time, Sreeram Chaulia signals new initiatives, such as a diplomatic forum led by India and Indonesia for 'Asian Alternative Security', that explicitly keeps out the US and China, and promotes intra-Asian conflict mitigation solutions and builds strategic trust.

Yet, there is not the suggestion of a single approach that fits all. If India has sought a more diversified plan that moves away from the anticipated strategic partnership with the US, but does not openly antagonise Trump, President Recep Tayyip Erdogan's Turkey has chosen a more confrontational approach: building new ties with Iran and Russia as part of an illiberal anti-Western geopolitical axis in the Middle East. In complete contradiction, the far-right, anti-establishment populist Brazilian President Jair Bolsonaro has tacked the other away: swiveling with certainty from a wary rivalry to a close partnership with the US. And as Sreeram Chaulia concludes, the implications for Nigeria are stark: as an isolationist US president calls for the 'self-reliance' of Africa, there is a need for Nigeria to drop any remnants of dependence on the US, and use this disruption as a catalyst for 'Pax Africana'.

Only a scholar and thinker as confident as Sreeram Chaulia could produce such a detailed book, and maintain such conceptual coherence and narrative drive. Moreover, notwithstanding his optimism that the emerging powers he focuses on in this compelling book have the capacity to navigate through all the disruption of the Trump years, he recognises the obstacles that they face. Above all, he argues that for their differences, they cannot take their own backyard for granted. Doing so is an immense strategic blunder. He warns quite rightly that leaders, notably Erdogan and Bolsonaro, do not appreciate the risks before them, with the adoption of extreme positions.

Overall, *Trumped: Emerging Powers in a Post-American World* is a big ambitious book that deserves a big wide-ranging audience. It builds on a keen sense of scholarship but is written in an accessible fashion. It might not be the last book on the Trump age, but it will remain unique in its insights outside of the conventional US–China–European Union framework.

Andrew F. Cooper, DPhil
Professor, the Balsillie School of International Affairs
and the Department of Political Science, University of Waterloo, Canada
Associate Research Fellow-UNU CRIS
(Institute on Comparative Regional Integration), Bruges, Belgium

Acknowledgements

The inspiration to write this book came on the night of 8 November 2016, when the world watched slack-jawed at the results of the US presidential election. The established Democratic candidate Hillary Clinton, the universally assumed shoo-in, lost to an upstart Republican who we all assumed was unwinnable. It was one of the greatest political upsets in history that shattered received wisdom and comfortable assumptions about America and its role in the world.

I kept wondering for months after Trump took office and shook the foundations of Pax Americana. Nagging questions bobbed up as I absorbed the unimaginable shifts Trump was embarking on.

How could a great power like the US suddenly invert itself from being omnipresent and actively involved in every corner of the world into a distant and declining power? Where and when have we seen these kinds of reversals before? How is the domestic political turbulence in America going to be read in regions of the world where it has historically been heavily involved? How long will this retreat go on and what kind of new world order will we see as a result? Do we really need an engaged and domineering America at all to make the world peaceful and prosperous, as Trump's innumerable liberal critics in the West are asserting?

This book derives from a fundamental aspect of international politics—shifts in world orders. I have written it both for academicians whose whole lives revolve around these matters and for non-specialists who are wondering what the sum total of the Trump phenomenon will add up to. My plain vanilla verdict is that Trump may be distasteful on many counts, but he and the strain he represents in American foreign policy are unique windows of opportunity for regional powers to rise up and fill the vacuums America leaves behind.

In the journey of writing this counter-intuitive book, I owe debts to Western and non-Western intellectuals and policymakers who share my belief in the efficacy and change-making power of countries like India, Turkey, Brazil and Nigeria.

Andrew Cooper, the leading Canadian scholar on global governance and rising powers, has written a thought-provoking Foreword to set the tone. Amitav Acharya, the Indian-Canadian theorist of international relations, has written many gems on regionalism and regional powers. His endorsement on the back cover is much appreciated. The prominent South African advocate for the Global South Elizabeth Sidiropoulos is a perpetual source of motivation to me. Her blurb is not just for this book but to the idea that the time has come for non-Western powers to take the lead. The distinguished Chilean diplomat and writer Jorge Heine is unmatched in his vision for Latin America's collective emergence on the world stage. I am fortunate to have his blessings. The Lebanese political scientist Karim Makdisi offered insights into Trump's impact on the Middle East. I value his endorsement. British historian Brendan Simms influenced me with his pioneering book on Trump's worldview. It is a fillip to have his thumbs-up too.

Special thanks to Chris Eze, the High Commissioner of Nigeria to India; Gustavo Westmann, the Political Counsellor of the Embassy of Brazil to India; and Ambassador Mohan Kumar, Chairman of Research and Information System for Developing Countries (RIS), for sharing valuable time and insights into the way Trump has challenged and incentivised regional powers around the world. My mentor and *Mwalimu*, pan-African scholar Professor Horace Campbell, also offered key pointers to sharpen the argument of this book. Thanks to my two Nigerian colleagues, Williams Iheme and Kasim Balarabe, who shared thoughts on Nigeria's role in Africa, and to my Indian colleague, Deepanshu Mohan, who helped formulate my argument on the economics of regional integration.

Three outstanding students of the Jindal School of International Affairs (JSIA) deserve praise for doing background research, digging out quotes, statistics and summaries for each of the chapters. This book belongs to Tahhira Somal, Megha Gupta and Nitin Arya. I see bright futures for these industrious, upcoming young talents. My Executive Assistant, Lalit Kumar, tirelessly procured books, journals and electronic materials at short notice as I was writing. Without his services, I would be crippled.

Acknowledgements

A big thank you to Professor C. Raj Kumar, the Vice Chancellor of O.P. Jindal Global University (JGU). Under his overall guidance and leadership, I have tried to steer JSIA to prominence. His friendship has been a personal and institutional backbone of my scholarship over the years.

Writing a book every few years has become second nature to me. The main driver of this habit is my best half, the artist and screenwriter Usha Rani Damerla. For more than two decades, she saw in me vast potential and stood by me as my biggest emotional pillar. She is already prodding me about my next book project! I owe more and more to her love.

My two children, Debarchan Vishnu Chaulia and Ahaana Kranti Chaulia, were ideal distractions during the months-long writing of this manuscript. In their innocent eyes and playful energies, I found relief from the stressful effect of monumental transformations in the international order. If I am a better father to them, it matters more to me than how well this book is received by readers.

My parents, Chandrakala Chaulia and Prafulla Kumar Chaulia, have believed so much in me and my chosen path of studying and commenting on world affairs that it is impossible to thank them in a few words. Their dream of raising me to be a voice in the field of international relations has been a permanent spur.

This is my second book each with Bloomsbury and I.B. Tauris. To be an author for such prestigious international publishers is a badge of honour I wear proudly. The Bloomsbury managerial and editing team of Praveen Tiwari, Nitin Valecha and Shreya Chakraborti is super professional and prompt. I cannot ask for more as a writer.

As this book is about contemporary international current events transpiring right before our eyes, there is a risk of some portions being overtaken by events. Possible errors that readers may spot due to any such jumps in global developments are entirely mine because of my choice of writing a book on a subject, which is in motion. Yet, I have tried to direct readers to the future in a way that this book stands the test of time. If a decade down the line someone picks it up and feels I had been on to something few foresaw, it would be my ultimate reward.

Sonipat
20 June 2019

Introduction

In our disillusionment after the last war we preferred international anarchy to international cooperation with Nations which did not see and think exactly as we did. We gave up the hope of gradually achieving a better peace because we had not the courage to fulfil our responsibilities in an admittedly imperfect world. We must not let that happen again, or we shall follow the same tragic road again—the road to a third world war.[1]

—President Franklin Roosevelt, 6 January 1945

America will always choose independence and cooperation over global governance, control, and domination... America will always act in our national interest. We will never surrender America's sovereignty to an unelected, unaccountable, global bureaucracy. America is governed by Americans. We reject the ideology of globalism, and we embrace the doctrine of patriotism.[2]

—President Donald Trump, 25 September 2018

Goodbye Governor America

It is a cliché to say that the world is in flux. The world and the order on which it rests are dynamic; they have always been evolving and will remain so. Nothing is permanent except change.

But then, we sometimes reach inflection points where the nature of change is drastic and dramatic and the most basic assumptions are upturned. We are at such a revolutionary point in time today, thanks to US President Donald Trump accelerating the demise of the post–Cold War or even the post–World War II international order by yanking America out of its decades-long project of ruling, policing and governing the planet. When the architect of an open system withdraws into a closed shell, undermines the structures it once created, calls it quits and opts 'out of the world order business', it is no less than a 'decisive break'[3] that heralds a new order.

The cover illustration of *The Economist* magazine in February 2017, right after Trump assumed America's highest office, conveys this historic shock best. He is lobbing a petrol bomb at the established order with a militant scowl and rioter's disdain on his face. The accompanying caption, 'An Insurgent in the White House', sums up the nature of this truly Black Swan phenomenon, which few observers, including myself, had seen coming.

If Trump's monumental upset win over Hillary Clinton in the November 2016 US presidential election was an unbelievable outcome, his tradition-busting rhetoric and actions since assuming office have been surreal. In foreign policy, he has done exactly what no one expected a sitting US president to do—extricate America from the race to maintain its number one hyperpower stature in the international system. If rival nations with the potential to equal the US or overtake it had thought it would be a tough grind, here was America apparently willingly forfeiting its global leadership under an out-of-the-box and out-of-whack president. The path to a multipolar world never seemed less imminent than when Trump arrived on the scene.

Yet, I will also demonstrate in this book that Trump presents a double-edged sword to emerging powers. On one hand, he is happy to relinquish America's controlling grip over regions around the world, thus providing space for emerging nations to rise to the occasion and take on governance and stabilisation of their areas into their own hands. But on the other hand, he is also upsetting the pre-existing balances of power in different regions and impairing emerging powers by leaving them alone to grapple with immediate obstacles from within their respective regions as well as a globally expansive and aggressive China. In his incoherent and self-contradictory way, Trump is at once a blessing and a curse for emerging nations.

This book centres on a principal consequence of the Trump presidency—the opening of the door for non-Western emerging powers to fill the vacuum in the world order left by an America in retreat. It focuses on the power shift that Trump is hastening and the variety of adjustments in tactics and strategy he is forcing upon rising powers in different corners of the world. Trump's refusal to allow the US to continue being the impresario that maintains regional balances of power, economic arrangements and political norms has vacated the field for new kinds of leadership, permutations and anxieties to mushroom in Asia, the Middle East, Africa and Latin America.

As representative emerging powers from each of these continents of the Global South, I have chosen for this book India, Turkey, Nigeria and Brazil, each of which had distinctive relationships with the US but find themselves in terra incognita since Trump's shake-up. China is not in this list for an objective reason. By notching up spectacular economic growth, military modernisation and global influence, China has already transcended the club of 'emerging' powers and is today a genuine superpower. The power gap between China and the aforementioned four emerging nations is vast on most indicators, albeit estimated to shrink in the next decade, even as the gap between China and the US is narrowing, and is roughly comparable to the gap between the Soviet Union and the US at the commencement of the Cold War in 1947.[4]

Still, by no means can a book on emerging powers afford to ignore China—it is now akin to an 800-pound gorilla, so much so that all the emerging powers I am covering deal with it profusely. How these nations find their feet and mojos in their respective regions and the wider global sphere depends on individual equations with both China and the US. So, China is a recurring theme in this book. I will analyse how Trump has approached the China problem in US foreign policy later in this Introduction, and triangulate China in subsequent chapters while analysing how each emerging power is tackling the Trump curveball.

Like China, Europe is another intersecting factor in this saga of emerging powers in a post-American world. I have omitted detailed individual case studies of European countries in this book even though they are dismayed and gobsmacked by Trump's apathy and hostility to America's trans-Atlantic allies. Like the emerging powers, the Europeans are discombobulated and endeavouring to wean away from dependence on the US for security and economic prosperity.[5] While none of the members of the European Union (EU) qualifies as an emerging power, the group has been jilted by Trump and is looking afresh at alternative partnerships. Wherever relevant in the following chapters, I will introduce Europe insofar as it affects bilateral ties between specific emerging powers and Trump's receding America.

An Emergent Force

Some background on emerging powers and their international experiences before Trump's arrival is pertinent. When Fareed Zakaria posited a 'post-American world' in 2008, he noted that while the US was still the military top gun in the international system, 'in every other dimension—industrial, financial, educational, social and cultural—the distribution of power is shifting, moving away from American dominance'.[6] His focus on the 'rise of everyone else' was justified because, at that time, America appeared strategically distracted and bogged down by President George W. Bush's global war on terror (GWOT) on non-state Islamist fundamentalists (2001–08); it was unable to focus on the long-term challenge of emerging states that were growing relatively fast, reducing the gap with the US and demanding revisions in the global power balance that had been skewed in America's favour since the end of the Cold War.[7]

A few months after Zakaria's widely read thesis hit the stands came the Wall Street crash and global financial crisis, which seriously set back the US economy even as China, and Brazil and India to a lesser extent, were humming and growing. In my estimation, the global economic crisis was a fatal blow to the US-ruled world not only by further narrowing the power difference between America and its nearest competitors, but also weakening 'Western capabilities to determine political and economic choices in the non-Western parts' and hollowing 'the influence of Western models of political economy as templates for the rest'.[8] Japanese Prime Minister-in waiting Yukio Hatoyama's comments in August 2009 reflected the tectonic shift:

> The recent financial crisis has suggested to many people that the era of American unilateralism may come to an end… I also feel that as a result

of the failure of the Iraq war and the financial crisis, the era of US-led globalism is coming to an end and that we are moving away from a unipolar world toward an era of multipolarity.[9]

The projection of a multipolar world with several power centres, or at least a bipolar world in the near future where the US has no option but to concede its primacy and share the podium with China, has gained currency since the 2008 crash. While America remained powerful in absolute yardsticks of hard power and regained soft power during the presidency of Barack Obama, its relative decline vis-à-vis other nations is a secular trend that has not been reversed. In light of this transition, many scholars and policymakers turned their attention to the phenomenon of emerging powers and how they will shape the contours of a post-American world.

Optimists often hailing from non-Western backgrounds painted emerging powers as positive actors of change who can improve international relations and make the world fairer and more democratic.[10] Pessimists, mainly American and European thinkers, asserted that more power accumulating in the hands of non-Western powers will undermine cooperative internationalism, stability and progress in democracy and human rights motored by America's 'liberal hegemony' and supremacy over the world.[11]

The seminal intellectual debate between these two camps—one eager to speed up the ascent of emerging powers and shatter empire, and the other nostalgically pining for the aura of American invincibility and liberal global governance—mirrored aspirations and forebodings in the real world of policymaking and praxis. Leaders of emerging powers and China, in tandem with nationalistic public opinion in their countries, welcomed the global power shift, heralding it as an inevitable marker of their civilisational greatness and a historical restoration of their lost glory at the pinnacle of world order.[12]

On the other hand, Western heads of government and strategic planners vowed that no stone would be left unturned and all policy levers would be utilised to maintain the post-Cold War status quo of an American-dominated and European-invested liberal international order.

Obama's signature initiatives like the Trans-Pacific Partnership (TPP) and the 'pivot' or rebalance to Asia were explicitly conceived to halt the movement of global economic and military power in China's favour.[13]

Obama insisted on 'an undeniable truth' that 'America must lead' and stressed that 'strong and sustained American leadership is essential to a rules-based international order'.[14] He questioned the wisdom of using excessive military force abroad but kept America diplomatically hyperactive across the globe by touting 'civilian power' and 'smart power' strategies of strengthening alliances and partnerships with regional and emerging nations.[15]

Critics slammed Obama for meekly surrendering US primacy in the international order by downsizing American military presence overseas, pacifistically accommodating strategic rivals like China and Russia, and disengaging to permit other capable states to displace the US and render it irrelevant.[16] Obama's diplomatic cautiousness ('don't do stupid shit'[17]) and apologetic self-criticism of America's past neo-imperialism ('the United States is still working through some of our own darker periods in our history'[18]) riled foreign policy hawks and militarists as giveaways of American toughness and preponderance.

In retrospect, while Obama was tactically different from Bush, he was very much wedded to the mainstream bipartisan American foreign policy tradition of believing in the US as an exceptionally righteous actor whose enlightened hegemony is worth preserving. He continued the 'dominant hegemonic role conception' of the US as a special superpower, which pursues its self-interests but simultaneously lifts the rest of the international community through provision of global public goods.[19] His parting advice to Trump before remitting office was that the US 'really is an indispensable nation in our world order' and that 'if we're not making the argument and fighting for it… then it collapses. There's nobody to fill the void.'[20]

The forty-fourth president was clearly worried about his successor's zero-sum-game 'America First' sloganeering that promised to discard the core strategic and moral principles guiding US leaders since Franklin Roosevelt. Obama's advice fell on deaf ears and, as emerging powers are realising, the rest is history in the making.

Enter the Enfant Terrible

Trump is a stormy petrel. An iconoclast who has thrown every known platitude and convention of American politics and foreign policy out of the window, the forty-fifth president of the US revels in sticking it to domestic and foreign foes with a candour that defies norms of civility and prudence associated with high offices.

Combative and impolitic in his mannerisms, ideological convictions and policy preferences, he is a polarising figure like no other, both inside the US and on the world stage. He forces everyone to either be with him or against him and defines dividing lines on issues as varied as race, class, gender, identity, nation and planet. A survey of 320 experts belonging to both the right and the left from the American Political Science Association ranked Trump as the most polarising of all US presidents, ahead of Abraham Lincoln and way above modern era predecessors like Obama, Bush, Bill Clinton and Ronald Reagan.[21]

The phrase 'disrupter-in-chief' has been widely applied to Trump, and this holds equally for domestic and foreign policies.[22] He stormed into office in January 2017 riding on the sweeping populist promise to 'drain the swamp' of a rigged American political system structured to favour the ultra-rich and dispossess the working classes.[23] On international affairs, he struck a chord with angry and sullen American have-nots by vowing to pose a 'true existential threat' to a sinister 'global power structure that is responsible for the economic decisions that have robbed our working class, stripped our country of its wealth and put that money into the pockets of a handful of large corporations and political entities'.[24]

Domestic interests and foreign policy are of course interconnected and inseparable, no matter who the American president is.[25] This fact of life has also operated worldwide and across time since the advent of the nation-state system.[26] But to Trump, these two categories which used to be bifurcated by the concept of an internal sphere where a sovereign state governs monopolistically with laws and rules over a fixed territory and given population, and an external sphere where states interact with other states in a competitive and less regulated environment, have coalesced now into a single oppressive whole. The 'nation' has been enslaved to the 'global' and it must be rescued from this cage.

Trump sees the global order, which both Democrat and Republican American presidents conceived and shaped since World War II, as a conspiracy concocted by liberal American elites to impoverish and suppress ordinary American people. When Trump bellows to his social base of the white American working class that 'those who control the levers of power in Washington' partner with 'the global special interests that don't have your good in mind'[27] it shows how radical and heterodox his agenda is.

His twin mission is to deconstruct and unravel the American state apparatus and break the world order to free American people. The influential Trump ideologue and former White House Chief Strategist Steve Bannon succinctly summed up his revolutionary motto: 'The post-World War II political and economic consensus is failing and should be replaced with a system that empowers ordinary people over coastal elites and international institutions.'[28]

On numerous occasions, Trump has revealed a fundamental parochial distrust and dislike for the outside world, which he treats as alien, hostile and exploitative of good and hardworking American common folk. To fully comprehend his Weltanschauung, consider his speech to non-American corporate titans at the Asia-Pacific Economic Cooperation (APEC) summit in Da Nang, Vietnam, in November 2017. After a perfunctory mention of the internationalist idea of a 'free and open Indo-Pacific' that earlier American presidents swore to prop up with US military and diplomatic commitments, he attacked the liberal ethos of the 'world as one big family' and refuted expectations that America would remain the prime upholder of a cooperative and converging global community.

> Let us never forget the world has many places, many dreams, and many roads. But in all of the world, there is no place like home. So, for family, for country, for freedom, for history, and for the glory of God, protect your home, defend your home, and love your home today and for all time.[29]

Protect home from whom? From Trump's perspective, the Pax Americana, which established a US-dominated 'Long Peace' and cooperative order among Western great powers after 1945,[30] and the web of economic globalisation deliberately spun by the US to preserve its status as the sole superpower in the world after 1991,[31] are constructs to cheat and mug average Americans. As he starkly stated the problem in a rally before working class Pennsylvanians:

> Our politicians have aggressively pursued a policy of globalization… Globalization has made the financial elite who donate to politicians very wealthy. But it has left millions of our workers with nothing but poverty and heartache… Our politicians took away from the people their means of making a living and supporting their families… This wave of globalization has wiped out our middle class.[32]

Anti-globalisation is the metanarrative underlying Trump's worldview. It colours his perceptions of all countries, especially China and emerging powers, which he believes are leveraging unfair global trade and investment rules to rip off the American people. As we'll see throughout this book, Trump does not make the customary US foreign policy distinction between allies and partners on one side and antagonists and enemies on the other. He lumps them together as threats to American health and considers his mission to fight and coerce them into making economic concessions. His July 2018 interview following a frigid summit with North Atlantic Treaty Organization (NATO) allies deserves detailed quotation here.

> I think we have a lot of foes. I think the European Union is a foe, what they do to us in trade. Now, you wouldn't think of the European Union, but they're a foe. Russia is foe in certain respects. China is a foe economically, certainly they are a foe. But that doesn't mean they are bad. It doesn't mean anything. It means that they are competitive… they've really taken advantage of us and many of those countries are in NATO and they weren't paying their bills.[33]

Trump's visceral economic nationalism and neo-mercantilism is the sine qua non for understanding how his foreign policy is affecting emerging powers. The economic dimension is, after all, raison d'être for a country to be classified as emerging. The phrase 'emerging markets' has been in circulation since 1981,[34] long before political transition toward multipolarity and talk of emerging powers came along. Consciousness of emerging market economies (EMEs), including clusters like the BRIC (Brazil, Russia, India and China) countries, later expanded to BRICS in 2010 with South Africa's entry, was spread by Western financial institutions and consultants for stock market investing and outsourcing of manufacturing to developing countries in search of cheap labour, low regulatory standards, high rates of return and profits.[35] As a purely economic proposition, EMEs were central pillars of post-Cold War globalisation, which Trump wants to bury. EMEs grew into powerhouses by virtue of attracting trillions of dollars' worth Western and Japanese inward capital since the 1980s,[36] and subsequently rose to the ranks of capital exporting nations through their outward foreign direct investment (FDI) in other countries.[37]

Trump's vow to bring back manufacturing to America through browbeating and cajoling American capitalists[38] is informed by a grudge that China and the emerging powers made hay while the sun of globalisation was shining. His vitriolic charge that outsourcing and free trade agreements are pushed by special interests who want a 'continuing rape of our country'[39] is factually dubious. Most economists find that American working class jobs have been lost largely due to automation rather than foreign trade or immigration.[40] But objectivity has never been Trump's strong suit and his propaganda that all countries are milking and fleecing the US has takers among his base of American voters who are the losers of globalisation.

Scapegoating emerging powers and blaming immigrants and free trade for America's ills resonate when there has been secular wage stagnation, mounting economic inequality and loss of upward social mobility in American society. The white working-class hillbillies from rural and small-town America, whom Trump famously tagged as the 'forgotten men and women'[41] with depressed fortunes, subscribe to xenophobic antipathy towards outsiders and all things foreign and global. For these have-nots in American society, expending American resources on protecting or stabilising foreign countries or giving them concessions to stand up against America's historic rivals is a senseless elitist enterprise that has done them immense harm.

The causal connection Trump's populist messaging has made between liberal foreign policies of preceding presidents and woes of ordinary Americans is arguable. But there is no smoke without fire. One empirical conclusion is undeniable. Globalisation benefited middle classes in emerging nations and the ultra-rich in developed nations, while leaving behind the middle and poorer classes in poor and rich countries at the bottom.

Branko Milanovic has compiled data to show that globalisation's losers include the very poor of Africa and the rest of the developing world, whose incomes remained unchanged from 1988 to 2008, as well as lower middle class citizens of developed nations in Europe and North America, who also suffered stagnating incomes. Those who moved up the socioeconomic ranks under globalisation were the middle classes in EMEs, the upper crust in other developing countries, and the fabulously rich in the industrialised West. The 'global middle class' especially from China and 'resurgent Asia', and the 'global plutocracy' from the topmost layer of social classes in the US, Europe, Japan and EMEs never had it so good as under the system of neoliberal globalisation. In contrast, the bulk of society in the least developed countries (LDCs) and the working class in the US and Europe have not enjoyed upward mobility.[42]

This juxtaposition lends credence to Trump's theory of a nexus between special interests in the US and emerging powers, which is pauperising American workers. The reality, however, is far more complex that his simplistic painting of China, Mexico, India and developing countries in general as villains. Globalisation has increased within-country inequalities in many EMEs too and it is a fallacy to argue that emerging powers as monolithic entities are the cause of ordinary Americans' misery. Nonetheless, Milanovic's finding that the global middle class from EMEs are gaining, plus his formulation of a '92-8 world', that is, a division of the pie where half of the world's income is controlled by the top eight per cent in the global class hierarchy,[43] add to the hatred against foreigners and other countries that Trump is stirring up in America through his populist mix of class angst and patriotism.

Back to the Future of Populism

To properly appreciate the Trump effect on emerging powers, it is instructive to dig deep into the strain of populism he symbolises and its antecedents, where pressure from below in American society sharply impinged upon American foreign policy. Mark Twain is attributed with the adage, 'History doesn't repeat itself, but it does rhyme'. Trump is neither the first nor the only American politician to use the formula of economic nationalism, isolationism and abandonment of foreign commitments for domestic electoral gains. Despite his personal background as an outgoing real estate tycoon with sprawling global business interests,[44] and in spite of belonging to the right-wing Republican Party (touted as the 'globalisation and opportunity party' since Reagan[45]), many elements of Trump's critique of foreign countries and the international order resemble those of contemporary and yesteryear socialists and populists.

F.H. Buckley, a Trump speechwriter and self-described right-wing Marxist, has noted stark similarities in the outlooks of Trump and the anti-globalisation leftist Democratic presidential candidate in the 2016 US presidential election, Bernie Sanders. Buckley argues the difference was only in method but not in objective: 'Sanders would have employed socialist means to achieve socialist goals, while Trump proposed capitalist means to do so.'[46] Sanders's foreign policy line was to berate the 'increasingly globalized economy, established and maintained by the world's economic elite for failing people everywhere'. He vowed to 'fundamentally reject our "free trade" policies and defeat the TPP'. As a socialist who sounded like Trump's twin, he tried to differentiate himself by rebuffing the latter's narrow nationalism and pledging to enhance 'international cooperation and help poor countries develop'.[47]

In the end, Trump's far-right conservatism carried the day in the election season as he could mobilise white working Americans using the lethal combination of cultural and economic insecurities. His populism came out on top over Sanders's socialism and

Hillary's confused liberalism because he pinpointed domestic and foreign enemies and had more clarity in his rhetoric. That said, it is no exaggeration that the 2016 presidential primaries proved the proximity of the far-right and far-left, which have always shared common tendencies and nostrums.[48]

Trump is part of a longer legacy of American conservatives whose domestic and international themes and positions bear more than a passing resemblance to those from the left. The history of right-wing populism in rich nations has comparable politicians in eras past who came from privileged backgrounds but sounded the bugle of class conflict, redistribution, rolling back free trade and free markets, and defending the 'nation' from globalisation-type foreign processes, immigrants and entangling international commitments that benefit elites.

There have been earlier American populists in times of economic distress who are uncanny ancestors to Trump, even though they failed to take power and enter the White House. The People's Party aka Populists in the America of the 1890s was led by William Jennings Bryan, who contested the 1896 presidential election criticising the robber baron capitalists, banks, railroads and mega corporations of that age. Extreme income inequality, farmer distress and low wages in fin de siècle America combined to provide fertile ground for Bryan's rise; he was dubbed The Great Commoner. Apart from progressive attacks on big business houses like the Morgans, Rothschilds, Carnegies and Rockefellers, Bryan strictly opposed immigration into the US from 'Asiatic races' to protect American labour and prevent foreigners from coming in and 'endangering our civilization'.[49]

In the 1930s, with America caught in the throes of mass unemployment during the Great Depression, Huey Long launched a populist Share Our Wealth campaign against the rich and big corporations to redistribute income from the elite to the masses. He attacked Wall Street banks and the US Federal Reserve and positioned himself as a crusader for justice, far beyond Franklin Roosevelt. In foreign policy, Long was an economic protectionist and isolationist who contended that the Spanish-American War of 1898 and World War I were 'murderous frauds waged for the benefit of Wall Street'.[50] His assassination in 1935 cut short a possible match with Franklin Roosevelt in the 1936 presidential election, but he remains one of the icons of populism.

Barry Eichengreen's research shows that neither Bryan nor Long could succeed beyond a point at the national level in the US because incumbent mainstream political parties and presidents like William McKinley, Theodore Roosevelt and Franklin Roosevelt understood grass-roots anger in American society, co-opted populist ideas for equity and implemented reforms that ameliorated working class frustrations. The populist threat was also contained by state elites responding in foreign policy by prioritising domestic considerations over international ones and blowing the trumpet of economic nationalism by resorting to protective trade tariffs.[51]

It is worth recalling here that Franklin Roosevelt entered the pantheon of US foreign policy legends for his liberal internationalism and vision to shape the post-World War II international order through a US-initiated system of cooperative global institutions, democracy and capitalism underpinned by military alliances and bases. But before World War II, when he was confronting radical populist opponents like Long and facing widespread isolationist public opinion in America, Roosevelt opportunistically took a leaf out of the populist playbook. He downplayed advocacy for the US joining the Permanent Court of International Justice in 1931,[52] disavowed his earlier backing of the League of Nations and of lower trade tariffs during the 1932 presidential election,[53] and detached the dollar from the international gold standard in 1933 to inflate American incomes at the cost of the global economy and to the detriment of foreign allies.[54]

Had it not been for the force majeure of the rise of fascism and World War II, Franklin Roosevelt's now-famed liberal internationalism may never have won traction to overwhelm populist and isolationist feelings that prevailed in America during the inter-war period. Even as Hitler, Mussolini and Japanese militarists were running amok in Europe and Asia, the US witnessed an anti-interventionist and anti-internationalist 'America First' conservative movement backed by small businesses, farmers and average workers who thought a German victory over Europe would do less harm to the US economy than America entering the war.

The populist America First leader Charles Lindbergh used anti-Semitic rhetoric to warn in September 1941 that American Jews who wanted Roosevelt to plunge into the war and defeat Hitler represented 'the greatest danger to this country by virtue of their large ownership and influence in our motion pictures, our press, our radio, and our government'.[55] In other words, 'them' special interests and elites have a vested interest in foreign military campaigns while 'us' ordinary Americans would be the losers if the US tried to rescue European allies.

It was only the enormity of the blow from Pearl Harbor that pulled the rug from under the feet of these insular advocates and put the US on what turned out to be an almost permanent path of internationalist action, responsibility and ambition. The failure of the America First movement in the 1940s provides a key insight into the strength of populism in the history of US foreign policy and explains why Trump is daring to turn seven decades of said policy orthodoxy on its head. Unless America is staring at an existential threat from overseas to its very capitalistic way of life, physical safety and security, its default diplomatic predilection has been nationalistic, isolationist and deferential to populism.

The historic phases that witnessed large-scale US military missions overseas, promotion of democracy, human rights and free trade, participation in international coalition-building, investment in global institutions, maintenance of alliances and provision of global public goods through security guarantees, commitments and aid coincided with dread about being overrun or annihilated by all-consuming generational threats like fascism, communism and Islamist terrorism. Melvyn Leffler has argued that 'heightened threat perception' since World War II has tempted the US to 'overcommitments', 'overassertion of American power', arrogance and abuse in international affairs driven by assumed 'universality and superiority of American values'.[56]

Dominic Tierney divides American history into 'eras of threat' and 'eras of safety' based on the degree of external threats. The former are characterised by an ethos of competition, crusading war and pushback against 'the enemy out-group', all of it buttressed by national cohesion at home of the 'American in-group' and strong public support for internationalism and interventionism. In contrast, the latter periods are marked by the US 'losing its preoccupying focus', turning attention to domestic affairs, social fractiousness and blurring of in-group and out-group boundaries. In such times, even if the American state undertakes military and non-military interventions abroad against 'amorphous threats' for humanitarian rescue, economic development, democracy promotion or peacekeeping, they 'tend to be unpopular'.[57]

It so happened that the three illiberal ideologies of fascism, communism and Islamist fundamentalism appeared on the horizon in quick succession, with minor interregnums, from the 1930s until the 2000s, making it look like a globally involved and hegemonic America was there to stay forever in actively moulding the international system and imposing its values in the name of freedom and liberty. But this chain of successive globalist foreign policies only held true until Bush's presidency, which was inspired in its GWOT by America's World War II and Cold War exploits of trouncing illiberal demons. Richard Immerman's study of Bush's neoconservative hyper-interventionist aide Paul Wolfowitz reveals the psyche that pervades 'eras of threat'. To Wolfowitz, 'destroying monsters was the prerequisite for establishing an American empire, and an American empire was the prerequisite for an Empire for Liberty.'[58]

Once the fervour of the GWOT ended with Bush, Obama grasped the war-fatigue and public desire for avoiding costly overseas commitments. His view ('just because we have the best hammer does not mean that every problem is a nail') and his principle that 'the threshold for military action must be higher', that is, 'when our people are threatened; when our livelihood is at stake; or when the security of our allies is in danger',[59] echoed the American public's habitual will to withdraw from the world and stop the quest for global supremacy during 'eras of safety'. As mentioned earlier, Obama was still wedded to liberal internationalism and only took America's foot off the pedal in its militaristic aspect. Robert Kagan has correctly portrayed Obama as a transitional figure slowly moving away from the post-World War II and post-Cold War traditions of US exceptionalism and liberal mission to dominate the world.[60]

In this sense, Trump is a completion of the Obama-initiated transition towards shredding full-spectrum global hegemony as the former's presidency falls within an 'era of safety' in the minds of many American citizens. Trump's contempt for alliances, international institutions and responsibilities appear sacrilegious to liberals, but it is a reflection of the fact that most of the US public does not feel imperilled by any great diabolical menace from a single foreign country these days. Eliot Cohen argues that Trump has 'accelerated a trend—that of Washington's retreat from its global responsibilities—that was already developing by the time he took office due to extinction of the living memory of World War II... that revolutionised US foreign policy'. The 'awareness of just how terrible the world could become if the United States chose not to lead' has evaporated and Trump is reflecting it in his foreign policy.[61]

A public opinion survey of more than 1,000 Americans in July 2018 by the Eurasia Group consultancy confirms how close Trump's isolationism and populism is to the majority's foreign policy preferences: 44 per cent respondents chose an 'independent America' worldview, which translates into America must focus more on its domestic challenges than on the challenges that come with international leadership. About 19.5 per cent went for a 'moneyball America' worldview, that is, foreign policy should be driven by a focused calculation of costs and benefits to national interest. Barely 9.5 per cent opted for an 'indispensable America' worldview, spelt out as American leadership is necessary for global stability and therefore American peace and prosperity. These figures were reversed when the same survey was administered to 45 randomly selected US foreign policy experts and strategic elites; 47 per cent ascribe to indispensable America while only 9 per cent thought independent America was the better way.[62] Trump rails incessantly against the liberal establishment because of his instinctive grasp of the gulf between experts and the laity. The total contempt he has shown for liberal internationalism is not due to whimsical or idiosyncratic beliefs of his own. As a politician, he is channelling the public's clarion call for a globally restrained and narrowly self-interested foreign policy.

Allies, partners and emerging powers with mixed feelings about the US should no longer take the old America—which instinctively and automatically pressed all levers to set up economic and regional regimes and police conduct in the world—as a given because liberal internationalism is today disconnected from the domestic American milieu and suffers a legitimacy deficit. To cite Doug Stokes, we are at a stage of history where 'the benefits of American elites' preferred global model, suited as it is to powerful sectors both within the country and also globally, become a much harder sell to those who feel acutely the economic costs to themselves and their families'.[63] John Ikenberry has elaborated the point that the 'connection between progressivism at home and liberal internationalism abroad has been broken' in developed countries. The days when internationalism went hand in hand with domestic economic well-being and social mobility in the West are over and we are now witnessing a 'crisis of legitimacy and social purpose' of the liberal order in its former bastions of the US and Europe.[64] Barring another epochal attack on the American homeland like the September 11 strikes on New York and Washington, the new normal is of an America stepping back and withdrawing from remote control management of the international order.

To be sure, Trump does frequently inveigh against radical Islamic terrorism, portrays an alarming picture of the tremendous onslaught or invasion of hordes of immigrants from Mexico, and also paints China's export colossus as a mortal threat to American workers. During the 2016 presidential campaign, he even referred to the serialised trifecta of communism, fascism and jihadist extremism:

> In the 20th Century, the United States defeated Fascism, Nazism, and Communism. Now, a different threat challenges our world: Radical Islamic Terrorism. We will defeat Radical Islamic Terrorism, just as we have defeated every threat we have faced in every age before.[65]

But absolute white-knuckle fear about fascism, Soviet communism or Al Qaeda terrorism has long passed in the American popular imagination. Getting voters to endorse global commitments to contain a buoyant China, maintain balances of power in Eurasia and defend foreign alliances forged in bygone eras of crisis is akin to boiling the ocean at present. As to the war against Islamist extremism, Trump declared in December 2018 (not even two full years in the White House) that the Islamic State (ISIS) had been neutralised. To justify withdrawal of US forces from Syria, he tweeted in his trademark boastful tone, 'When I became President, ISIS was going wild. Now ISIS is largely defeated and other local countries, including Turkey, should be able to easily take care of whatever remains. We're coming home!'[66]

I will elaborate the strategic repercussions of American military withdrawal from Syria in Chapter II on Turkey–US relations, but here it suffices to note that Trump has often revelled in classic populist buck-passing and jettisoning of America's previous self-appointed role as the guardian of global security. His explicit disavowal that 'the United States cannot continue to be the policeman of the world' and that he will deliver a 'harsh response' to jihadists only if the American homeland itself faced another terrorist attack,[67] left American mainstream internationalists, security pundits, allies and partners around the world shaking their heads. The rebuttal from Mitch McConnell, the Senate Majority Leader from Trump's own Republican Party, that the US may not be the world's policeman but is the 'leader of the free world', which must sustain a global coalition against terrorism and stand by allies,[68] conveyed in a nutshell the gulf between globalism and nationalism, elitism and populism.

Abandonment of international obligations and multilateralism has not upset Trump's base in America. An opinion poll conducted days after Trump's Syria pull-out announcement showed that 43 per cent Americans thought quitting Syria was the right decision, while 45 per cent thought it was a mistake. On the partisan scale, 58 per cent of Republican-leaning citizens and 30 per cent of Democrat-leaning citizens approved of this move.[69] In a polarised political environment, Trump's foreign policy of isolationism has a sizeable catchment area. As a populist, he cares much more for this grass-roots consent than the expert advice or pressure of the establishment.

The ideal receptive moment for radical conservatives like Trump to find traction for their nativist, narrow nationalistic and anti-establishment foreign policies is peacetime with no almighty external enemy of the US in sight but seething economic insecurities of working classes at home. Interestingly, Trump was foreshadowed by the conservative populist Pat Buchanan who attempted to latch on to one such 'normal' period in the 1990s after the end of the Cold War. His two quixotic bids for the Republican Party nomination to the US presidency in 1992 and 1996 fizzled, but his enlightened nationalism comprising reduction of US foreign aid, avoiding humanitarian interventions, withdrawing the US from the United Nations and the North American Free Trade Agreement (NAFTA), stemming the flood of immigrants, winding up foreign military bases and devoting budgets to domestic needs, presented at least a theoretical alternative to liberal internationalism, which was the credo of the Bill Clinton presidency.[70]

Buchanan's motto of 'America First—and Second, and Third'[71] ended up being ridiculed as a zany prescription. He could not generate momentum because the US economy was roaring under Bill Clinton, who also implemented social safety nets and left little room for widespread economic distress in society to rally populist isolationism and snowball. But there is one period in early twentieth-century history that Buchanan kept harking back to as an ideal when foreign policy populism and isolationism had been in vogue. In the 1920 US presidential election, the Republican candidate Warren Harding campaigned on a manifesto of return to normalcy after the end of the Great War, with catchphrases like 'not heroics, but healing' and 'not submergence in internationality, but sustainment in triumphant nationality'.[72]

For a war-weary America disillusioned with European rivalries and eager to recover economically at home, it was music to the ears and Harding won a landslide victory. Once in power, Harding was lobbied by American capitalists and internationalist bankers to seek cancellation of debts owed by European allies to the US so that European economies could revive and purchase American exported products. But the isolationist US Congress struck down such proposals and interest rate reductions and debt cancellation dragged on.[73] In 1922, Harding signed the Fordney-McCumber Bill that raised trade tariffs to the highest level in US history and deprived struggling European allies easy access to the US market. Harding's Republican successors as president, Calvin Coolidge and Herbert Hoover, also hewed carefully to the prevalent mood of domestic prioritisation at the cost of financial generosity and military commitments to stabilise Europe. Hoover held the widely shared belief of the time that the US 'was sufficiently self-contained to withstand upheaval and even revolution abroad' and that his country had a robust internal market and domestic demand to sustain itself 'regardless of events elsewhere'.[74] In 1930, Hoover signed the Smoot-Hawley Tariff Bill, which was again a concession to populist and isolationist forces and a blow to America's foreign trading partners. And as discussed earlier, even Franklin Roosevelt could not disregard the trail blazed by his populist and economic nationalist predecessors. While it is debatable as to what extent American isolationism and appeasement of fascism in Europe in the inter-war years were responsible for the rise of Hitler and Word War II,[75] for our purpose it is worthwhile to see that Washington was mean, tight-fisted and self-centric in that era. It behaved as an unexceptional country in supposedly normal times.

Trump has not alluded to the isolationist Republicans of the 1920s with nostalgia, but his America First foreign policy inherits pieces of their legacy. Peter Beinart elaborates that

> what links Trump and the conservative presidents of the 1920s is their view of all foreign governments, regardless of ideology, as alien and predatory, and their desire not to bind America to any of them. In both eras... the insistence that foreign governments have cheated America is bound up with the insistence that foreign people have cheated Americans.

And in both eras, there was 'obsession with American sovereignty', an uptick in racism and xenophobia, and 'panic about immigration'.[76]

One major difference between then and now is the meaning of the world, which has expanded vastly for America today. When isolationists and populists were calling to shun international responsibilities and withdraw into a domestic cocoon in the inter-war years, the hegemonic power of the US was limited to Latin America and the range of its interactions only included Europe and parts of East Asia. Stephen Ambrose has shown how America's conception of foreign interests and zones of influence expanded hugely in the second half of the twentieth century:

> On the eve of World War II... America had no entangling alliances and no American troops were stationed in any foreign country. The dominant political mood was isolationism. America's physical security... seemed assured... because of the distance between

America and any potential enemy. A half century later, the United States had a huge standing Army, Air Force and Navy... had military alliances with fifty nations... and no matter how far outward America extended her power, America's national security was constantly in jeopardy.[77]

Barring Brazil, which was at the core of America's hemispheric backyard delimited in the nineteenth century Monroe Doctrine, none of the emerging powers covered in this book had substantial links with America in the old populist and isolationist era. So, when a Bryan, Long or Harding sought to avoid international commitments or extract America's pound of flesh from allies, it did not constitute global disengagement as per our contemporary parlance. The American empire and its economic companion, globalisation, which Trump is attempting to unravel are far more spread out and entrenched structures with multiple stakeholders, implying that his insurrection is against a bigger beast and the effects of his militancy will be felt on a wider scale than was the case in the earlier instances of American isolationism and populism. Subsequent chapters in this book illustrate how emerging powers will reap the maximum benefits and also bear the maximum brunt of Trump's anti-globalist turn.

Unmooring from the Anchor

Liberal internationalists and interventionists cite past isolationist and populist itches in US foreign policy to critique Trump and forewarn of imminent disaster and chaos in the international order if America does not strive to prolong its centrality as an anchor state. Kagan argues that democracy, capitalism and general peace, which are the bedrocks of what liberals consider progress, could not have been mainstreamed after 1945 if not for the 'geographical and geopolitical space created by American power'. He adds that 'deeply etched patterns of history' like fascism, totalitarianism and destructive wars were interrupted over the next seven decades thanks to the moderate American stabilising hand. If America went home, there would be no special state to save the garden of a universally beneficial liberal order from dark forces of nature.[78]

A similar trepidation keeps liberals from across the Atlantic awake at night. Anders Rasmussen, the former Danish Prime Minister and unabashed pro-American, writes that 'if the United States retrenches and retreats, or even if the world thinks that American restraint reflects a lack of willingness in preventing and resolving conflicts by using military force if need be, it leaves a vacuum that will be filled by the bad guys,' that is, Russia and China, which are acting in aggressive 'nineteenth-century fashion'.[79]

The construct of American hegemony as the last backstop against anarchy in the international system, and American abandonment as a fatal error that would cause apocalyptic outcomes, is a powerful one that has motivated generations of national security elites and foreign policy professionals. Like the civilising mission and white man's burden metaphors that provided justification for European colonialism in Asia, Africa and Latin America, the liberal mission of using American military, economic and diplomatic power to make the world a better place is embedded in the American foreign policy self-conception cutting across political affiliations of Democrats and Republicans. Irrespective of the tags, liberal and conservative, in domestic policy debates and positions, most mainstream lawmakers, policymakers and thinkers since Woodrow Wilson and Franklin Roosevelt have made sustenance of a US-led liberal international order an article of faith. It is rooted in the myth received from the British settlement of North America in the seventeenth century that the US is an exceptional, providentially chosen nation with a manifest destiny to spread good and fight evil.[80] As the shining city upon a hill, the US is apparently born to lead and bound to do so for the greater good of humanity.

Acknowledging the strength of this discourse in 2010, William Pfaff wrote, 'It has become somewhat of a national heresy to suggest the US does not have a unique moral status and role to play in the history of nations and therefore in the affairs of the contemporary world. In fact it does not.'[81] Missionary-style conceit about America having found truth, light and God first, then setting about to proselytise and succour heathen lands and regions mired in misery accord complete agency to the US as the sheriff that is a force for betterment of international relations and treats other powers around the world as immoral and undesirable, if not incapable. This spirit was reflected in a quip attributed to Hillary: 'I don't want my grandchildren to live in a world dominated by the Chinese.'[82]

From the parameters of legitimacy and efficiency in setting rules and policing the world, the liberal internationalist camp assigns automatic primacy to the US. The rest of the world has the choice of dutifully tagging along as allies, junior partners and client states, or counterbalancing the US and paying a heavy price for opting to be the bad guys.[83] American proponents of hegemonic stability cannot countenance a world order where China and emerging powers can singly or in some form of concert be autonomous builders, monitors and enforcers of benign regional and global architectures. Armed with an infinite superiority complex, or what John Mearsheimer labels 'crusader mentality' that is hardwired and hard to restrain,[84] liberal internationalists and interventionists assume the US has a divine and earned prerogative to rule and that it is irreplaceable.

Sympathisers of American economic hegemony and global military footprint interpret the historical record in ways that burnish the US. For example, Hal Brands labels America's post-Cold War performance as pretty successful and parades a long list of its presumed achievements.

> … democracy continued its advance… global living standards continued to rise… the maintenance of US military presence and alliances in Europe and East Asia helped tamp down potential instability and security competitions… With the US presence still in place, there was no need for these or other key countries to provide fully for their own security, which markedly reduced the incentives for them to engage in arms-racing and other kinds of destabilizing behavior… the extension of American alliance commitments to eastern Europe helped smother incipient conflicts… and reduced incentives for nuclear proliferation or major military buildups by historically insecure states.[85]

Such language leaves little to extrapolation. American global interventionism and alliance systems deliberately take the agency out of the hands of regional powers and adversary nations, foster local dependencies on the US, and lock out potential challengers that might upstage US hegemony. Emerging powers, which have ambitions of stepping in and shouldering responsibilities to carve a more just international system, do not accept versions that vest in the US a birthright monopoly over global leadership.

From the critical lenses of rising nations today, the liberal international order had never been so liberal to them or to smaller and weaker states whom it pretended to be shielding from regional bullies. Chafing at the iniquitous results of the US-dominated liberal world order has been a constant feature of emerging powers' self-consciousness and promotion of equitable models of 'South-South' cooperation. From the inaugural summit of the BRIC countries in 2009, joint declarations have reiterated demands for 'a more democratic and just multipolar world order based on the rule of international law, equality, mutual respect, cooperation, coordinated action and collective decision-making of all states'.[86] These diplomatic communiques leave little ambiguity about what the emerging powers think of the liberal content of the US-led world order.

Hardeep Puri, who served as India's Ambassador to the UN, unmasked the true face of US and European liberal interventionism and manipulation of multilateral institutions during the Bush and Obama presidencies. Far from ensuring order, stability and liberal peace, he wrote, the Western 'desire for geopolitical domination, unseating undesirable or inconvenient regimes and establishing dependent ones in their place… invariably led to the rise of terrorists and non-state military actors' and created 'unprecedented chaos and unravelling of countries'.[87] In similar vein, Celso Amorim, who was Brazil's Minister of External Relations, argued that far from the rosy imagery of a US-led new world order after 1991, what developing countries got was a globalisation that 'increased inequalities among and within States. The promise of a better and fairer world that would result from the triumph of "Western" political values and of market economy was not fulfilled. Contrary to Francis Fukuyama's predictions, History did not meet its end.'[88]

Criticism of the US-structured liberal order comes not only from the political left within emerging nations, but also from the nationalist right-wing sections. Chapter II of this book reveals the fundamental unease and misgivings the Islamist ruling class in Turkey has about the role of the US and its imposed order in the Middle East. Emerging powers that have ambitions to enter the league of great powers have been hemmed in as a result of long-term American presence and arrangement of local relations among neighbours. The political and economic conditionalities and caveats the US introduces in various regions for disbursing foreign aid, providing market access to exports, security assistance and other forms of capacity building are onerous and not necessarily in the best interests of emerging powers.

As discussed, US-enabled globalisation after 1991 did generate positive effects for middle and upper classes in several emerging nations. The very rise of these countries as economic stars of the future was possible because of their integration into the liberal capitalist world order. But simultaneously, such nations have felt frustrated by the limitations and infringements on their strategic autonomy that the US put in place by virtue of being the orchestrator of the whole show around the world. Moreover, the stark distinction the US generally makes between friendly 'client states' on one hand and enemy states on the other in each region leaves little room for creative, inclusive and endogenous coalitions to emerge under the leadership of locally able emerging powers. Divide and rule is as old as the hills and empires have always resorted to it. The Pax Americana since 1945 was less direct and brutal compared to European colonial empires, but it too practised and perfected the art of dividing regions and subregions.

David Sylvan and Stephen Majeski have noted that even if a particular country is allied as part of America's empire of client states, it is subjected to intense political surveillance by Washington to make it behave as per grand strategic designs. As to the enemy states targeted by the US, the reason for their being outcaste and pressurised has less to do with whether they are democratic, authoritarian, socialist or free-market economies, and more about their alignment preferences, that is, which great power or superpower they wish to partner with. To Sylvan and Majeski, this explains why 'during the Cold War, the US could back a single-party Communist state (Yugoslavia), and why today, an important US client is a fundamentalist Islamic regime (Saudi Arabia)'.[89]

Geopolitical control by the US supersedes liberal values and ideals in the ironically named liberal international order—a reality that at times benefits emerging powers but also hampers their efforts to remake their respective regions along different organising methods. In the first chapter, I will demonstrate how Pakistan's long-time status as a US client state has posed insuperable hurdles to India's strategic growth and rise in Asia. In Chapter III, I will further elaborate this point by examining how Brazil clashed with the US over the latter's hegemony by default status and had to work hard to prioritise the Southern Common Market (Mercosur) model of regional economic integration over Washington's brainchild of the Free Trade Area of the Americas (FTAA). And in Chapter IV, I reveal how Nigeria has found its own role in taking the lead for countering terrorism, maintaining order and regime stability in West Africa constrained by American hegemony.

Global interventionism by the US since 1945 has been described by historians as an empire by invitation rather than imposition[90] because many countries (elites and the general public) in Europe, the Middle East, Asia and Latin America voluntarily sought US military presence and economic aid in pursuit of their national interests and lobbied Washington to take charge of their destinies. Given this wilful delegation of authority by allies to the US to police their regions and Washington's modus operandi of indirect control through economics, ideological appeal and steering global institutions, Robert Keohane has taken exception to the usage of the word empire for US-dominated liberal order. In his reckoning, America's forms of rule were quite different from those of the Soviet Union or European colonialist states and hence better characterised as just hegemony,[91] that is, a hierarchical ordering of states where the dominated consent to the domination.

I will elucidate throughout this book that, even today, emerging powers do realise that when the US remains active in their regions, it has some practical utility in specific geopolitical situations. But by the nature of their emergence and their unwillingness to be played around like puppets, these rising powers do not want full-blown Pax Americana, with all its encumbrances. As aspirants to great power or superpower status, they perceive the US competitively instead of acquiescingly and focus more on the negative consequences of the liberal international order to push the envelope and achieve a multipolar world. LDCs, which are the weakest in material power, may have no choice but to willy-nilly submit to superpowers or resist them at their own risk. But emerging powers belong to a middle layer and their horizon has multipolar world written on it. They have the will and wherewithal to attenuate US liberal internationalism, which poses barriers to fairer distribution of power in the world.

Geir Lundestad has listed several imposed interventions by the liberal American empire and warned against 'taking the invitational aspect too far'.[92] Emerging powers, which retain memories of America's reckless use of unilateral force, covert coups for regime change and economic blackmail, which were applied on them or broadly in their neighbourhoods, do not buy the touted liberality of American globalism. As revisionist states wanting equity and justice, they would echo Inderjeet Parmar's verdict on the liberal international order as 'a system of hierarchy and inequality whose bosses cannot yet comprehend an order… on the basis of something approaching equality of the broad mass of people—citizens—at home, let alone the non-Western peoples of the Global South, or even their elites'.[93]

This book explains how the quest for an alternative order by emerging powers has found an unlikely bedfellow in the figure of Trump, who is undermining the liberal order from within its sanctum sanctorum. His mission of turning American foreign policy on a dime has inadvertently opened a window of opportunity for emerging powers to take the reins of their destinies into their own hands. As an anti-establishment rebel who unexpectedly obtained executive power in America by a quirk of fate, Trump has punctured the founding myth of US exceptionalism and deflated the country's political will to keep leading the world.

While previous presidents poured liberal scorn on authoritarian nations and juxtaposed them with America's purported good nature, Trump the populist directed fire at domestic political opponents and institutions. Notwithstanding his notorious penchant to insult foreign leaders on economic transactional grounds, he refrained from judgemental rhetoric against countries for their lack of democracy or human rights. During the presidential campaign in 2016, he rejected the liberal internationalism of the previous Republican president Bush, and stated categorically: 'When the world looks at how bad the United States is, and then we go and talk about civil liberties, I don't think we're a very good messenger… We're not in a position to be more aggressive. We have to fix our own mess.'[94] As president, in a famous interview with Fox News in February 2017 that vexed the mainstream foreign policy establishment, Trump was asked why he respected his Russian counterpart Vladimir Putin despite knowing the latter was 'a killer'. His unreserved reply was, 'You got a lot of killers. What, you think our country's so innocent?'[95] It was a telling blow to liberal internationalism and America's smugness about its democratic rectitude and natural responsibility to run the international system. It tore the veil off the dark side of Pax Americana, which previous presidents had swept under the carpet of a morally upbeat foreign policy identity.

Since the 1940s, the American grand strategy was premised on preventing formidable non-democratic states like Nazi Germany, Russia or China from gaining supremacy over land and resources of Eurasia, which could endow them with gigantic power and threaten the mainland from the Atlantic or the Pacific sides.[96] After the Cold War ended, American presidents modified this doctrine to apply to any authoritarian enemy (not necessarily a humungous one) that posed a threat to US hegemony in a region. In 1991, Defense Secretary Dick Cheney pleaded to the Congress that America must not become complacent after the fall of the Soviet Union and retrench from forward military deployments, cutting-edge weapons production and far-flung alliances because 'we want to ensure that non-democratic powers will not dominate regions of the world critical to us or come to pose a serious global challenge'.[97]

The spectre of authoritarian rogue states was reiterated by the Bush administration, this time with Cheney as the Vice-President, in 2001. Its stated purpose of remaining engaged in the world for shaping a balance of power that favours freedom and confronting 'enemies of liberty and our country'[98] kept the binary of good democracies and bad dictatorships intact in American foreign policy. The Obama administration made fresh diplomatic overtures to formerly estranged authoritarian countries like Cuba, Myanmar and Iran, but it too stood by the dogma that 'threats to our security arose from authoritarian states opposed to democratic forces while our greatest opportunities came from advances for liberty and rule of law'.[99]

As discussed earlier, the US has had countless tyrannical client states during and after the Cold War. It never truly and indiscriminately countered authoritarianism worldwide. So, to justify unilateral regime change operations and other controversial acts of meddling, manipulation and pressure on geopolitical antagonists, the liberal internationalist trope of promoting liberty in the world came in handy. During the invasion and occupation of Iraq, even as the US was violating international laws rampantly, President Bush rehashed America's moral calling by saying, 'I believe we have a duty to free people. I hope we wouldn't have to do it militarily, but we have a duty.'[100]

Trump, the radical populist, has had enough of this liberal values-based categorisation of the world as consisting of democratic saints and undemocratic sinners. His strange affinity for Putin and gushing praise for the autocrat as 'a man so highly respected within his own country and beyond'[101] is ideological but from an obverse illiberal prism. Putin is the ultimate bugbear and villain for Western liberals. His forceful foreign policies in Europe remind them that remnants of the Cold War are still around. He irritates them no end with his stubborn defiance of liberal sacred cows like globalisation, secularism, human rights, environmentalism, cross-border migration, free speech and multiparty democracy. Ceaseless Democratic allegations and confirmations by US intelligence agencies that Putin covertly intervened in the 2016 US presidential election to favour Trump against the torchbearer of liberal internationalism, Hillary, have turned the Russian president into a larger-than-life nemesis of the mainstream establishment in America.

But to Trump, Putin's conservative, religious and nationalistic credentials are inspiring, and he feels empathetically connected. Trump's former White House adviser and strategist, Bannon, is on record stating, 'We, the Judeo-Christian West, really have to look at what Putin is talking about as far as traditionalism goes, particularly the sense of where it supports the underpinnings of nationalism'.[102] The American Alt-Right movement, which is part of Trump's domestic voter base, finds in Putin a paragon because he has been negating what they consider as effeminate and deracinated liberalism for nearly two decades. Trump's personal soft corner for Russia, his unconventional willingness to upturn entrenched bipartisan American hostility towards Putin, and his scepticism about the anti-Russian EU and NATO are best understood in the context of this ideological camaraderie.

Is there a tactical or strategic reasoning as well behind Trump's openness to friendship and deal-making with the authoritarian Putin? The doyen of American realpolitik, Henry Kissinger, advised Trump during his presidential transition to adopt a 'reverse Nixon strategy of work with Russia to contain a rising China', a proposal reported to have found receptive ears among some of Trump's top advisers.[103] But if prising Russia away from China to prevent an anti-Western axis of authoritarians is a clever Machiavellian stroke of genius, Trump has not particularly warmed up to it or been mindful of it in the course of his erratic foreign policymaking. Non-stop investigations and insinuations of his collusion with Russia during the 2016 presidential campaign have hung like a Damocles' sword over his head, raising the domestic political risks of teaming up with Russia to isolate China.

If grand manoeuvres with Russia against China remain unfulfilled, Trump has had more success in enlisting Russian support against second-order threats like jihadist terrorism. Shortly after taking office, Trump said he wanted to 'get together with Russia to knock the hell out of ISIS, because that's the real sickness'.[104] Disregarding liberal establishment howls that cooperating with Russia would entrench dictatorial regimes and undermine democratisation, Trump has coordinated closely with Putin for 'enhanced de-confliction efforts' of the US and Russian militaries in Syria and a political solution to the war there,[105] and even in the decision to pull American forces out from that hotspot.[106]

If Western liberal revulsion towards Putin created fissures in the international community, which were exploited by ISIS during Obama's second term, Trump has had no compunctions in partnering with Putin to ostensibly save the Judeo-Christian civilisation from jihadists. As we shall see in Chapter II on Turkey, Trump did not mind handing Syria over to Russian and Iranian hegemony and violating the cardinal rule of American foreign policy of disallowing authoritarian rival states from dominating any region of the world. This drastic change in approach was possible because Trump is daring to redefine America's identity as the antithesis of authoritarianism and challenging the dogma in the US foreign policy establishment that Russia should, by default, be treated as an inveterate foe.

America's national interests and how they relate to the world are being sought to be reinvented by Trump. He is trying to ram through a structural makeover of a non-receptive foreign policy and national security bureaucracy imbued in the liberal hegemonic tradition. It is no coincidence that the sensational anonymous op-ed by a senior official within the Trump administration, claiming a steady state within Trump's government is undermining him from within, devotes so much space to his illiberal foreign policy instincts. Its message of a two-track presidency deserves lengthy quotation:

> In public and in private, President Trump shows a preference for autocrats and dictators, such as President Vladimir Putin of Russia and North Korea's leader, Kim Jong-un, and displays little genuine appreciation for the ties that bind us to allied, like-minded nations… the rest of the administration is operating on another track, one where countries like Russia are called out for meddling and punished accordingly… the president was reluctant to expel so many of Mr. Putin's spies as punishment… He complained for weeks about senior staff members letting him get boxed into further confrontation with Russia, and he expressed frustration that the United States continued to impose sanctions on the country for its malign behavior. But his national security team knew better—such actions had to be taken, to hold Moscow accountable.[107]

In subsequent chapters, I will uncover how the two-track presidency engendered by a tug-of-war between what Trump loyalists deem deep state and his populist base is at once a source of trouble for emerging powers and also leverage for their own power buildups in their respective regions. America is socially and economically more divided than ever before in modern times, a fact that is being reflected in the chaotic flip-flopping and wobbly decision-making of the Trump administration. But this does not mean Trump is having no impact at all on foreign or domestic policies or is being tied down or smothered to the point of irrelevance on the world stage. His contrarian acts of omission and commission emanate from political and ideological substructures, which must be thoroughly dissected in order to make intelligent estimates about the future landscape for emerging powers.

What should be absolutely certain to rising powers is that Trump's brand of America First narrow nationalism or patriotism is not going to vanish, no matter how his own political career graph evolves. Mearsheimer, the guru of realism in the academic discipline of International Relations, has been an inveterate critic of liberal internationalist US foreign policy and a defender of nationalism, which shuns interventionist wars, is non-intrusive vis-à-vis sovereignty of other countries and concentrates on maintaining a balance of power with rival states. In his opinion,

> With the rise of China and the resurrection of Russian power having put great power politics back on the table, Trump eventually will have no choice but to move toward a grand strategy based on realism, even if doing so meets with considerable resistance at home.[108]

Trump's December 2017 National Security Strategy (NSS) did float the phrase 'principled realism', vowing that 'we are not going to impose our values on others' and undertaking to push back against 'the revisionist powers of China and Russia'.[109]

But it is a fatal error to pigeonhole Trump by pronouncements and doctrines in the context of the two-track presidency. In December 2018, Trump's liberal internationalist Defense Secretary Jim Mattis resigned and made public his disagreements with the president. A newspaper reported the crux of the matter as follows:

> Mr. Mattis's core complaint was that Mr. Trump had lost sight of the importance of the competition for global power with Russia and China, who want 'a world consistent with their authoritarian model'. Mr. Mattis was the primary author of a new American defense strategy whose central goal was to take on 'revisionist' powers—an approach that some of Mr. Trump's former advisers say the president never fully comprehended.[110]

This competition for global power is what matters most as emerging nations scan their surroundings and wonder about the unheralded path the US is traversing under Trump. They must not err by conflating the NSS of the Trump administration with Trump himself or his populist camp within the government. Theorists like Mearsheimer are trapped within the intellectual confines of the world as it used to be (great powers vying for influence with other great powers in an anarchic world), and lack consciousness of the domestic churning in America and of revolutionary breaks in history. As emerging powers are realising, the Trump effect of sapping the US empire from inside is a break from the past and adjusting to his foreign policy requires one-of-a-kind juggling, recalibration and repurposing of their strategies.

Although Trump is a democratically elected president, there is merit in drawing parallels between him and emperors over the centuries who voluntarily gave up the business of imperial domination and conquest through self-realisation. In the third century BC, Ashoka, the emperor of the Indian subcontinent, underwent an atypical change of heart after the bloody conquest of Kalinga. He expressed public remorse for the carnage, eschewed military aggression henceforth and switched to a pacifist order based on non-violence. Nayanjot Lahiri has described his transformation as 'triumph recorded as a disaster and defeat snatched from the jaws of victory'. In an era when other empires were expanding ferociously around the world, it was 'a staggering reversal of the very conception of kingship'.[111] Ashoka still wanted to preserve his vast territorial dominion but lost the will do so through imperialist instruments. The Mauryan empire began declining in his twilight years due to rebellions, family squabbles and fiscal stress. It disintegrated under his successors, possibly partly as an outcome of his legacy of pacifism and administrative failure.

In late nineteenth-century Brazil, emperor Dom Pedro II who had waged victorious wars on Latin neighbours and consolidated a vast domain, grew weary, loosened the monarchical grip and released the foot off the pedal of despotism, which had sustained the imperial system. His indifference to absolute rule culminated in a *coup d'état* and dissolution of the institution of monarchy in the 1890s. Some historians assign to Pedro II 'prime, perhaps sole, responsibility for his own overthrow' and the collapse of the Brazilian empire.[112]

Empires are complex structures and cannot be dismantled solely by the whims of a single ruler. As in the case of the Mauryan empire, the Brazilian crown's fall had to do with social churning and economic undercurrents. The needs of urban capitalism, disaffection of key classes and institutions like the military, and the advent of a republican ideology were all underlying causes. But Pedro II's wilful rejection of the burdens of empire was a striking individual defiance of customary imperial ways. His apathy for maintaining the empire and cryptic republican inclinations are well reflected in his statement, 'Let the country govern itself as it thinks best and consider right whoever may be right.'[113]

Such offbeat individualism was witnessed again in the late 1980s as the Soviet Union crumbled. President Mikhail Gorbachev was no less than an emperor in terms of the expanse of his territory and inherited influence over the Eastern Bloc. His new thinking on foreign policy was a stunning retreat from the Soviet totalitarian playbook of repression and ideological control. By ruling out use of force and violence to control Moscow's vassal states in Eastern Europe and even republics within the Soviet Union (the so-called Sinatra Doctrine), he brought about 'the sharpest break of all with tradition… that glorious ends justify the most repugnant means'.[114] Economic decline, military overstretch and factionalism in the Kremlin were clearly the long-term factors behind the demise of the Soviet Union, but the collapse may not have occurred at the time it did if not for Gorbachev.

Was Gorbachev a liberal in communist sheepskin? Could the Soviet Union have survived if a militaristic hardliner was at the helm of the Soviet Communist Party in the decisive 1989–91 period? Counterfactuals are innately difficult to prove, but Gorbachev's example of an anti-systemic mind happening to be in charge of an empire and shrugging as it dissolves in front of his own eyes is instructive because Trump too belongs to the cadre of maverick rulers who catalysed imperial or superpower suicide.

In July 2017, Trump was given an elaborate presentation in the Pentagon by America's national security and foreign policy officialdom. After being lectured about the virtues of US-forged 'rules-based post-war international order, the military side of our alliance structures', trade agreements and American global leadership, the angry populist president shot back at his puzzled briefers: 'This is exactly what I don't want.' He then regurgitated his familiar broadsides, 'The Europeans are deadbeats, our allies are taking advantage of us, we're paying for everyone else.'[115] Wherever Trump turns, he sees a 'broken international system and unfair practices' being abused by other countries to hurt American people,[116] an inversion of the long-time grievances heard in developing countries that the US and other rich nations had been exploiting and plundering them through the rules and institutions of neocolonial globalisation.

Whether Trump's cocktail of populist isolationism and economic nationalism will irretrievably demolish the liberal international order and finish off American hegemony depends on domestic and international structural and relational factors that transcend his own personality and populist ideology. But it is undeniable that Trump as a person is playing the protagonist in the drama of a maturing post-American world. Individual personalities have mattered at fateful bends in the history of US foreign policy. Frank Costigliola's research throws light on how differences in emotions, sensibilities, life experiences and personal politics of Franklin Roosevelt and Harry Truman caused the US to transit from a relatively warm friendship with Stalin's Russia to the bitterness of the Cold War. Costigliola's counterfactual, 'If Roosevelt had lived a little while longer… he might have succeeded in bringing about the transition to a post-war world managed by the Big Three [the Soviet Union, the US and Britain],'[117] is a tantalising one. But Truman happened to become president after Roosevelt's untimely death and the world got locked into a terribly conflicted bipolar system.

Had Hillary won the presidential election in 2016 (she got 48.2 per cent of the popular vote compared to Trump's 46.1 per cent), we would not be contemplating the coda for Pax Americana and this book would never have been written. We must give Trump his due as the wrecker who is leading the charge and precipitating the decline of US hegemony. Historian Alfred McCoy argues that even before Trump entered office, negative, long-term trends of America's loss of influence had been evident. These included 'a declining share of the global economy, an erosion of US technological primacy, an inability to apply its overwhelming military power… on an ever more recalcitrant planet, and a generation of increasingly independent national leaders, whether in Europe, Asia, or Latin America'. Yet, McCoy contends, a semblance of the fundamentals of American hegemony was kept intact under Obama. Once Trump came on the scene, he 'has done a remarkable job of demolishing these very pillars of US global power'. The populist president made '70 years of global dominion go crumbling in a matter of months'.[118]

Trump's rapid effect on the international order can also be understood through the words of the perceptive Chinese scholar Jia Qingguo, who says, 'The US is not losing leadership. You're giving it up.

You're not even selling it… the change happened too fast to digest.'[119] Letting go of empire, that too in a hurry, is an unsettling and disturbing process if one wants to defend the status quo. It is also an exhilarating once-in-generations opportunity for new wannabe great powers that fancy their chances of a revised world order in a post-imperial space. This book is a guide to how emerging powers are struggling to minimise the downsides and maximise the upsides of the Trump earthquake.

Halting or Propelling China?

The number one geostrategic quandary that will make or break emerging powers' quest for a multipolar world that gives them their due is how the two current superpowers—the US and China—will square up to each other. Is Trump really a tough nut nemesis for China or a blowhard paving the way for it to overtake the US? Will his reign revitalise America to stay ahead of China, or is his America First philosophy inadvertently making China great again? The answers lie in an assessment of geopolitical/military, economic, diplomatic/institutional and ideological aspects of US policy towards China.

Trump has blown hot and cold on China since his win over Hillary, who was much reviled in Beijing for her liberal human rights and democracy hobby horses, and strategic intent to push back Chinese expansionism in the Indo-Pacific.[120] As president-elect, Trump rattled Beijing in December 2017 by upending protocol and talking to Taiwanese President Tsai Ing-wen as if she were the head of an internationally recognised nation-state. His 10-minute chat with Tsai was the first any US leader had conducted with the head of Taiwan since Washington ended diplomatic ties with Taipei and forged relations with Beijing in the late 1970s. Trump followed this act of touching China's raw nerve on what it considers a core issue of Chinese sovereignty by asking, 'I don't know why we have to be bound by a One China policy unless we make a deal with China having to do with other things, including trade.'[121] He later backtracked from cancelling America's adherence to the One China principle, but the Trump administration signed the Taiwan Travel Act in March 2018, permitting senior American officials to interact with Taiwanese counterparts.[122] American weapons sales to Taiwan to defend itself from a possible Chinese invasion have been kept up under Trump. To boot, Trump has also signed a Reciprocal Access to Tibet Act, banning US visas to Chinese officials who deny American citizens access to Tibet—another ultra-sensitive sovereignty concern for Beijing.[123]

In retrospect, these mostly symbolic hostile steps do not add up to a sustained aggressive China-containment strategy. Trump's anti-globalisation economic nationalism and unidimensional obsession with wringing concessions from China on trade have left gaping holes in America's Indo-Pacific strategy. The populist's prioritisation of a trade win over China and his passion for a nuclear disarmament settlement with North Korea with Chinese assistance have provided plenty of room for Beijing to advance its overall worldwide power projection. Trump's businessman persona and itch for transactional deals with China that let up geopolitical pressure in return for trade concessions mean that China's rise is unstoppable.

On trade, it is true that China has faced tangible duress from Trump. The neo-mercantilist American leader for whom trade deficits imply that the US is losing while trade surpluses mean the US is winning, slapped tariffs on Chinese exports worth $250 billion by the end of 2018 and threatened to immediately impose tariffs on an additional $267 billion, that is, 100 per cent of Chinese exports to the US, unless China changes its 'unfair practices and gives fair and reciprocal treatment to American companies'.[124] Further, Trump demanded that Beijing end its controversial 'Made in China 2025' industrial policy for global domination in hi-tech manufacturing fields through massive state subsidies.

In the initial stages of the trade war, the hyper-nationalistic Chinese did not blink and retaliated with tariffs on US exports to China. Targeted Chinese tariffs, which hurt local economies in Republican-ruled states, visibly riled Trump as they carried risks of blowback from his own white working class voter base. Enraged Chinese nationalists egged their government on to go further and restrict the supply of intermediate goods on which American domestic manufacturers rely, or squeeze American investors in the vast Chinese domestic market and make life hell for them if Trump kept harassing China on trade.[125]

Ultimately, whether or not any settlement with China on trade is signed or holds, the fact is that China had more to lose than the US from battling Trump. Total Chinese exports to the US amounted to $517 billion as of 2018, while the US exported goods worth just $130 billion to China. The trade war ate into China's GDP growth, striking at the Communist Party's domestic economic targets and dictatorial hold over society. Stimulus packages by the government to boost domestic consumption and reduce dependence on trade did mitigate the worst impact of Trump's economic war on China, but again, 19 per cent of China's GDP comes from exports and adjustment pains are not easy. Quiet, face-saving accommodation of at least some American demands on trade was thus inevitable for China. Trump often claimed he was winning the trade war, and for once, these boasts were not hyperbole.

On the geopolitical plane, however, Trump has no victory to show against China. Beijing's assertive and combative foreign policy under President Xi Jinping is most obvious in the military and political influence domains, and it is in these arenas that Trump has been trumped. Beijing's ambitious defence spending of approximately $250 billion per year and its multipronged pursuit of pushing the US military out of the Indo-Pacific maritime region had already upended the balance of power in Asia against Washington by the time Trump was settling into office. In May 2018, the head of the US Indo-Pacific Command, Admiral Philip Davidson, admitted that 'China is now capable of controlling the South China Sea in all scenarios short of war with the United States'.[126]

China's deployment of sophisticated anti-ship missiles and the progress of its A2/AD (Anti-Access Area Denial) naval strategy to prevent the US military from intervening for long enough until China establishes a fait accompli have unsettled American military planners and conveyed signals to countries in East Asia that China is the decisive force. The ease with which China commandeered the Scarborough Shoal from the Philippines as the Obama administration watched passively in 2012, and the rapid speed with which China dredged over 3,200 acres of artificial islands in the South China Sea and converted many of them into de facto military bases, leave no doubts that China has muscled itself into an favourable position vis-à-vis the US.

Brushing off warnings from the US Vice-President Mike Pence that the US military 'will not be intimidated and will not stand down' in the South China Sea,[127] Xi's China is displaying self-assurance based on its relative military upper hand. It is true that Trump has raised American defence expenditure in keeping with his NSS goal of facing down long-term strategic competition from China and Russia. There have also been frequent Freedom of Navigation Operations (FONOPs) by the US Navy close to Chinese-controlled de facto military bases in the South China Sea.

But China has an edge here as its primary sphere of influence and military operations is the Indo-Pacific, while the US remains thinly stretched due to its legacy of commitments in Asia, the Middle East and Europe. Trump's obsessive antagonism towards Iran (more on this in Chapter II) and the ever-present clouds of war and terrorism over the Middle East, which tie down the US in that troubled region, open room for China to metastasize across Asia. Chinese strategist Wang Jisi has astutely noted:

> Despite labeling China as the United States' principal rival, the Trump administration has fixed its attention on the world of disorder (especially the Middle East and North Korea), and that shouldn't change as long as China does not commit any blunder that might draw the United States' focus away from more imminent troubles.[128]

Xi is also getting a free pass from Trump on geopolitical competition because of the latter's unwillingness and failure to shore up America's alliance system in Asia. Trump's indiscriminate trade war and tight-fistedness towards allies and strategic partners have weakened the web of friends with which previous US administrations used to try and contain China's rise. Trump's allergy to multilateralism and his inability to look at key Asian countries like Japan, South Korea, India, Vietnam and Indonesia as part of a bigger strategic counterbalancing coalition against China have unshackled Xi and sowed doubts into the minds of countries that had earlier banked on American backing to resist Chinese inducements and threats. The phenomenon of weakening US alliance bonds had started during Obama's tenure, but is booming under the isolationist and transactional Trump. China is loving this trend, which is synchronously sending out a sobering chill to emerging powers. I will elaborate this phenomenon in Chapter I on India's dilemmas.

Trump's flat rejection of globalism and embrace of patriotism is another factor benefiting China as it seeks the mantle of world leadership. Xi's triumphant posturing at international forums as the new champion of multilateral cooperation and his presentation of China as a constructive good guy on the world stage presents a perfect foil to Trump's image of an 'ugly American' with a mean attitude.[129] China's narrative is that it is spearheading globalisation 2.0 through inclusive mega-connectivity corridors like the Belt and Road Initiative (BRI).[130] It amounts to redesigning the world's diplomatic and institutional architecture while Trump is withdrawing the US into a corner for bilateral hardball bargaining to win short-term gains or satisfy the anger of his far-right constituents.

When Trump pulled the US out of the TPP immediately after being sworn in as president, China celebrated as this coalition had been cobbled together by Obama to isolate China. Beijing is evidently relieved to see that the US under Trump has neither the generosity nor the resources to compete with it in trade agreements, development assistance, foreign aid and connectivity corridors. The excess capacity that China has accumulated in manufacturing and construction is so vast that it can literally remake the entire developing world to suit its geopolitical goals even as the US steps aside as a bystander. For decades, under the rubric of liberal internationalism, the US had posed as a do-gooder, which economically and militarily stabilised Latin America, Africa and Asia. It cultivated ties with elites and citizens in poor nations and determined their fates through Bretton Woods lending institutions. Today, as Trump refuses to hand out free lunches to any country, that liberal swagger of America has disappeared. There is only one big money-spinner in sight—China.

Trump is also a blessing in disguise for China at the level of ideational struggle. The liberal democratic values with which the West used to anoint itself as morally superior to authoritarian China and Russia are passé today. Liberal free markets and cosmopolitan discourses about a borderless and interdependent world may have generated prosperity in the West at one time, but they are increasingly being blamed as unjust and unfair since the economic crisis began in 2008. Trump capitalised on this illiberal sentiment to win the 2016 election and since assuming office, has deleted promotion of democracy and human rights abroad as a US foreign policy principle.

The advocacy and soft power lead the US enjoyed over China until Obama was in office is gone with Trump. A survey by the Pew Research Center in 2017 showed that America's favourability around the world had shrunk drastically and was practically equal to that of China.[131] By 2018, polls placed Xi ahead of Trump by 7 per cent in global confidence 'to do the right thing in world affairs'.[132] With democracy regressing internationally, the China model of a long-horizon authoritarian developmental state is inspiring and incentivising poorer developing countries. China's ascent and vastly expanding influence in the Global South, contrasted with the troubled and inwardly focussed Western democracies, are indicators for developing nations as to which way the wind is blowing. We will revisit this shift in Chapter IV on Nigeria.

It is premature to declare liberal democracy or even the liberal internationalist foreign policy tradition of the US dead in the water. Comebacks do happen. But the founder of China's state-guided capitalism, Deng Xiaoping, sounds far more prophetic today than the American scholar Francis Fukuyama, who had launched the doctrine of Western liberal domination in the 1990s but is now chastened by democracy's decline.[133] Of course, there are limits to how far and deep the Beijing Consensus will penetrate and replace Pax Americana. Blowback against Chinese hegemonic conduct and debt trap diplomacy is gathering in the Global South. But Xi has a distinct advantage as he seeks to fulfil his Chinese dream of prosperity at home and influence abroad.

There is no global equivalent to China in economic, institutional and diplomatic capabilities anymore. In Asia, as India and smaller countries are discovering, the military deterrent to China is also diminishing. Except the injury that Trump temporarily inflicted through his trade war, the rest of his actions and policies have enabled rather than disabled China. It would be a mistake to get carried away by Trump's aggressive tone and pugilistic style of rhetorically punching China. A thorough evaluation of his record shows he has been more bark than bite, and Beijing is thankful for it. Chinese scholar Xu Guoqi's reading of Trump as 'a gift for the current regime in China' and his prediction that 'because of Trump, Xi Jinping's Chinese Dream could be achievable now' are credible.[134]

Towards Multipolarity

If Trump's America First entails the US sliding in the global power configuration, letting slip its lead and handing over the initiative to China, where do emerging powers stand amid this unfolding transition? Many commentators and strategists in the West are so used to posing the US and China as the contenders for world supremacy that they neglect the motivations and possibilities involving third, fourth and fifth countries, which see themselves as also running in a race where the finish line has great power status written over it. Elsewhere, I have lamented the paucity of a Sino-US binary vision, which elides the critical contingent of emerging powers and is blind to power shifts occurring inside regions of the world.

> Whenever one talks of power transferring from one nation-state to the other in the twenty-first century, the popular notion is that the United States is in relative decline and will be overtaken by China... Yet power is also changing hands within the most dynamic continent of the world—Asia... A long-term strategic view of the next two decades requires us to take a multipolar rather than a bipolar view, and to thereby reimagine the world order as comprising numerous other agents—especially from within fast-growing and modernising Asia—besides China and the United States.[135]

The story of how Trump, the proverbial curate's egg, is boosting and curtailing the power of emerging nations is as important as the saga of how he is changing calculus for China. When one looks at America from New Delhi, Ankara, Brasilia and Abuja, it is primarily from the angle of each national capital's self-interest. Contrary to the snobbish liberal Western assumption that all countries, especially the people living in them, are bound to benefit from partnering or allying with a benign hegemon like the US, emerging power centres evaluate America via raison d'état and human welfare benefits that interacting with it bring. They resent American double standards, hypocrisy and high-handedness when these qualities restrict emerging powers' freedom of action and maximisation of wealth, power and security.

Christopher Coyne and Abigail Blanco have pointed to the illiberal tendency of US liberal internationalists to strongly condemn interventions or human rights abuses by non-ally governments while not holding allies or the US itself accountable for disastrous military misadventures. US liberal interventionists 'view their own actions as noble, righteous and justified, but similar actions by others as exactly the opposite'.[136] When America uses force, subterfuge or blackmail, it is branded as leadership. If China, Russia or the emerging powers resort to the same methods, they are castigated as brutish and destabilising troublemakers. Apart from conceit, the instrumental use of liberal values to hold back emerging powers that do not belong to the US camp is a serious problem I will keep coming back to in this book.

However obnoxious Trump is in his transactional and pugnacious foreign policy towards one and all, there is a refreshing departure in his eschewing of America's holier-than-thou mentality. His lack of pretence and America's loss of appetite to lord over every region of the world are no minor blips of history. Russian analyst Vladimir Frolov has depicted Trump as 'God's gift that keeps on giving' and declared that, irrespective of 'some degree of unpredictability and mercurial policies on the tactical level', the big picture for Russia is 'in Trump we trust… to do the right thing'.[137] Likewise, Major General Jin Yinan of China's People's Liberation Army (PLA) has said, 'Trump has given us a grand gift, though he does not know it. We are quiet about it. We repeatedly state that Trump harms China. We want to keep it that way. In fact, he has given China a huge gift.'[138]

As to emerging powers, Peter Schechter has argued that the Trump doctrine of abdicating global leadership and abandoning indirect US economic control through multilateral institutions is a dizzying shift, which will push them to adopt 'alternative models to achieve growth and prosperity, bask in this brave new moment when non-Western powers and systems are beginning to look more attractive by the day, and express a broad range of discretion in how they manage domestic affairs'. But ultimately, he sees the 'engines of tomorrow's economy shifting their development strategies within China's orbit';[139] that is, emerging powers will have to gravitate towards Beijing and be subsumed under some variant of Pax Sinica.

I will demonstrate in following chapters that exchanging the tired and withdrawing American master for a resurgent and striding Chinese master need not be the fate of emerging powers if they correctly appraise the Trump opportunity and build endogenous, non-American and non-Chinese structures of cooperation, unity and collective action. Subservience and servility have never been intrinsic qualities of emerging nations. Brazilian scholars Pedro Fonseca, Lucas Paes and Andre Cunha have synthesised concepts of middle, semi-peripheral or intermediate powers to come up with a set of attributes that are found in emerging nations. They define an emerging power as 'a country that observes a positional improvement in the distribution of global wealth and converts it into political power'. This conversion involves 'acquisition of military capacities, regional leadership formation and activism in the international order' to make it normatively favourable to them.[140] Without such a string of revisionist activities, the country will remain economically significant but politically insignificant. In other words, it may be an EME but cannot be counted as an emerging power. Chasing political power with ambition and acuity is in the DNA of emerging nations, meaning that they would not be comfortable with the proposition of either American or Chinese suzerainty.

'Emergence' is a condition of fulfilling dreams of power and influence through appropriate means. It allows for tactical compromises and partnerships as per the existing configuration of global power, but not to the extent of allowing oneself to be yoked to a superior power. Small states might practise 'bandwagoning' or aligning with adversarial great powers because the former are too weak and lack any option to counterbalance the latter. It is a form of capitulation and acquiescence to inferiority. Stephen Walt has outlined the consequences when a weak states enlists as a junior partner of a superpower:

> Bandwagoning involves unequal exchange; the vulnerable state makes asymmetrical concessions to the dominant power and accepts a subordinate role… Bandwagoning is an accommodation to pressure (either latent of manifest)… Most important of all, bandwagoning suggests a willingness to support or tolerate illegitimate actions by the dominant ally.[141]

With the US progressively disinterested and unwilling to live up to security assurances and guarantees in the Indo-Pacific under Obama and Trump, small powers in Asia like the Philippines, Cambodia and Malaysia have tilted towards China for survival instead of posturing to stand up to it. Ted Carpenter has enumerated the reasons:

> The recognition of China's growing power and a belief among some smaller states that attempting to counter it is both more hazardous and costly than learning to live with it... resentment against the United States and its allies as the incumbent hegemonic network... fading confidence in Washington's willingness and ability to protect small security clients in East Asia...[142]

Even a pillar of the US alliance system like South Korea has dithered and flirted with moving into China's embrace. Trump's desperate quest for a solution to the North Korea imbroglio and his compulsive global cost-cutting spree have brought to the fore hitherto sacrilegious ideas like the US withdrawing some or all of its 28,500 troops from South Korea, forcing South Korea to shell out more money in return for American protection, and letting South Korea and Japan defend themselves against regional threats by developing indigenous nuclear weapons.[143] Trump's threat to terminate the 'horrible' KORUS trade agreement with South Korea and his tough renegotiation of the deal to advantage US manufacturers have further dented trust between Seoul and Washington. The South Korean Trade Minister Kim Hyun-chong frankly let out that the two treaty allies had 'heated discussions' and that 'if President Trump becomes a two-term president... I believe there will be continuous (trade) risks during that time'.[144] While not daring to venture as far as bandwagoning with Beijing for security, South Korea has already donned a 'reluctant pro-China bandwagoning position' on economic cooperation and connectivity.[145] A top aide to South Korean President Moon Jae-in openly mooted long-term plans to 'get rid of the alliance' with the US and 'construct a new security community in Northeast Asia where we don't have to take sides either [with] China, either [with] the United States. We can maintain very friendly relationships with both great nations.'[146]

The emerging powers I am covering in this book, especially India, also face a crunch as an inwardly coiling US under Trump falters as opposed to an expansionist China. But being larger nations than South Korea with geopolitical ambitions to be stewards of their regions and architects of the new world, these emerging powers are aiming higher than merely surviving by staying neutral in an ocean of big sharks. They want to be sharks, or less lethal but weighty whales themselves and are looking to counter hegemonic superpowers, be they occidental or oriental, standing in their way.

Philip Nel avers that the emerging powers of today are more capable carriers of the baton of an 'unfinished struggle against disrespect and humiliation', which animated first-generation post-colonial leaders. 'They share the general distrust of their predecessors towards the way in which the global order operates, but they have much more confidence in their ability to *reform* and exploit this order to meet their domestic and global visions.'[147] Emerging powers are difficult customers for any hegemon because they are unwilling to play second fiddle. Patrick Stewart notes that however hard Bush and Obama tried co-opting emerging nations into the US-dominated liberal order under the rubric of responsible stakeholders, they met resistance. The ideal scenario for Western liberal internationalists was 'for the rising powers to embrace Western principles, norms and rules'. But emerging states were 'intent on altering existing rules, not adopting them hook, line and sinker'. The conviction that 'they are entitled to reshape international arrangements to suit themselves' collides with liberal imperialism's objectives of converting them to suit Western interests.[148]

Obama's bet was that a reformed, accommodative liberal order that brings emerging powers into the room can ensure US primacy and continuation of capitalist globalisation. The institution of the G20 heads of state summit since 2008 reified this strategy and emerging powers did indeed warm up to this hybrid multilateral institution and contributed to its effectiveness. But rising powers have not been satiated by the G20 alone and they are still questioning the hierarchical, discriminatory and apartheid-like features of the liberal order. Amrita Narlikar has observed that rising powers display 'a revisionist tendency' and are inclined to form counterbalancing coalitions against established powers, even as the latter have tried to use integrative strategies with the former like 'offering places at the high tables of various international institutions'.¹⁴⁹ Thus, the liberal internationalist project and rising powers have a fundamental conflict of interest, which cannot be papered over.

But what happens if established Western powers themselves kick away the scaffolding of liberal internationalism, as we have seen in the US and Europe with the surge of far-right populism? Is the conflict of interest between emerging powers and the West going to vanish or will it morph into a fascinating matrix of competition-cum-cooperation, where emerging powers fill up the post-American leadership vacuum in their respective regions and coalesce multilaterally around the banner of withstanding creeping Chinese illiberal hegemony?

In early 2016, before the Trump tsunami slammed into American shores and the populist plague permeated Europe, liberal analyst Ted Piccone clustered powerful countries into three camps. The first had states dominated by autocratic leaders and closed political systems, that is, China and Russia, which side with authoritarian governments and defend traditional state sovereignty. The second camp consisted of the US and other powerful democracies of the West, which 'underwrite most international activities to protect and promote human rights and democracy'. The third camp existed between the two and featured imperfect rising democracies growing into stars on the international stage while following constitutional democracy and market economics. Piccone put India, Brazil, South Africa, Turkey and Indonesia in this basket and professed hope that they would develop into an antidote to the model spearheaded by China and Russia.¹⁵⁰

Fast forward to 2026. These three camps are still distinct groups, but the ideological solidity of the Western liberal caucus is shaky as it tries to recover from the far-right nationalist and isolationist spells in the US and Europe. Members of the third camp have grown more powerful but none of them is yet able to equal China in might. What should they do, sidle up to the Chinese tent and shelter under it? Wait for the aftermath of the Trump wave to bottom out in America and hope for the liberal international order to resume under future US presidents? Or think for themselves rather than through the received wisdom of Western liberalism and Chinese statism, live up to their ambitions, take regional and global problems by the scruff of the neck and reconstruct the world order in a third way?

This book is the story of emerging powers at the crossroads having to rise to the occasion at a rare uncertain juncture, when an American president 'contradicts everything that has been US foreign policy since the end of World War II'.[151] The liberal Leviathan is shuttering up behind walls and a brave new world is out there to be carved by those who dare.

Endnotes

1. Franklin Roosevelt, *State of the Union Addresses* (Frankfurt: Outlook Verlag, 2018), 107.
2. 'Remarks by President Trump to the 73rd Session of the United Nations General Assembly,' issued 25 September 2018, UN Headquarters, New York, https://www.whitehouse.gov/briefings-statements/remarks-president-trump-73rd-session-united-nations-general-assembly-new-york-ny/.
3. Robert Kagan, 'Trump Marks the End of America as World's "Indispensable Nation",' *Financial Times*, 19 November 2016, https://www.ft.com/content/782381b6-ad91-11e6-ba7d-76378e4fef24.
4. Øystein Tunsjø, *The Return of Bipolarity in World Politics: China, the United States and Geostructural Realism* (New York: Columbia University Press, 2018).
5. Samuel Osborne, 'Angela Merkel Again Says "Europe Must Take Fate into Own Hands" and Step Up as a Diplomatic Player,' *The Independent*, 30 May 2017, https://www.independent.co.uk/news/world/europe/angela-merkel-europe-donald-trump-us-germany-ties-eu-india-a7762811.html.
6. Fareed Zakaria, *The Post-American World* (New York: W.W. Norton, 2008), 5.
7. Harry Kazianis, 'Why 9/11 Spared China from a Dangerous Duel with America,' *The National Interest*, 14 March 2016, https://nationalinterest.org/blog/the-buzz/why-9-11-spared-china-dangerous-duel-america-15488.
8. Sreeram Chaulia, *Politics of the Global Economic Crisis: Regulation, Responsibility* (Abingdon: Routledge, 2014), 142.
9. Yukio Hatoyama, 'Japan Must Shake Off US-Style Globalization,' *The Christian Science Monitor*, 19 August 2009, https://www.csmonitor.com/Commentary/Opinion/2009/0819/p09s07-coop.html.
10. Amitav Acharya, *The End of American World Order* (Cambridge: Polity Press, 2014); Oliver Stuenkel, *Post-Western World: How Emerging Powers are Remaking Global Order* (Cambridge: Polity Press, 2016).
11. Richard Haas, 'The Unraveling: How to Respond to a Disordered World,' *Foreign Affairs*, Vol. 93, Issue 6 (November/December 2014): 70–79; Robert Kagan, *The World America Made* (New York: Vintage, 2013).
12. Sreeram Chaulia, *Modi Doctrine: The Foreign Policy of India's Prime Minister* (New Delhi: Bloomsbury, 2016); David Mares and Harold Trinkunas, *Aspirational Power: Brazil on the Long Road to Global Influence* (Washington DC: The Brookings Institution Press, 2016); Soner Cagaptay, *The Rise of Turkey: The Twenty-First Century's First Muslim Power* (Lincoln: Potomac Books, 2014); Liu Mingfu, *The China Dream: Great Power Thinking and Strategic Posture in the Post-American Era* (Beijing: CN Times, 2015).
13. Chi Wang, *Obama's Challenge to China: The Pivot to Asia* (Farnham: Ashgate, 2015).
14. *National Security Strategy*, Obama White House, February 2015, https://obamawhitehouse.archives.gov/sites/default/files/docs/2015_national_security_strategy_2.pdf.

15. Hillary Clinton, 'Leading Through Civilian Power: Redefining American Diplomacy and Development,' *Foreign Affairs*, Vol. 89, Issue 6 (November/December 2010): 13–24.
16. Colin Dueck, *The Obama Doctrine: American Grand Strategy Today* (New York: Oxford University Press, 2015).
17. David Rothkopf, 'Obama's 'Don't Do Stupid Shit' Foreign Policy,' *Foreign Policy*, 4 June 2014, https://foreignpolicy.com/2014/06/04/obamas-dont-do-stupid-shit-foreign-policy/.
18. Nile Gardiner and Morgan Roach, 'Barack Obama's Top 10 Apologies: How the President has Humiliated a Superpower,' *WebMemo*, no. 2466 (2 June 2009): 3, The Heritage Foundation.
19. Peter Rudolf, 'Liberal Hegemony and US Foreign Policy Under Barack Obama,' *SWP Comments* 40 (August 2016), German Institute for International and Security Affairs.
20. Shawn Donnan and Andres Schipani, 'Obama Urges Trump to Regard US as an Indispensable Nation,' *Financial Times*, 21 November 2016, https://www.ft.com/content/643f6c9c-af84-11e6-a37c-f4a01f1b0fa1.
21. Gregory Eady et al., 'Comparing Trump to the Greatest—and the Most Polarizing—Presidents in US History,' Brookings Institution, 20 March 2018, https://www.brookings.edu/blog/fixgov/2018/03/20/comparing-trump-to-the-greatest-and-the-most-polarizing-presidents-in-u-s-history/.
22. Linda Feldmann, 'Disrupter in Chief: How Donald Trump is Changing the Presidency,' *The Christian Science Monitor*, 4 January 2018, https://www.csmonitor.com/USA/Politics/2018/0104/Disrupter-in-chief-How-Donald-Trump-is-changing-the-presidency; Zach Wade, 'Disruptor in Chief: How Trump is Changing World Order,' CNN, 17 September 2018, https://edition.cnn.com/2018/09/16/world/world-order-under-president-trump/index.html.
23. Trevor Hughes, 'Trump Calls to "Drain the Swamp" of Washington,' *USA Today*, 18 October 2016, https://www.usatoday.com/story/news/politics/elections/2016/2016/10/18/donald-trump-rally-colorado-springs-ethics-lobbying-limitations/92377656/.
24. Chris Cillizza, 'Donald Trump Says There is a Global Conspiracy Against Him,' *The Washington Post*, 13 October 2016, https://www.washingtonpost.com/news/the-fix/wp/2016/10/13/donald-trump-leans-in-hard-to-the-conspiracy-theory-of-the-2016-election/?noredirect=on&utm_term=.906ffe61a180.
25. Helen Milner and Dustin Tingley, *Sailing the Water's Edge: The Domestic Politics of American Foreign Policy* (Princeton: Princeton University Press, 2015).
26. Robert Putnam, 'Diplomacy and Domestic Politics: The Logic of Two-Level Games,' *International Organization*, Vol. 42, Issue 3 (Summer 1988): 427–60.
27. Cillizza, 'Donald Trump Says.'
28. Philip Rucker and Robert Costa, 'Bannon Vows a Daily Fight for "Deconstruction of the Administrative State",' *The Washington Post*, 23 February 2017, https://www.washingtonpost.com/politics/top-wh-strategist-vows-a-daily-fight-for-deconstruction-of-the-administrative-state/2017/02/23/03f6b8da-f9ea-11e6-bf01-d47f8cf9b643_story.html?utm_term=.8e17ce2c165c.
29. 'Remarks by President Trump at APEC CEO Summit,' issued on 10 November 2017, Da Nang, Vietnam, https://www.whitehouse.gov/briefings-statements/remarks-president-trump-apec-ceo-summit-da-nang-vietnam/.
30. Charles Mee, *The Marshall Plan: The Launching of the Pax Americana* (New York: Simon and Schuster, 1984).

31. Jonathan Kirshner, 'Globalization, American Power, and International Security,' *Political Science Quarterly,* Vol. 123, Issue 3 (Fall 2008): 363–89.
32. Al Weaver, 'Trump Vows to Scrap TPP, NAFTA, Clinton Trade Deals,' *Washington Examiner,* 28 June 2016, https://www.washingtonexaminer.com/trump-vows-to-scrap-tpp-nafta-clinton-trade-deals.
33. Jeff Glor, '"I think the European Union is a Foe," Trump Says Ahead of Putin Meeting in Helsinki,' CBS News, 15 July 2018, https://www.cbsnews.com/news/donald-trump-interview-cbs-news-european-union-is-a-foe-ahead-of-putin-meeting-in-helsinki-jeff-glor/.
34. Special Reporter, 'What's in a Name? Defining Emerging Markets', *The Economist,* 5 October 2017, https://www.economist.com/sections/special-reports.
35. Jim O'Neill, 'Building Better Global Economic BRICs,' Goldman Sachs Global Economic Paper No. 66, 30 November 2001, https://www.goldmansachs.com/insights/archive/archive-pdfs/build-better-brics.pdf.
36. Michael Enright, *Developing China: The Remarkable Impact of Foreign Direct Investment* (Abingdon: Routledge, 2017); Narayan Sethi and Sanhita Sucharita, *FDI and Economic Growth in India* (Jaipur: Rawat Publications, 2013).
37. Lael Brainard and Leonardo Martinez-Diaz, eds., *Brazil as an Economic Superpower? Understanding Brazil's Changing Role in the Global Economy* (Washington DC: The Brookings Institution Press, 2009).
38. AFP, 'Donald Trump Threatens GM Over Plant Closures, Takes Shot at Carmakers Push into China,' *South China Morning Post,* 28 November 2018, https://www.scmp.com/news/world/united-states-canada/article/2175337/donald-trump-threatens-gm-over-us-plant-closures.
39. Jose DelReal and Sean Sullivan, 'Trump: TPP Trade Deal "Pushed by Special Interests Who Want to Rape Our Country",' *The Washington Post,* 28 June 2016, https://www.washingtonpost.com/news/post-politics/wp/2016/06/28/trump-tpp-trade-deal-pushed-by-special-interests-who-want-to-rape-our-country/?utm_term=.c94bb1724389.
40. Claire Miller, 'The Long-Term Jobs Killer Is Not China. It's Automation,' *The New York Times,* 21 December 2016, https://www.nytimes.com/2016/12/21/upshot/the-long-term-jobs-killer-is-not-china-its-automation.html.
41. David Savage, 'At Alabama Rally, Trump Promises Hope for the "Forgotten Men and Women",' *Los Angeles Times,* 17 December 2016, https://www.latimes.com/nation/politics/trailguide/la-na-trailguide-updates-trump-promise-hope-for-the-forgotten-1482020798-htmlstory.html.
42. Branko Milanovic, *Global Inequality: A New Approach for the Age of Globalization* (Cambridge: Belknap Press, 2016), 3.
43. Branko Milanovic, 'Global Inequality by the Numbers: In History and Now—An Overview,' Policy Research Working Paper 6259, Poverty and Inequality Team, Development Research Group, The World Bank (November 2012): 8.
44. Curt Devine, 'Trump's Foreign Business Interests: 144 Companies in 25 Countries,' CNN, 29 November 2016, https://edition.cnn.com/2016/11/28/politics/trump-foreign-businesses/index.html.
45. Allan Golombek, 'On the Subject of Globalization, Dems and GOP Exchange Hats,' *RealClear Markets,* 4 December 2018, https://www.realclearmarkets.com/articles/2018/12/04/on_the_subject_of_globalization_dems_and_gop_exchange_hats_103519.html.
46. F.H. Buckley, *The Republican Workers Party: How the Trump Victory Drove Everyone Crazy, and Why It was Just What We Needed* (New York: Encounter Books, 2018), 12.

47. Bernie Sanders, 'Democrats Need to Wake Up,' *The New York Times*, 28 June 2016, https://www.nytimes.com/2016/06/29/opinion/campaign-stops/bernie-sanders-democrats-need-to-wake-up.html.
48. For the horseshoe theory on this strange fellowship, see Jean-Pierre Faye, *Le siècle des idéologies* (Paris: Armand Colin, 1996).
49. Willard Smith, 'William Jennings Bryan and Racism,' *The Journal of Negro History*, Vol. 54, Issue 2 (April 1969): 131.
50. Jerry Sanson, 'What He Did and What He Promised to Do… Huey Long and the Horizons of Louisiana Politics,' *The Journal of the Louisiana Historical Association*, Vol. 47, Issue 3 (Summer 2006): 275.
51. Barry Eichengreen, *The Populist Temptation: Economic Grievance and Political Reaction in the Modern Era* (New York: Oxford University Press, 2018); Joanne Reitano, *The Tariff Question in the Gilded Age: The Great Debate of 1888* (University Par: Penn State University Press, 1994).
52. Robert Accinelli, 'The Roosevelt Administration and the World Court Defeat, 1935,' *The Historian*, Vol. 40, Issue 3 (May 1978): 466.
53. Robert Dallek, *Franklin D. Roosevelt and American Foreign Policy, 1932–1945* (New York: Oxford University Press, 1995), 19–20.
54. Jeannette Nichols, 'Roosevelt's Monetary Diplomacy in 1933,' *The American Historical Review*, Vol. 56, Issue 2 (January 1951): 295–317.
55. Paul Holbo, 'Wheat or What? Populism and American Fascism,' *The Western Political Quarterly*, Vol. 14, Issue 3 (September 1961): 734.
56. Melvyn Leffler, *Safeguarding Democratic Capitalism: US Foreign Policy and National Security, 1920–2015* (Princeton: Princeton University Press, 2017), 300–01.
57. Dominic Tierney, 'Does America Need an Enemy?' *The National Interest*, 19 October 2016, https://nationalinterest.org/feature/does-america-need-enemy-18106.
58. Immerman, Richard. *Empire for Liberty: A History of American Imperialism from Benjamin Franklin to Paul Wolfowitz* (Princeton: Princeton University Press, 2010), 221.
59. 'Remarks by the President at the United States Military Academy Commencement Ceremony,' 28 May 2014, US Military Academy–West Point, New York, https://obamawhitehouse.archives.gov/the-press-office/2014/05/28/remarks-president-united-states-military-academy-commencement-ceremony.
60. Kagan, 'Trump Marks the End.'
61. Eliot Cohen, 'America's Long Goodbye: The Real Crisis of the Trump Era,' *Foreign Affairs*, Vol. 98, Issue 1 (January/February 2019): 144–45.
62. Mark Hannah, 'Worlds Apart: US Foreign Policy and American Public Opinion,' Eurasia Group Foundation (February 2019): 16–17.
63. Doug Stokes, 'Trump, American Hegemony and the Future of the Liberal International Order,' *International Affairs*, Vol. 94, Issue 1 (January 2018): 147, Oxford University Press.
64. John Ikenberry, 'The End of Liberal International Order?' *International Affairs*, Vol. 94, Issue 1 (January 2018): 19, 21, Oxford University Press.
65. 'Donald Trump's Speech on Fighting Terrorism,' *Politico*, 15 August 2018, https://www.politico.com/story/2016/08/donald-trump-terrorism-speech-227025.
66. Bloomberg, 'Trump Says Turkey Should Easily Be Able to Mop Up ISIS in Syria,' *The Straits Times*, 23 December 2018, https://www.straitstimes.com/world/united-states/trump-says-turkey-should-easily-be-able-to-mop-up-isis-in-syria.
67. PTI, 'US Can't Be World's Policeman: Trump to US Troops in Iraq,' *The Times of India*, 27 December 2018, https://timesofindia.indiatimes.com/world/us/us-

cant-be-worlds-policeman-trump-to-us-troops-in-iraq/articleshow/67268197. cms.
68. 'McConnell Warns Against Early Exit from Syria, Afghanistan,' AP News, 29 January 2019, https://www.apnews.com/97fd806160094dd280e92adec608f3b7.
69. Amina Dunn and Bradley Jones, 'Americans Divided Over Decision to Withdraw from Syria,' Pew Research Center, 18 January 2019, https://www.pewresearch.org/fact-tank/2019/01/18/americans-divided-over-decision-to-withdraw-from-syria/.
70. John Judis, 'The Buchanan Doctrine,' *The New York Times*, 3 October 1999, https://www.nytimes.com/1999/10/03/books/the-buchanan-doctrine.html.
71. Patrick Buchanan, 'America First—and Second, and Third,' *The National Interest*, Vol. 19 (Spring 1990): 77–82.
72. Carl Hodge and Cathal Nolan, eds., *US President and Foreign Policy: From 1789 to the Present* (Santa Barbara: ABC Clio, 2006), 226.
73. Leffler, *Safeguarding Democratic Capitalism*, 28–46.
74. Leffler, *Safeguarding Democratic Capitalism*, 74.
75. Arnold Offner, *American Appeasement: United States Foreign Policy and Germany, 1933–1938* (Cambridge: Belknap Press, 1969).
76. Peter Beinart, 'Trump Takes His Party Back to the 1920s,' *The Atlantic*, 14 June 2018, https://www.theatlantic.com/ideas/archive/2018/06/the-death-of-cold-war-conservatism/562811/.
77. Stephen Ambrose, *Rise to Globalism: American Foreign Policy Since 1939* (New York: Penguin, 1997), XI.
78. Robert Kagan, *The Jungle Grows Back: America and Our Imperiled World* (New York: Alfred Knopf, 2018), 9–10.
79. Anders Rasmussen, *The Will to Lead: America's Indispensable Role in the Global Fight for Freedom* (New York: HarperCollins, 2016), X, 4.
80. Anders Stephanson, *Manifest Destiny: American Expansion and the Empire of Right* (New York: Hill & Wang, 1996).
81. William Pfaff, *The Irony of Manifest Destiny: The Tragedy of America's Foreign Policy* (New York: Bloomsbury, 2010), p. Blurb.
82. Jeffrey Goldberg, 'The Obama Doctrine,' *The Atlantic*, April 2016, https://www.theatlantic.com/magazine/archive/2016/04/the-obama-doctrine/471525/.
83. Mahmood Mamdani, *Good Muslim, Bad Muslim: America, the Cold War, and the Roots of Terror* (New York: Harmony, 2005).
84. John Mearsheimer, *The Great Delusion: Liberal Dreams and International Realities* (New Haven: Yale University Press, 2018), 2.
85. Hal Brands, *American Grand Strategy in the Age of Trump* (Washington DC: The Brookings Institution Press, 2018), 9–10.
86. 'Joint Statement of the BRIC Countries' Leaders,' Kremlin, 16 January 2009, http://en.kremlin.ru/supplement/209.
87. Hardeep Puri, *Perilous Interventions: The Security Council and the Politics of Chaos* (New Delhi: HarperCollins, 2016), 7.
88. Celso Amorim, 'Brazilian Foreign Policy Under President Lula (2003–2010): An Overview,' *Revista Brasileira de Política Internacional*, Vol. 53, Special Edition (December 2010): 215.
89. David Sylvan and Stephen Majeski, *US Foreign Policy in Perspective: Clients, Enemies and Empire* (Abingdon: Routledge, 2009), 25–26.
90. John Gaddis, *Strategies of Containment: A Critical Appraisal of American National Security Policy During the Cold War* (New York: Oxford University Press, 2005), 384–85.

91. Robert Keohane, 'The United States and the Postwar Order: Empire or Hegemony?' *Journal of Peace Research*, Vol. 28, Issue 4 (November 1991): 437.
92. Geir Lundestad, '"Empire by Invitation" in the American Century,' *Diplomatic History*, Vol. 23, Issue 2 (April 1999): 213.
93. Inderjeet Parmar, 'The US-led Liberal Order: Imperialism by Another Name?' *International Affairs*, Vol. 94, Issue 1 (January 2018): 172.
94. 'Transcript: Donald Trump on NATO, Turkey's Coup Attempt and the World,' *The New York Times*, 21 July 2016, https://www.nytimes.com/2016/07/22/us/politics/donald-trump-foreign-policy-interview.html.
95. Christopher Mele, 'Regarding Putin, Trump Suggests U.S. Isn't "So Innocent",' *The New York Times*, 5 February 2017, https://www.nytimes.com/2017/02/04/us/politics/putin-trump-bill-oreilly.html.
96. Melvyn Leffler, *A Preponderance of Power: National Security, the Truman Administration, and the Cold War* (Stanford: Stanford University Press, 1992).
97. Congress, *The Future of US Foreign Policy in the Post-Cold War Era* (Washington DC: Government Printing Office, 1992), 320–21.
98. 'President George W. Bush's Inaugural Address,' 20 January 2001, The White House, https://georgewbush-whitehouse.archives.gov/news/inaugural-address.html.
99. Obama White House, *National Security Strategy*, 19.
100. Bob Woodward, *Plan of Attack* (New York: Simon & Schuster, 2004), 89.
101. David Remnick, 'Trump and Putin: A Love Story,' *The New Yorker*, 3 August 2016, https://www.newyorker.com/news/news-desk/trump-and-putin-a-love-story.
102. Bob Dreyfuss, 'Is Steve Bannon Trump's Link to Putin and the European Far Right?' *The Nation*, 19 March 2018, https://www.thenation.com/article/is-steve-bannon-trumps-link-to-putin-and-the-european-far-right/.
103. Bethany Allen-Ebrahimian et al., 'Henry Kissinger Pushed Trump to Work with Russia to Box in China,' *Daily Beast*, 25 July 2018, https://www.thedailybeast.com/henry-kissinger-pushed-trump-to-work-with-russia-to-box-in-china?ref=scroll.
104. PTI, 'Trump Wants to "Knock the Hell Out of ISIS" with Putin,' *The Asian Age*, 28 January 2017, https://www.asianage.com/world/americas/280117/trump-wants-to-knock-the-hell-out-of-isis-with-russias-putin.html?fromNewsdog=1&utm_source=NewsDog&utm_medium=referral.
105. 'Joint Statement by the President of the United States and the President of the Russian Federation,' 11 November 2017, Office of the Spokesperson, Washington DC, https://www.state.gov/joint-statement-by-the-president-of-the-united-states-and-the-president-of-the-russian-federation/.
106. Kim Hjelmgaard, 'Russia's Putin Hails Trump's Decision to Withdraw U.S. Troops from Syria,' *USA Today*, 20 December 2018, https://www.usatoday.com/story/news/world/2018/12/20/russia-president-vladimir-putin-annual-news-conference/2373305002/.
107. Anonymous, 'I Am Part of the Resistance Inside the Trump Administration,' *The New York Times*, 5 September 2018, https://www.nytimes.com/2018/09/05/opinion/trump-white-house-anonymous-resistance.html.
108. Mearsheimer, *The Great Delusion*, 6.
109. *National Security Strategy of the United States of America*, The White House, December 2017, https://www.whitehouse.gov/wp-content/uploads/2017/12/NSS-Final-12-18-2017-0905.pdf.
110. Helene Cooper, 'Jim Mattis, Defense Secretary, Resigns in Rebuke of Trump's Worldview,' *The New York Times*, 20 December 2018, https://www.nytimes.com/2018/12/20/us/politics/jim-mattis-defense-secretary-trump.html.

111. Nayanjot Lahiri, *Ashoka in Ancient India* (Cambridge: Harvard University Press, 2015), 117.
112. Roderick Barman, *Citizen Emperor: Pedro II and the Making of Brazil, 1825–1891* (Stanford: Stanford University Press, 1999), 399.
113. Mary Williams, *Dom Pedro the Magnanimous: Second Emperor of Brazil* (New York: Octagon Books, 1966), 297.
114. William Taubman, *Gorbachev: His Life and Times* (New York: Simon & Schuster, 2017), 218.
115. Robert Worth, 'Can Jim Mattis Hold the Line in Trump's War Cabinet?' *The New York Times*, 26 March 2018, https://www.nytimes.com/2018/03/26/magazine/can-jim-mattis-hold-the-line-in-trumps-war-cabinet.html.
116. PTI, 'Donald Trump Says China No Longer in Race to Supersede US as Top Economic Power,' *The Economic Times*, 8 November 2018, https://economictimes.indiatimes.com/news/international/world-news/donald-trump-says-china-no-longer-in-race-to-supersede-us-as-top-economic-power/articleshow/66545223.cms.
117. Frank Costigliola, *Roosevelt's Lost Alliances: How Personal Politics Helped Start the Cold War* (Princeton: Princeton University Press, 2011), 4.
118. Alfred McCoy, 'Trumping the Empire,' *TomDispatch*, 16 July 2017, http://www.tomdispatch.com/blog/176308/tomgram:_alfred_mccoy,_trumping_the_empire/
119. Evan Osnos, 'Making China Great Again,' *The New Yorker*, 1 January 2018, https://www.newyorker.com/magazine/2018/01/08/making-china-great-again.
120. Didi Tatlow, 'Hillary Clinton, as Seen Through a Chinese Prism,' *The New York Times*, 10 July 2016, https://www.nytimes.com/2016/07/11/world/asia/hillary-clinton-as-seen-through-a-chinese-prism.html.
121. Tom Phillips, 'China "Seriously Concerned" after Trump Questions Taiwan Policy,' *The Guardian*, 12 December 2016, https://www.theguardian.com/us-news/2016/dec/12/donald-trump-questions-us-commitment-to-one-china-policy.
122. Daniel Lynch, 'Playing the Taiwan Card,' *Foreign Affairs*, 19 March 2018, https://www.foreignaffairs.com/articles/china/2018-03-19/playing-taiwan-card.
123. PTI, 'China Warns of "Forceful Measures" as Trump Signs New Law on Tibet,' *The Economic Times*, 21 December 2018, https://economictimes.indiatimes.com/news/defence/china-warns-of-forceful-measures-as-trump-signs-new-law-on-tibet/articleshow/67192813.cms.
124. Richard Partington, Dominic Rushe and agencies, 'Trump Hits China with $200bn of New Tariffs as Trade War Escalates,' *The Guardian*, 18 September 2018, https://www.theguardian.com/us-news/2018/sep/17/donald-trump-united-states-threatens-to-impose-200bn-import-tariffs-on-china-in-trade-war.
125. Reuters, 'Beijing Won't Just Play Defence in Trade War with US, Says Chinese Tabloid,' *Business Standard*, 17 September 2018, https://www.business-standard.com/article/international/beijing-won-t-just-play-defence-in-trade-war-with-us-says-chinese-tabloid-118091700148_1.html.
126. Hannah Beech, 'China's Sea Control Is a Done Deal, "Short of War with the US",' *The New York Times*, 20 September 2018, https://www.nytimes.com/2018/09/20/world/asia/south-china-sea-navy.html.
127. PTI, 'Mike Pence Warns of Chinese "Aggression" in the South China Sea,' *The Week*, 5 October 2018, https://www.theweek.in/news/world/2018/10/05/Mike-Pence-warns-of-Chinese-aggression-in-the-South-China-Sea.html.
128. Wang Jisi, 'Did America Get China Wrong? The View from China,' *Foreign Affairs*, Vol. 97, Issue 4 (July/August 2018): 184.

129. Jamil Anderlini and Wang Feng, 'Xi Jinping Delivers Robust Defence of Globalisation at Davos,' *Financial Times*, 17 January 2017, https://www.ft.com/content/67ec2ec0-dca2-11e6-9d7c-be108f1c1dce.
130. 'Belt and Road Initiative Strives to Reflect "Globalization 2.0",' *China Daily*, 26 March 2017, http://www.chinadaily.com.cn/business/2017-03/26/content_28683281.htm.
131. Margaret Vice, 'In Global Popularity Contest, US and China—not Russia—Vie for First,' Pew Research Center, 23 August 2017, https://www.pewresearch.org/fact-tank/2017/08/23/in-global-popularity-contest-u-s-and-china-not-russia-vie-for-first/.
132. Adam Taylor, 'Global Confidence in Trump Lower than for China's Xi, Poll Shows,' *The Washington Post*, 1 October 2018, https://www.washingtonpost.com/world/2018/10/01/global-confidence-trump-lower-than-chinas-xi-poll-shows/.
133. Francis Fukuyama, 'Why is Democracy Performing So Poorly?' *Journal of Democracy*, Vol. 26, no. 1 (January 2015): 11–20.
134. Benjamin Carlson, 'Why China Loves Trump,' *The Atlantic*, March 2018, https://www.theatlantic.com/magazine/archive/2018/03/trump-china/550886/.
135. Sreeram Chaulia, 'Power and Peril in the Asian Century: Prospects for Stability,' *The Fletcher Forum of World Affairs*, Vol. 41, Issue 1 (Winter 2017): 80.
136. Christopher Coyne and Abigail Blanco, 'Empire State of Mind: The Illiberal Foundations of Liberal Hegemony,' *The Independent Review*, Vol. 21, Issue 2 (Fall 2016): 243. Vol. 21, No. 2
137. Neil MacFarquhar, 'Glee in Russia Over Trump's Foreign Policy Largess,' *The New York Times*, 21 December 2018, https://www.nytimes.com/2018/12/21/world/europe/russia-trump-foreign-policy.html.
138. 'A PLA General's Speech on How China Should Deal with Trump,' Chinascope, 28 February 2017, http://chinascope.org/archives/11357.
139. Peter Schechter, 'Emerging Powers See Opportunities Under Trump Doctrine,' *Geopolitical Monitor*, 11 September 2018, https://www.geopoliticalmonitor.com/emerging-countries-see-opportunities-under-trump-doctrine/.
140. Pedro Fonseca et al., 'The Concept of Emerging Power in International Politics and Economy,' *Revista de Economica Politica*, Vol. 36, Issue 1 (January–March 2016): 65.
141. Stephen Walt, 'Testing Theories of Alliance Formation: The Case of Southwest Asia,' *International Organization*, Vol. 42, Issue 2 (Spring 1988): 282.
142. Ted Carpenter, 'What are the Philippines and Malaysia Doing When It Comes to China?' *The National Interest*, 5 November 2016, https://nationalinterest.org/feature/what-are-the-philippines-malaysia-doing-when-it-comes-china-18298.
143. Mark Landler, 'Trump Orders Pentagon to Consider Reducing U.S. Forces in South Korea,' *The New York Times*, 3 May 2018, https://www.nytimes.com/2018/05/03/world/asia/trump-troops-south-korea.html.
144. Hyunjoo Jin and Joyce Lee, 'US, South Korea Revise Trade Deal, Korean Steel Faces Quota,' Reuters, 26 March 2018, https://www.reuters.com/article/us-southkorea-trade-usa/u-s-south-korea-revise-trade-deal-korean-steel-faces-quota-idUSKBN1H206V.
145. Chung-in Moon and Seung-chan Boo, 'Coping with China's Rise: Domestic Politics and Strategic Adjustment in South Korea,' *Asian Journal of Comparative Politics*, Vol. 2, Issue 1 (March 2017): 3.
146. Uri Friedman, 'A Top Adviser to the South Korean President Questions the US Alliance,' *The Atlantic*, 17 May 2018, https://www.theatlantic.com/international/archive/2018/05/moon-south-korea-us-alliance/560501/.

147. Philip Nel, 'Redistribution and Recognition: What Emerging Regional Powers Want,' *Review of International Studies*, Vol. 36, Issue 4 (October 2010): 951–52.
148. Patrick Stewart, 'Irresponsible Stakeholders? The Difficulty of Integrating Rising Powers,' *Foreign Affairs*, Vol. 89, Issue 6 (November/December 2010): 46–47.
149. Amrita Narlikar, 'Negotiating the Rise of New Powers,' *International Affairs*, Vol. 89, Issue 3 (May 2013): 567.
150. Ted Piccone, *Five Rising Democracies: And the Fate of the International Liberal Order* (Washington DC: The Brookings Institution Press, 2016), XII–XIII.
151. Matt Kelly, 'Leffler: Trump Upends 100 Years of US Foreign Policy,' *UVA Today*, 29 September 2017, https://news.virginia.edu/content/leffler-trump-upends-100-years-us-foreign-policy.

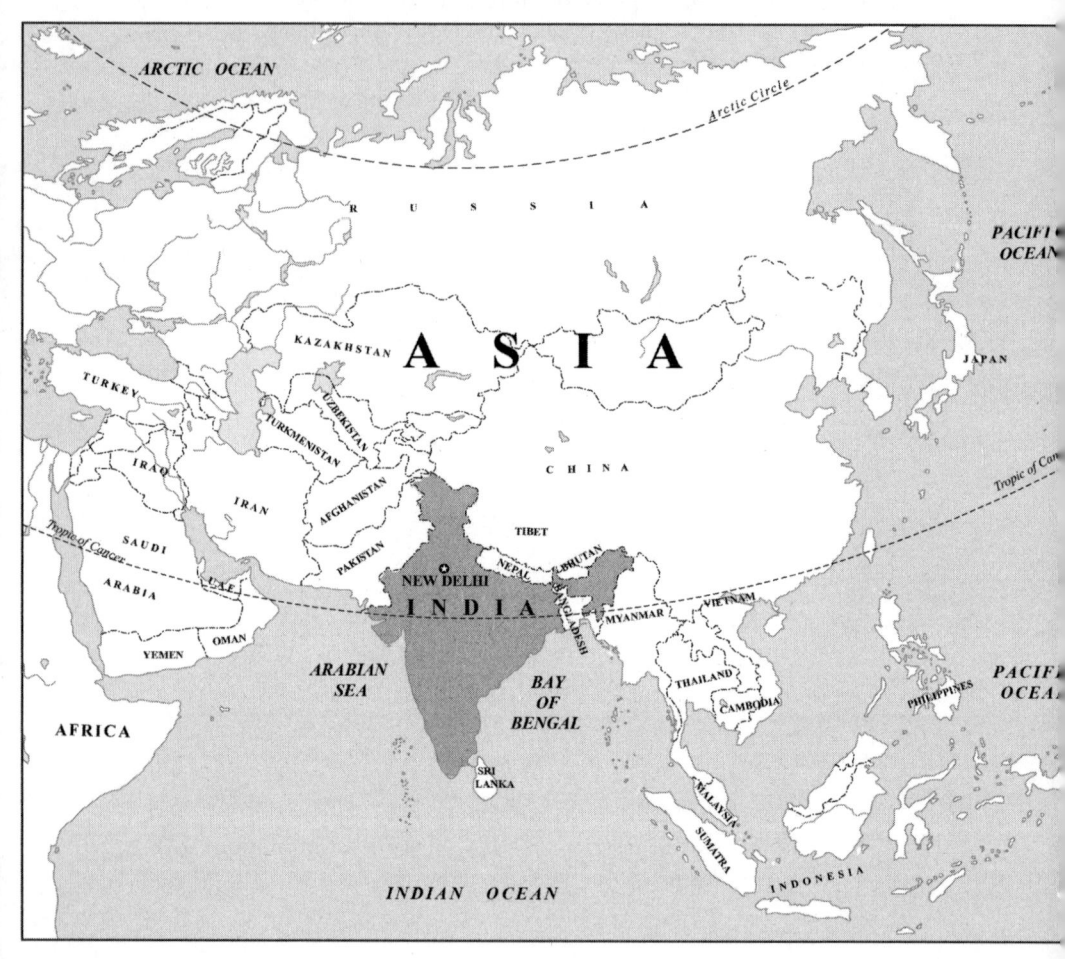

Map not to scale.

I
India: Strategic Neglect to Strategic Assertion

We have some of these countries that are considered growing economies. Some countries that have not matured enough yet, so we are paying them subsidies. Whole thing is crazy. Like India, like China, like others we say, 'Oh, they're growing actually,' they call themselves developing nations and under that category they get subsidies. We have to pay them money. We're going to stop it. We have stopped it. We are a developing nation, too, OK? We are. As far as I'm concerned, we are a developing nation.

—President Donald Trump, 8 September 2018[1]

It feels like the opposite of globalisation is happening. The negative impact of this kind of mindset and the wrong priorities cannot be considered less dangerous than climate change or terrorism. In fact, everyone is talking about an interconnected world but we will have to accept the fact that globalisation is slowly losing its lustre. The solution to this worrisome situation is not isolationism. Its solution is understanding and accepting change and formulating agile and flexible policies for these changing times.

—Prime Minister Narendra Modi, 23 January 2018[2]

A New Context

On 21 November 2014, Indian Prime Minister Narendra Modi tweeted that he had invited then US President Barack Obama to be the Chief Guest for India's marquee Republic Day celebration, scheduled just two months hence. The same day, the White House responded:

> The President will travel to India in January 2015 to participate in the Indian Republic Day celebration. This visit will mark the first time a US president will have the honour of attending Republic Day. The President will… strengthen and expand the US–India strategic partnership.[3]

It happened like clockwork with perfect coordination between the two sides and signalled that the Washington of that time treated India as a bulwark and pillar in the liberal international order.

Senior Obama administration officials 'appreciated' Modi's 'very political gesture' of wanting a US president as the guest of honour at an occasion where India displayed its military might and national progress to the world. The word from Washington was that Obama's acceptance represented a 'judgement call about India, India's prospects and what kinds of relationship US should have with India'.[4]

However, friction in bilateral relations between the world's two largest democracies was not entirely absent in the Obama era. India voted against American positions in the UN General Assembly and Security Council on a variety of issues, ranging from human rights violations in Iran and the Israel–Palestine dispute to the US embargo on Cuba and reaffirming faith in a New International Economic Order.[5] The Obama administration was disappointed when India awarded big-ticket military acquisition deals to Israeli, French or Russian weapons manufacturers as opposed to American competitors.[6] Throughout the Obama presidency, the US Trade Representative (USTR) also fretted and complained bitterly about lax intellectual property rights (IPR) protection for American corporations in India and other barriers to American exports.[7]

Yet, in spite of these irritants, Obama steadily expanded a strategic relationship with India, which Bill Clinton seeded and George W. Bush tapped into in the new millennium. Clinton was the first to rediscover India. He hailed the US and India as 'natural allies' in 2000.[8] Bush described the two as 'brothers in the cause of human liberty' in 2006.[9] Obama often reiterated that India and the US formed the 'defining partnership of the twenty-first century'.[10] All three post-Cold War presidents placed a premium on the fact that India was a rare stable democracy in the developing world, which also had a vast rising middle class that could consume American products and services. Unlike during the Cold War, when India and the US were 'estranged democracies'[11] as New Delhi stuck to a foreign policy of non-alignment and followed an economic model of autarkic socialism, American leaders from both Democratic and Republican parties warmed up to India from the late 1990s because it satisfied the two principal needs of liberal internationalism—expansion of capitalist opportunities and furtherance of civil and political freedom.

India also grew in estimation by fulfilling a crucial third need for the US, viz. geopolitical. As I explained in the Introduction, American custodians of the liberal world order since the 1940s have considered it essential to prevent any non-democratic hegemon from dominating Eurasia and posing an existential threat to the US homeland and its core democratic capitalist values. Over the past two decades, American policymakers have grown progressively more anxious about authoritarian China's spectacular rise and debated how this juggernaut can be halted or, at least, managed so it does not upset the applecart of liberal internationalism. The realist strategy of offshore balancing, wherein a great power strengthens favoured regional powers to check the advances of another hostile great power, was in the back of the mind whenever Bush or Obama eyed India. Bush overcame non-proliferation dogmas and inked a landmark civilian nuclear agreement with India in 2007 as part of a 'contain-China-by-building-up-India strategy'.[12] Obama's Defence Secretary Leon Panetta commented in 2012 that 'defence cooperation with India is a linchpin' of the strategy of the pivot or rebalancing of the US military in Asia, whose unstated but obvious goal was to contain China.[13]

Taken together, the three foundations of the US–India strategic partnership, a phrase the two countries have officially used since 2004—mutual economic gain, geopolitical alignment and democratic affinity—have not always been realised comprehensively. American businesses have often soured at restrictions in accessing the Indian market and complained about the unrealised potential in trade and investment the world's second-largest middle class was supposed to generate. Yet, Clinton, Bush and Obama prioritised geopolitical and democratic aspects of ties with India and accepted some degree of economic dissonance as inherent in the fact that India is a democratic country whose internal political compulsions would not permit maximal American commercial demands on cutting trade subsidies or tariffs, raising IPR protections and purchasing defence equipment.

A consensus of enlightened self-interest informed the liberal internationalist establishment's treatment of India, warts and all. Even if corporate America was unable to extract the highest possible profit out of India, it still stood apart as a shining example to the US foreign policy mainstream. Indian-American scholar Ashley Tellis argues that because India was presumed precious for 'maintaining a balance of power that advantaged the liberal democracies', the liberal establishment in Washington 'justified acts of extraordinary US generosity toward India'. Calculated altruism imbued the liberal American mission to 'bolster India's national capabilities without any expectations of direct recompense'.[14] Obama's claim that 'the United States not only welcomes India as a rising global power, we fervently support it, and we have worked to help make it a reality',[15] underscored the point that liberal internationalist elites looked at the big picture and overall strategic benefit of enabling India's ascent. The totality of India's pricelessness was best summed up by Republican Senator John McCain, one of the gurus of the bipartisan liberal internationalist camp:

> When it comes to the defence relationship, I believe there is no limit to our potential. I see an India that provides critical stability in a rapidly changing Indian Ocean region. I see an India that maintains regional balance against expansionist adversaries in the Pacific. And I see an India that is a stronger, more capable ally in the struggle against global terrorism and piracy.[16]

Having grown accustomed to the bipartisan American consensus that India is a force for good, New Delhi never imagined nor expected a serious departure or rupture. Trump arrived, smashed the complacency and altered the context. Saying India was caught unawares by the Trump revolution is an understatement. New Delhi wished for continuity from Washington after the November 2016 presidential election, and instead got a transactional America First leader who had little regard for the democratic and geopolitical dimensions of the US–India relationship; what emerged was all-consuming neo-mercantilist passion for forcing every American partner and ally to cough up money, open markets and return jobs it had 'stolen' from the US homeland through a globalisation-fuelled outsourcing spree.

At a generic level, Trump's challenge to India is his lifelong conviction that America had for decades been overly magnanimous to relatively strong countries and ended up getting 'ripped off by everybody in the world'. His March 2016 diagnosis of what was wrong all along and how he intends to fix it put forth the issue starkly.

> I'm 'America First.' We have been disrespected, mocked, and ripped off for many, many years by people that were smarter, shrewder, tougher. We were the big bully, but we were not smartly led. And we were the big bully who was the big stupid bully and we were systematically ripped off by everybody... We will not be ripped off anymore. We're going to be friendly with everybody, but we're not going to be taken advantage of by anybody.[17]

As we saw in the Introduction, Trump's ultra-suspicious economic nationalism and wariness about other countries are not concoctions out of thin air. There is a basis to them—the souring of American middle and working class attitudes to globalisation and a US foreign policy centred on globalism. The doom-and-gloom scenario of American carnage that Trump has portrayed as the bitter fruit of the US offering too many concessions to foreign countries while neglecting the economic plight of American workers derives from fear of the US becoming uncompetitive in trade and losing markets to rivals. David Jacoby has aptly described the structural transition undergirding Trump's trade protectionism and 'unapologetically selfish' rejection of generosity to any country.

> With the unusually rapid pace of globalization, and especially the rapid rise of Chinese exports into their home markets, the countries that import large amounts of these products feel deluged and competitively attacked... In the 1980s, the United States was known and respected worldwide for its manufacturing strength, and the economy grew at 3.8% to 4.7% from 1994 to 1997. However, the United States was gradually losing its competitive advantage in manufactured goods... it was becoming more competitive in selling raw materials and natural resources like oil. The United States was beginning to resemble the trade profile of a country like Chile, which has historically been stuck in a rut of selling commodities like copper and other metals, rather than a country

like Germany, which has been revered for its engineering expertise. The United States was beginning to look like a less developed country.[18]

India is, of course, not China. As a far less industrialised country where large-scale manufacturing has not yet taken off, India should not have been much of a bother for Trump. Objectively, it is not a principal offender in his hit list of countries amassing gigantic trade surpluses from the US and allegedly fleecing it. India's trade surplus with the US, just shy of $25 billion as of 2018, was minor compared to China's nearly $350 billion, or even Japan's $69 billion, Germany's $65 billion and Mexico's $63 billion. And yet, trade hawks in the Trump administration went on an offensive against India and slapped steel and aluminium tariffs worth $240 million, followed by a withdrawal of non-reciprocal Generalised System of Preferences trade benefits worth $5.6 billion in early 2019 that had hitherto accrued to India as special treatment due to developing countries under the World Trade Organization (WTO) rules. The Trump administration also filed a suit against India at the WTO in March 2018 for export subsidies, the first such complaint since 2013. Trump's hawkish trade representative Robert Lighthizer castigated India's trade policies as instruments 'to sell their goods more cheaply to the detriment of American workers and manufacturers'.[19]

These were not minor hostilities. The US has been India's largest trading partner with the two-way flow in goods and services totalling more than $120 billion annually by 2018. Trade makes up 40 per cent of India's GDP and Trump's protectionist threats and policies spread considerable worry in New Delhi that the US president is out to spike India's economic boom, reduce outflows of American foreign direct investment (FDI) into India, and pose hurdles to Modi's signature Make in India manufacturing initiative. Modi's bid to transform India into a manufacturing power depends on the free flow of capital from the US and other advanced economies as well as the openness of global markets—the very conditions Trump is hell-bent to destroy. The contradiction between Make in India and Make America Great Again is unmissable.

The other problem Trump has set up for India is his uncompromising opposition to the movement of skilled Indian personnel to the US in the software services sector. Trump and the Republican-led Congress cracked down hard on the previously relatively easy route for Indian information technology workers into the US under the H1B visa scheme. More stringent conditions, scrutiny, high rejection rates, deportations and barriers to US citizenship for Indian IT professionals have spread fear of a fall in services trade between India and the US. Silicon Valley giants, which depend on relatively cheaper Indian techies on short-term visas in the US, petitioned and lobbied the Trump administration not to mix up the phenomenon of illegal immigration of low-skilled Latinos via the border with Mexico and the hiring of talented software workers from across the globe to boost US corporate bottom lines.[20]

But Trump has been impervious to pleas. His populist conviction that local American jobs are being displaced by unscrupulous Indians who are gaming the US immigration system is one more threat to the symbiotic link between the Indian and American economies, which had been built up over two decades. To decipher Trump's 'Buy American, Hire American' animus against outsourcing of services to India, his rant against back offices for American companies manned by Indian professionals during the 2016 presidential race is a classic.

> 'So I called up, under the guise I'm checking on my card, I said, 'Where are you from?', Trump said and then he copied the response from the call center in a fake Indian accent. 'We are from India,' Trump impersonated the response. 'Oh great, that's wonderful,' he said as he pretended to hang up the phone. 'India is great place. I am not upset with other leaders. I am upset with our leaders for being so stupid,' he said. 'You can't allow policies that allows China, Mexico, Japan, Vietnam, India. You can't allow policies that allows business to be ripped out of the United States like candy from a baby. The manufacturing jobs are being stolen. Our jobs are being taken. We are losing at every front. There is nothing good. Our country does not win anymore. The jobs are being stripped. Factories are closing. We are not going to let this happen anymore.'[21]

If the liberal internationalist establishment, backed by corporate America, perceives America's partnership with India as a win-win, Trump and his populists look at it as a zero-sum game where America is getting a raw deal.

Facing headwinds in economic relations from Trump's aggressive and uncompromising economic nationalism, Modi's government delayed retaliatory tariffs and countervailing measures until June 2019 in the hope of softening Trump's anger. New Delhi attempted to juxtapose India with China and reasoned that the former poses 'no such thing as a security threat to the US'.[22] The Make in India programme is far more modest than the Made in China 2025 hi-tech industrial policy under which China aspires to surpass the US in strategic fields like semiconductors, artificial intelligence and aircraft manufacturing through massive subsidies from the Chinese government. Unlike China, which is breathing down America's neck in cutting-edge sectors, Indian industrialisation is still relatively immature and not top-of-the-line. Some Indian strategists speculated that a full-blown US-China trade war would benefit India, as friction between Washington and Beijing might redouble New Delhi's value in Washington's eyes as a less confrontational actor.[23]

Given the existential dread with which India views the hegemonic rise of its giant neighbour China, Modi's government toned down the criticism of Trump's trade harshness so as not to alienate the US completely in other dimensions of the bilateral partnership. India's rhetorical reaction was muted compared to other participants in Trump's spiralling trade war. India did sue the US at the WTO for trade damages in May 2018, but simultaneously tried to sort out trade differences with the Americans through quiet bilateral channels so that the economic bad blood did not spill over into other strategic domains. India sought to be conciliatory and catered to Trump's infamous transactional calculus. In October 2017, India started importing American crude oil for the first time and proffered assurances that it would provide more market access to US exporters to reduce the trade surplus. As part of this delicate dance, official communiques of conversations between Trump and Modi would vary, with the American versions harping on the trade surplus India enjoyed and how to further cut it, and the Indian ones stressing the strategic partnership aspect. Trump's impression that 'the Indian leader tries to smooth-talk him over differences, particularly on trade and commerce'[24] reveals how India tried to fly below his radar and avoid his negative gaze.

But New Delhi's damage control tactics did not succeed in dimming Trump's ideological zeal for an all-out, indiscriminate economic war with every trade partner and his determination to raze the WTO-based liberal multilateral order. Invocations of the strategic partnership between India and the US and Washington's designation of New Delhi as a 'major defence partner' did not move the needle on American tariffs and related punitive actions against India. Sophisticated suggestions, like that of Republican House Speaker Paul Ryan to deploy tailored tariffs that hamper China while avoiding broader harm to other partners, was music to Indian ears but found few takers in the White House.[25] To the populist president, India was the 'tariff king' with 'tremendously high tariffs' that he had to bring to heel through pressure. As in the case of China, Canada, Mexico and the EU, Trump branded India and Brazil as countries that have taken advantage of his lenient liberal American predecessors and must be coerced to pay back to the US. In October 2018, while announcing a revised North American Free Trade Agreement (NAFTA) into which he railroaded Canada and Mexico, he let loose on India as the next target.

> Nobody ever spoke to these people (Indians). He (Modi) said, nobody ever spoke to me. I am not trying to be overly dramatic. We have had presidents of the United States and (US) Trade Representatives, they never spoke to India. Brazil is another one. They charge us whatever they want.[26]

Slapping protectionist barriers at entry into the lucrative American market and wringing concessions from foreign countries to showcase to American workers as wins in his kitty are quintessential tricks in Trump's economic nationalist playbook. Much to New Delhi's discomfiture, Trump is barely cognisant of geopolitical nuances and overly concerned about getting even on trade and capital movements with all countries. Emerging market economies (EMEs), including India, have found themselves on the receiving end of the US Federal Reserve's monetary tightening and raising of interest rates, policies that serve Trump's goal of domestic economic growth but impair investment and liquidity in the developing world. In Chapter II, I will analyse how Turkey's economy was virtually decimated by Trump's wanton policies.

India was comparatively resilient. But its currency, the rupee, also plunged repeatedly due to capital flight away from EMEs as the

US dollar strengthened in 2017 and 2018. The contrasting impact of America First trade and currency policies was conveyed by economist Kevin Logan's observation in late 2018: 'In the global economy right now—the US is booming, while most of the rest of the world slows or even stagnates.'[27] For Trump, the zero-sum game of international economic relations has to be reversed in America's favour. He does not accept the liberal logic of interdependence under which the US tolerated unequal exchanges as long as its overall hegemony was intact. Trump could care less if US leadership and the liberal world order go for a toss, but America should not be cheated henceforward. The former Indian trade negotiator and diplomat Mohan Kumar aptly described the negative systemic effects of the Trump typhoon and how it contradicts India's interests:

> What he has done by way of punitive tariffs on foes (China), allies (EU and Canada) and friends (India) is quite unprecedented and constitutes a violent assault on the bedrock of the multilateral trading system i.e. the Most Favoured Nation (MFN) principle... he has also completely disregarded the dispute settlement mechanism of the WTO... India has a profound systemic interest in the functioning of the dispute settlement mechanism and, by extension, in the smooth functioning of the multilateral trading system.[28]

Geopolitical Blind Spot

If Trump implies trouble for India in economic terms, he is sheer apathy in the geopolitical domain. As we saw in the Introduction, Trump never consistently and coherently subscribed to the liberal hegemonic concept of geopolitically counterbalancing China, which had been the de facto foundation of the US–India strategic compact. With treaty allies of the US like Japan and South Korea themselves subjected to trade punishment and exorbitant demands to pay more to the US despite their crucial roles in countering China's military and economic domination of Asia, India has found that its own importance for the mercurial Trump is quite uncertain.

This shakiness was symbolically confirmed in October 2018, when the White House declined India's invitation to Trump to be the

Chief Guest at its Republic Day parade in January 2019 by citing his domestic commitments and packed schedule. The Modi government had apparently sought Trump's presence at the Republic Day months ago in July 2018. There was stony silence and speculation for a long time before Washington conveyed regrets. It was a snub that New Delhi, inured to star treatment under Bush and Obama, shrugged off but hard to go unnoticed in a sensitive nation like India. The contrast between the Trump invite and the Obama invite for the same occasion tells a tale of the revised approach to India under the new populist US dispensation.

America's strategic neglect of India under Trump was also reaffirmed in other symbolic ways. In 2018, Washington twice postponed 2+2 talks comprising defence and foreign ministers of both sides in a joint format. The alibis for the delays included the unending turnover of senior Trump administration personnel and prioritisation of the North Korea talks by the US over other business. That it took more than one year from commitment to implementation of the 2+2 dialogue (the first round was finally held in September 2018) suggested unresolved gaps and irritants in relations such as the trade war and economic sanctions on Iran.[29] I will return to the Iran problem wrought by Trump in US–India relations later in this chapter, but the point being made here is the vast noticeable difference in the manner in which Washington used to court India before Trump and since he took office.

The general chaos and inability to fill key administration posts, which defined Trump's first years in the White House also affected India, which had to conduct diplomacy without any American ambassador in New Delhi from January to November 2017. The serial resignation of liberal American career diplomats out of disgust for Trump's populist policies and his incapacity to replace them due to ideological and budgetary hiccups affected India too. There was no full-time Assistant Secretary for South Asia in the US State Department from June 2017 until the first half of 2019 when this book was written, an unprecedented hiatus since this crucial coordinating position was created at Foggy Bottom in 1992. The former US Deputy Secretary of State, William Burns, slammed Trump's deliberate hollowing of America's international presence as 'unilateral diplomatic disarmament'.[30] As one of many big countries puzzled by Trump's neglect, India was left scratching its head. Trump is a political animal through and through when he is battling domestic American affairs. He polarises Americans for or against each and every entity and institution in the US with vitriol and acerbic language. But in international relations, he is fairly isolationist and non-judgemental about specific foreign countries unlike any of his liberal predecessors since World War II. To fully comprehend his strategic neglect and disinterest in India, one must probe the principled disdain for America's allies and partners he has nurtured for more than 30 years.

Historians Charlie Laderman and Brendan Simms have demonstrated a steady mercenary streak in Trump's approach to countries friendly to US interests. During the 1980s, when the Soviet Union and the US were locked in intense Cold War rivalry and the whole American foreign policy establishment was geared to tackle what President Ronald Reagan called the 'evil empire', Trump contrapuntally ignored this threat and instead critiqued American allies like West Germany, Japan, Saudi Arabia and Kuwait for free riding on US security guarantees and prospering at America's cost. He denounced 'our so-called allies as a disaster for this country' and bemoaned how 'they have lifestyle because we give them their freedom and they give us nothing'.[31] Completely dismissing the liberal hegemonic maxim that America's provision of global public goods to allies like trade concessions and security of the sea lanes benefits the US and prolongs US hegemony, Trump argued that America should 'help our farmers, our sick, our homeless' by taxing allied countries. In an open letter published in 1987, he outlined what would become the essence of his mean and minimalist foreign policy as president:

> End our huge deficits, reduce our taxes, and let America's economy grow unencumbered by the cost of defending those who can easily afford to pay us for the defence of their freedom. Let's not let our great country be laughed at anymore.[32]

By the year 2000, Trump the isolationist was advocating that 'we can pull our troops out of Europe, protect Europe with our nuclear arsenal and use those funds for schools'.[33] In 2010, he launched a broadside against

Bush's nation-building and global war on terrorism (GWOT) as wasteful errors that deprived America of economic development at home.

> I don't want to build roads in Iraq. I want to build roads in New Jersey... I don't want to build schools in someplace when in St. Louis we can't build our own schools.[34]

India started figuring in Trump's foreign policy horizon more frequently after 2010 alongside China, Brazil and Mexico as wily fast-growing developing countries manipulating the US through globalisation and 'taking our jobs'. As India has never been a treaty ally of the US and is only an independent-minded strategic partner, Trump did not hold as much of a grudge against it for cashing in on American military protection. But there is an analogy between allies and partners. If alliances are costly and unnecessary for Trump unless they generate monetary profits through arms sales like those to Saudi Arabia, he wants partnerships to also yield concrete economic benefits to the US. A strategic partner that does not serve narrowly defined American material interests is no partner at all for Trump. An India that buys more American weapons and shoulders more burdens for regional security in Asia to free up American resources would win Trump's certification of a good partner. An India that purchases substitutes to American arms from competing countries or free-rides on US military presence and power projection in its regional environs, on the other hand, is an unworthy partner.

Modi's government struggled to handle this illiberal pecuniary pressure from Trump. Grasping that nothing satisfies Trump more than a country ordering and acquiring more American products and services that generate profits for US companies and jobs for American workers, Modi shed past Indian inhibitions about loss of sovereignty and signed the Communications Compatibility and Security Agreement (COMCASA) in September 2018, which opened the door for the US to sell encrypted communication systems and equipment to the Indian military. The Pentagon certified in early 2019 that defence sales to India had reached 'an all-time high' and that the 'strategic partnership continues to advance at an historic pace as we continue to increase our interoperability and information-sharing capabilities'.[35]

To Trump, the geopolitical advantages of militarily strengthening India's capabilities are immaterial. If it happens incidentally as more American hi-tech weapons are exported to India, he is happy. But from New Delhi's perspective, it has been chasing the dream of ending the buyer-seller model with all its foreign defence partners, including the US. Attaining self-reliance in defence through co-production and joint manufacturing with foreign defence majors in India is the mantra of Modi's Make in India drive. Indigenisation of core military manufacturing competencies has been a Holy Grail for India since the mid-1990s and it has made halting progress. As of 2018, imports still accounted for 60–65 per cent of India's defence requirements, with the US experiencing exponential growth in sales and supplying 15 per cent of India's arms, while Israel had climbed up to 11 per cent. Historically, India had been dependent on Russia for its military hardware, but its share fell to 62 per cent.[36]

American defence firms, aided by a push from the US government, have contributed to India's diversification from over-reliance on Russia. But diversification is small solace for India, which aims to be a leading power in the world under Modi. The final goal of indigenisation of defence manufacturing is yet to be achieved and the US has not been beneficial towards that end. Notwithstanding the signing of a US–India Defence Technology and Trade Initiative (DTTI) in 2012, there has not been any breakthrough in weapons co-manufacturing between the two countries. Unlike the Russia–India co-developed BrahMos supersonic cruise missile, the US and India have no notable cutting-edge showpiece item to boast of. Lockheed Martin and Boeing announced plans to manufacture F-16 fighter jets and Apache or Chinook helicopters in India, but these are yet to take off. Liberally attuned Trump administration officials have said they are keen on 'sharing some of our most advanced defence technologies with India',[37] but New Delhi is unsure whether the neo-mercantilist US president can be persuaded to transcend the crude mentality of a salesman.

An American leader who perennially counts his pennies and insists on America First in every interaction cannot be trusted to build the capacity of allies or partners. For India, one early test of whether Trump can be an asset in abetting its rise was his harsh response to its decision to buy the $5.4-billion S-400 anti-missile system from Russia. The chief of India's Air Force assessed this defensive shield as a 'booster dose' to the country's national security capabilities.³⁸ It is incomparable in range and precision, and technically far superior to the American Terminal High Altitude Area Defense (THAAD) system or the Israeli Arrow anti-missile system. India, which had relied on outdated anti-aircraft and missile strike capacities, felt that the induction of the state-of-the-art S-400 will make it impregnable and bolster its deterrence in possible wars with China or Pakistan. On grounds of quality and military utility, the S-400 was a no-brainer for India.

But this big ticket defence transaction got entangled in the crossfire between Russia and the US, which had threatened to impose economic sanctions on any country that fills Russia's coffers through significant new purchases. The Countering America's Adversaries Through Sanctions Act (CAATSA), passed in 2017 amid worsening US-Russia ties over election meddling and geopolitical tensions in eastern Europe and the Middle East, turned into a thorn in the flesh for India. For reasons unrelated to India, this American law imposed unwelcome constraints on India's freedom to choose its own defence pathway. Throughout 2018, the Trump administration threatened sanctions on India if it went ahead with acquiring the S-400 and warned that the US president would not be granting India any waivers. This happened in spite of liberal internationalists in Trump's cabinet like the then Defence Secretary Jim Mattis and Secretary of State Mike Pompeo wanting India to be given leeway to get hardware from whichever country that bolsters its military muscle.³⁹

That Trump was piling sanctions pressure India on S-400 as a bargaining chip to peddle more American weapons was obvious. In October 2018, it came to light that Washington offered a quid pro quo to New Delhi to grant the sanctions waiver on S-400 'if India were to give an assurance that it would buy the F-16 fighter aircraft from the United States'.⁴⁰ It was an impossible offer as India was not keen on buying a jet the US already gave to the Pakistan Air Force and which is incompatible with the Russia–India produced BrahMos missile. While trying to make nice with Trump and preserve the cumulative accomplishments of the last two decades in bilateral relations, Modi had red lines and the US was crossing one by repeatedly wagging its finger at the S-400 deal. As a staunch nationalist who balks at any hint of appeasement, the Indian Prime Minister had had enough. He went ahead and signed the anti-missile shield agreement with Russia, daring Trump to walk his talk on sanctions.

Discarding the Russian-made S-400 for less capable American alternatives like the Patriot would not wash in an India where preserving 'strategic autonomy' and an independent foreign policy had sacred status dating back to its proud post-colonial national identity. As I have shown in the Introduction, emerging powers like India are not malleable clients that will do the bidding of the US. India's self-image is of an independent actor whose geography and level of economic and military power drive it to prefer strategic linkages with countries like Russia and Iran, which Trump has demanded India must isolate by eschewing oil purchases from it. By standing firm on an 'India First' pedestal, Modi conveyed to Washington that he will not buckle under Trump's ultimatums, but instead find a path to retain India's strategic options.

Ideally, India wanted Trump to understand its compulsions on core national security choices and not harass it with threats of sanctions over Russian weapons or Iranian oil. It tried to do an end run around Trump by allying with globalist grown-ups in the Trump cabinet like Mattis and National Security Adviser H.R. McMaster—who were sympathetic to India's overall strategic value—to convince the populist president against sparring with India. If these liberal internationalists had final say on these matters, they might have concluded that there is an intrinsic advantage to the US from India getting more powerful without encumbrances. Just letting India grow economically and militarily and not posing hurdles to its rise as an emerging power should work wonders for the US, as democratic India could, whether intentionally or circumstantially, act as a counterbalance to authoritarian China that is flexing muscle across the Indo-Pacific.

Modi wants Trump to realise that there is no alternative to multilateral coalition-building to control China's ascent. Singly, the US is no longer capable of deterring or containing China. How craftily India plays the China card to convince the US is the crux of managing the friction that has developed between the world's two major democracies under the uncaring Trump. Forebodings in New Delhi about the US accommodating China and leaving India in the lurch in the Indo-Pacific are not newfound. When Obama took over from Bush in 2009, a similar wave of apprehension had coursed through Indian foreign policy elites.

At the time, the most dreaded idea in New Delhi was G-2, a suggested arrangement between Washington and Beijing to divide the world into two exclusive spheres and consign India to a subordinate role in Asia under Chinese oversight.[41] Mistrust of American intentions and opportunism in India predates Trump and there is a pedigree of lingering doubts in India from the Obama era about how reliable the US was as a strategic partner.[42]

But Obama at least had the liberal internationalist vision, if not the follow-through, for counterbalancing China. Trump's pivot is to the American homeland, not Asia. He wishes to Make America Great Again not via old-fashioned great power games. By ceaselessly lamenting the enormous economic costs the US bears in propping up NATO in Europe and the Pacific alliance structure in Asia, he has shown a populist businessman's instincts rather than liberal statecraft. From an Indian point of view, Trump's commercialised my-way-or-the-highway attitude and disrespect for India's sovereign choices signal lack of sagacity and reveal a US that's disoriented about what kind of Asia it really wants. Writing in 2008, when Bush had unambiguously plumped for India to counterbalance China, Indian scholar Brahma Chellaney observed that 'while China wants a multipolar world and a unipolar Asia, the US wants a multipolar Asia but a unipolar world'.[43] Under the populist Trump, India has reasons to conclude that the US would not mind letting the Chinese blueprint come true.

Willam Avery, who served in the US State Department under presidents Clinton and Bush, published a book with a captivating title in 2012—*China's Nightmare, America's Dream: India as the Next Global Power*. The Western liberal hegemonic yearning for democratic India moving to the top echelons of the world order and thereby stopping dictatorial China in its tracks has not vanished among US career bureaucrats, think-tank mavens and mainstream politicians. But Trump has superimposed on this template his populist programme, where America First might be achieved without propping up India or counterbalancing China. Which power dominates the Indo-Pacific is irrelevant to Trump who wants to score economic victories over all Asian countries so as to enrich the US and end their alleged exploitation. When an American president sees no heroes and only scores of villains in Asia, he is effectively excluding the US from determining the balance of power in the world.

Recalibrate or Perish

New Delhi's moment of truth about Washington's lack of commitment to checking China came during a two-month-long tense standoff in 2017 between the militaries of China and India over 34 square miles of disputed Himalayan land at the tri-junction with Bhutan known as the Doklam plateau. India faced a barrage of threats and warnings from Chinese state-owned media about the People's Liberation Army or PLA's 'overwhelming firepower and logistics' and capability of 'annihilating all Indian troops in the border region'.[44] Despite China's conventional superiority over India, Modi did not succumb to this psychological warfare and maintained a stoic strategic resolve not to pull out the Indian army until the Chinese agreed to halt road construction and simultaneously withdrew PLA presence from the tri-junction. In response to menacing Chinese references to India's humiliating defeat in the 1962 war, the Modi government stressed that times had changed and called China's bluff by quietly but firmly insisting that 'the situation in 1962 was different and India of 2017 is different'.[45]

In the end, armed hostilities did not break out and the row was settled through mutually agreed troop withdrawals and assurances. American security analyst Bonnie Glaser noted during the Doklam face-off that China had found in Modi 'a leader who is willing to stand up for Indian interests and work together with other countries in the region that are looking to impose constraints on China… and that's something Beijing is worried about'.[46] Although India sailed through unscathed by gutsily relying on its own strategic resolve, one striking aspect about the Doklam crisis was the muted and ambiguous stand of the Trump administration, which India would have wanted to take its side and tilt the scales against China. Barring anodyne statements urging 'direct dialogue aimed at reducing tensions' and hoping that 'India and China can find a negotiated solution to return to a peaceful state of affairs',[47] there was little to indicate that the US saw in Doklam a strategic opportunity to restrain Chinese expansionism and hegemony in South Asia.

Indian scholar Sumit Ganguly noted key lessons from the Trump administration's stand on Doklam as indicators for the future of New Delhi's quest for long-term balance of power in Asia.

> … the administration has yet to formulate a policy that would serve as a successor to the rebalancing effort of the Obama administration… from the standpoint of New Delhi, it simply has not fashioned any viable policy towards India and South Asia. The American avoidance of a decisive stance… may lead Beijing to believe that taking an unyielding stance on the dispute may not invite American disapproval. In turn, this could embolden it to stick to its guns.[48]

American academic Robert Farley speculated on reasons for Trump's neutral silence on Doklam, including his all-out effort to 'get Chinese cooperation on the North Korea issue' and his isolationist 'distaste for international entanglements'. But the larger conclusion Farley arrived at was that Trump lacked 'a coherent strategy towards the US–India relationship'.[49]

Until Obama was in charge, Modi pursued an unapologetic and uninhibited strategic partnership with the US, marking a departure from wary and guarded Indian governments of earlier periods. This US tilt was in no small measure motored by qualms about China's looming shadow. Invocations from Washington and New Delhi during the Obama era that they share a 'joint strategic vision for the Asia-Pacific and the Indian Ocean'[50] conveyed a strategic message to Beijing that there is an informal US–India axis to rein it in. Rhetorically, similar language of strategic alignment between the US and India continued to emanate under Trump. For instance, in August 2017, while the Doklam crisis was on, the two countries agreed to 'elevate their strategic consultations to enhance peace and stability across the Indo-Pacific region'.[51] But much of this pro-India tilt in Washington came from the globalists within the 'two-track presidency' I referred to in the Introduction, rather than Trump himself.

Concerned about Trump's inattention and uncertainty, India has tried to maintain strategic continuity by working behind Trump's back with the liberal steady state or deep state in the permanent US foreign policy and national security apparatus. The prime asset India had was Jim Mattis, 'one of the rare figures in the Trump White House who intuitively understood the intrinsic value of the US–India bilateral relationship and actively worked to expand it, advocating aggressively on its behalf particularly in the defense and strategic realms.' He also campaigned inside the US government for a country-specific waiver to India from CAATSA sanctions for buying the Russian S-400.[52] Sadly for India, Mattis was eased out of the Pentagon in December 2018 owing to fundamental foreign policy disagreements with Trump over the latter's neglect of allies and partners.[53]

An anecdote narrated by Bob Woodward about Modi's visit to the US in 2017 illustrates how the liberal internationalists in the Trump administration worked to continue special treatment of India, but ran into a sceptical Trump. India had requested for Modi and Trump to bond at the presidential retreat in Camp David, which has been historically reserved for diplomatic meetings with world leaders who were close to the US. Trump had already by then hosted Chinese President Xi Jinping for an informal tête-à-tête at his Mar-a-Lago estate in Florida. Modi was looking for something on an equal footing to show that India was no less a power than China. According to Woodward, the White House turned down the proposal and told US National Security Adviser at that time, McMaster, 'We're just going to do dinner here. It's what the president wants.' An exasperated McMaster, a liberal internationalist like Mattis, replied with an expletive-laden fit of anger at the slighting of Modi because 'he understood the strategic importance of India with whom outreach and strong relations were essential'. Trump, who did not understand and was possibly miffed at India over the bilateral trade deficit, prevailed and Modi received only a 'no-frills cocktail reception and working dinner at the White House'.[54]

Following the eyeball-to-eyeball showdown with China over Doklam, despite holding his own and not conceding to Xi, Modi realised he had to recalibrate India's counterbalancing strategy with its giant northern neighbour. While the political and defence establishment still had faith in the US and Modi found a certain personal rapport with Trump, there were questions about how reliable an ally Washington would be in the event that conflict with China in the Himalayas or the Indian Ocean grows hotter. In the Introduction, I touched upon how Trump's narrow America First ideology sent strong signals to America's treaty allies in Asia such as the Philippines, Thailand, Japan and South Korea that Washington might not stand by its commitments in a conflict. The liberal 'adults' in the Trump administration such as Mattis, McMaster and Rex Tillerson tried to assure them of continued commitment, but Trump's harsh words asking allies such as South Korea and Japan to pay up for the US security umbrella and his moves towards trade war with almost all Asian partners dampened spirits and prodded many of them to seek to 'bandwagon' with China. By the end of 2018, all the India hands in the Trump administration, including Mattis, McMaster and Tillerson, had quit after refusing to toe Trump's illiberal foreign policy.

India had to adapt. As the nationalist leader of an emerging power who wants India to emerge as a leading power in the world, Modi did not cave in to China's demands the way Philippine President Rodrigo Duterte did by refusing to further press the Philippines' territorial claims in the South China Sea after its landmark victory in an international court over disputed islands. Modi displayed his combative side by resisting Chinese threats of 'annihilation' during the border standoff at Doklam. Still, he was aware of India's vulnerabilities vis-à-vis a more powerful China and had no delusions that Trump will come to his aid in the event of new military face-offs with China. Moreover, as I have elaborated earlier in this chapter, Trump's economic czars also trained their guns on India as a problem-maker for American companies' commercial interests.

Caught in a bind where India felt jittery about Trump, Modi had no option but to embark on a thorough reimagining of Sino-Indian ties. He met Xi in a crucial informal summit at Wuhan in April 2018 and vowed to review relations with China 'from a strategic and long-term perspective'.[55] Modi never mentioned Trump at Wuhan, but the US president's lack of appreciation of India's role as a democratic stabilising force in Asia was well-understood and resented in New Delhi, and it formed a backdrop to India's moderation of approach towards China. The agreement at Wuhan by the two leaders to give 'strategic guidance'[56] to their respective militaries and avoid flare-ups at the border in the high Himalayas was implemented and there were subsequently fewer incidents between the two armies along their 4,057-kilometre-long Line of Actual Control (LAC). India also restrained political activism of the Tibetan refugees and government-in-exile whom it hosts as a sweetener to dial down tensions with China. Elsewhere, I have analysed how the Trump factor motivated the de-escalation between India and China.

> The unpredictability of US President Donald Trump's strategy toward China is adding to India's sense that it must reorganize its game plan toward China as per the changing international power equations. If Trump has no coherent plan or coalition to counterbalance China, New Delhi will look to avoid direct collisions with Beijing.[57]

Trump's unreliability has introduced interesting tactical rapprochement between India and China. State-owned Chinese news media have heralded the China-India Plus One model of cooperation, beginning with joint work on capacity-building and connectivity to link Uzbekistan and Afghanistan.[58] Beijing has proposed extending such trilateral projects with New Delhi to Myanmar and Nepal as well. With India flatly objecting to entering China's signature Belt and Road Initiative (BRI) owing to sensitivities of sovereignty and loss of control in its own backyard in South Asia and the Indian Ocean region, there is scope for workarounds where it could team up with China in specific developing countries lacking tugs-of-war for ascendancy between New Delhi and Beijing. In trade, Modi has called for fast-forwarding and early conclusion of the Regional Comprehensive Economic Partnership (RCEP) agreement that includes the Association of South East Asian Nations (ASEAN), China, Japan, South Korea, Australia, New Zealand and India.[59] While India is wary of RCEP exacerbating a surfeit of Chinese goods imports and worsening its trade deficit with China, regional economic integration within Asia holds the key to finding long-term alternatives to Western markets that could become more inhospitable owing to Trump-style populism and protectionism.

Both Beijing and New Delhi keenly follow US domestic politics and electoral cycles. Decision-makers in the two Asian capitals have kept a close eye on Trump's zigzagging fortunes in the US political arena. Instead of burning all bridges with Washington or going hammer and tongs at it, Beijing and New Delhi keep channels open to different layers of the complex US state establishment in the hope of riding out the Trump storm. Hypothetically, if Trump is ever impeached by the US Congress for alleged collusion with Russia and obstruction of justice, or his political career is derailed for other reasons, the old Sino-Indian underlying structural contradictions will probably re-emerge and prevent cooperation from blossoming. On the other hand, if the Trump effect lasts, an unintended byproduct of his political longevity could be a higher level of partnership and trust between China and India.

Yet, the geopolitical reality is such that even though Trump failed to check the threat of Chinese hegemony in the Indian and Pacific Oceans, New Delhi cannot altogether throw away the American card to pacify Beijing. In terms of military capabilities and forward troop presence, the US remains one of the key players, together with Japan and ASEAN, that India will need to march to what it sees as its destined spot as a great power. China does not receive any defence assistance, technology or sales from the US while US–India military ties have grown manifold. Hyperbole from China before the Wuhan summit that India was ready for a 'major shift' and a 'new course like never before'[60] could not mask the fact that China maintains an 'all-weather friendship' with India's sworn enemy Pakistan, which poses a direct national security threat to India through promotion of Islamist terrorism and secessionism in Jammu and Kashmir.

Apprehensions about China turning into a dominant global power keep not only Western liberal internationalists awake at night but also the Indian establishment, which has to survive right next door. India's population nurses suspicions about China's motivations and impact. During the Doklam episode, nationalistic calls for boycotting Chinese goods could be heard across India. A survey by Pew Research Center in 2017 showed that 41 per cent Indian citizens held an unfavourable view of China while only 9 per cent felt that negatively about the US.[61] So, in spite of Trump's economically belligerent and strategically incoherent approach, a national consensus of sorts persists in India that China is a competitor and rival that does not want India to rise in world affairs. There is a structural rootedness to this perception because India believes it alone among all the emerging nations has the size, demography and economic potential to become China's equal in the international power configuration. Just as China is looking to narrow the power gap with the US, India seeks to do the same with China.

By recalibrating with China, India is not returning to its Cold War-era policy of non-alignment to defend itself from the imperialistic pull and haul of a bipolar international system. What India did under Modi even before Trump came into the frame was to practise hard-nosed realpolitik, keeping in sight its own pledge to be a leading power and an independent power centre in the emerging multipolar international order, rather than conforming to the Western strategic image of a swing state opportunistically oscillating between China and the US or remaining equidistant from these two pre-eminent powers.[62] Trump's frigidity and callousness have accelerated this process and intensified the onus on India to pursue self-reliance in its national security and exhibit bolder regional leadership in its diplomacy.

Elder Brother, with or without Uncle Sam

In December 2018, Trump sprang another isolationist surprise that left India flabbergasted. He directed the Pentagon to start a drawdown of the US military from Afghanistan and reduce force levels from 15,000 to half that number in the longest war America has ever fought. It was a unilateral decision by a strategic commitment-weary Trump at a time when the Taliban were on the rampage and the weak Afghan state was losing territory and morale. An Indian journalist wrote that the move would 'effectively throw the Afghan government under the bus, and beyond that, endanger Indian presence, investment, and stakes in the country, since it is expected to open the floodgates for the return of Taliban and other Pakistani terrorist proxies'.[63] India had for years considered the US as a vital partner in Afghanistan with a shared goal of controlling jihadist extremism sponsored by Pakistan. New Delhi exulted in August 2017 when Trump announced a new South Asia strategy that promised no 'hasty withdrawal' of US forces, no deadlines for US troop reductions, total aid cut-off and ultimatum to Pakistan for 'housing the very terrorists that we are fighting', and a vow to 'further develop strategic partnership with India.'[64]

Just 16 months later, Trump the capricious populist tired of this interventionist path he had been persuaded to take by Mattis and company against his basic instincts. He announced the drawdown without bothering to consult Modi or any other NATO partner, which had soldiers stationed in Afghanistan. He also authorised direct peace talks with the Taliban as part of his 'cut and run' operation. Like the negotiations with North Vietnam in the early 1970s, Trump wanted a face-saving pact with the Taliban to justify the full withdrawal of all US troops. Much to New Delhi's discomfiture, Washington pursued the Taliban talks in Qatar behind a screen of total secrecy and relied on Pakistan to strike an accord with the Taliban. The Afghan government in Kabul, India's main ally, was relegated in this shadow dance,[65] rendering New Delhi's insistence on an 'Afghan-led and Afghan-owned' peace process wishful.

Adding insult to injury, Trump pooh-poohed India's cherished contributions to Afghanistan in a January 2019 cabinet meeting, rehashing his populist jeremiad about partner countries slyly free-riding at America's expense.

> I get along very well with India and Prime Minister Modi. But he is constantly telling me, he built a library in Afghanistan. Library! That's like five hours of what we spend (in Afghanistan). And he (Modi) tells me. He is very smart. We are supposed to say, 'Oh thank you for the library.' Don't know who's using it (the library) in Afghanistan. But it's one of those things I don't like being taken advantage of. What other countries have done for the last long period of time is given us some soldiers and then talk about it like it's the end of the world. And we are subsidising their military by billions and billions and billions of dollars, many, many, many times, what those soldiers cost that country.[66]

Trump's sardonic belittling of India's role in Afghanistan struck a raw nerve in New Delhi. It felt unfair and naïve to India, which had sacrificed so much for infrastructure and capacity-building of the Afghan state. It spelt out unmistakably that Trump can short-change or dump India for the sake of America First. In Chapter II, I will discuss how Trump dropped a similar unilateral bombshell on US allies and partners in the Middle

East by calling for a complete troop withdrawal from Syria. Here, what is instructive to glean from Trump's worldview is that he has steadfastly advocated avoiding land wars and US military deployments abroad. In 2011, after Obama had raised US troop levels in Afghanistan through a record-high surge, Trump declared, 'I believe in air power... You can knock [the] hell out of them without losing soldiers and losing lives.'[67] Avoiding economic costs of what Trump often castigates as America's 'world protection' duties, and redirecting taxpayer's money to rebuilding America domestically, are core isolationist themes Trump feels he must implement to keep the faith of his voter base.

As with so many other foreign policy about-turns, his intention to depart from Afghanistan was driven primarily by domestic political calculations at the cost of international allies and partners. He could not care less for America's superpower status or its global alliance systems. Only a radical isolationist like Trump could brashly rebuff the long-held consensus within the US liberal establishment in favour of sustained American military presence in hotspots. By calling it quits in Syria and winding down forces in Afghanistan, Trump channelled the average American Joe and Jane. White working-class voters, to whom Trump feels answerable, do not see sense in the liberal American strategy of maintaining costly overseas military commitments, bases and security alliances. Massive American geopolitical power projection to prevent the rise of regional hegemons in the Middle East, East Asia or Europe is a bewildering phenomenon to ordinary Americans. Western strategic pundits and allies tout a globally engaged US posture as necessary for maintaining international stability. But Trump and his upstart base believe it is a wasteful and elitist pursuit, which diverts precious resources from economic problems at home. The elitist 'system' tried but failed to tame Trump's prioritising of short-term politics over long-horizon policy.

In light of the cascading effects of Trump's abandonment of the historic American role as an arbiter, the onus is on negatively affected countries to regroup. India, which confined its role in Afghanistan to developmental assistance and military capacity-building without any boots on the ground, can no longer free-ride on a Trumped-up US to be the ultimate backstop against the collapse of the Afghan state. We are in a carpe diem phase that alert emerging powers like India have to seize and turn to their advantage. If Trump's populism is removing the US as an anchor or fulcrum from crucial conflict zones, the ensuing power vacuums have to be filled. As I demonstrated in the Introduction, we are truly entering a post-American world and astute players must re-strategise to make the best of US abdication.

The delicately poised situation in Afghanistan demands a new approach to preserve Indian interests there, which are two-fold. First, New Delhi wants to prevent the return of a jihadist 'emirate' under the Taliban (who ruled Afghanistan from 1996 to 2001), which again can become a staging ground for anti-India terrorist activities. The second goal is to forestall a Pakistan-dominated Afghanistan, which thwarts India's leadership in South Asia and access to Central Asia. Both these interests were rendered vulnerable by Trump's evacuation because the future make-up of the Afghan state and its foreign policy orientation have grown quite dicey. Since the war-weary and domestically preoccupied Trump was in a weak corner, the deal he pushed would have had to be to the Taliban's advantage and the Afghan state's disadvantage.

To India's dismay, Afghanistan is inevitably headed for a hybrid state with official co-sharing by both moderate Afghan politicians and Taliban hardliners. Extreme factionalism and lack of unity among moderate Afghan leaders have been the Achilles' heel of the state for decades. Once the Taliban enter government, or get autonomous dominion over regions of the country where they already have de facto control, it will become an even more fragmented and divided state. Pakistan would then have greater sway over parts of its apparatus, and will not hesitate to use its proxies there to boost military 'strategic depth' against India.[68] The only way to mitigate this scenario is for India to enter a broad-ranging coalition of regional states to bolster moderate elements in the post-American, post-war Afghanistan framework.

The first-ever India–Central Asia Dialogue in Tashkent, Uzbekistan, in January 2019 was a smart initiative by the Indian government to huddle with neighbouring countries that dread a jihadist resurgence in Afghanistan after US troops depart. As secular Muslim-majority nations close to ethnic minority communities inside Afghanistan, the Central Asians could be seconded by India to monitor and enforce ceasefires, and deploy boots on the ground if the Taliban violate the terms of the final peace deal. As China enjoys a financial and strategic choke hold over Pakistan via the China–Pakistan Economic Corridor (CPEC), New Delhi could also strive for an accommodation with Beijing to restrain Islamabad's promotion of anti-India jihadist proxies like the Haqqani Network in Afghanistan. If China demands a loosening of India's military partnership with the US in return for Beijing constraining Islamabad in Kabul, New Delhi should be open to such grand bargains. In any case, as mentioned earlier, US–India military and strategic coordination to counterbalance China is at best fitful under Trump.

Signals from Iran that it can use its influence on certain Taliban units to help India[69] offered another opportunity that New Delhi grabbed. Given that Iran and India have enormous stakes in the Chabahar Port and its connected Zaranj-Delaram Highway, New Delhi could use Tehran's facilitation to blunt the anti-India edge in sections of the Taliban. The Trump administration's abrogation of the Obama era nuclear deal with Iran (dealt extensively in Chapter II), and Washington's offensive to force regime change in Iran and compel all of Iran's Asian and European partners to desist from buying Iranian oil, have met a thumbs down in India. Just as Modi went ahead to defy Trump and buy the S-400 from Russia, he did not comply with Trump's pressure to join economic sanctions against Iran. New Delhi has a mind of its own based on India First and where this principle clashes with Trump's America First, the former wins hands down.

Apart from Iran, India also entered into consultations with Russia and Saudi Arabia, which have some Taliban constituencies of their own, and can offer their good offices.[70] Portions of the Taliban seethe at being dictated to by Pakistani intelligence agencies. Appealing to the Taliban's Afghan nationalism and proposing a 'no-hostility' agreement to independent-minded Taliban segments, will do no harm to New Delhi's long-term interests. Thanks to Trump's retreat, Afghanistan has been thrown into an epic scrum. India cannot afford to postpone hard decisions or remain a passive bystander. Proactively bolstering pro-India moderate forces inside the nascent hybrid Afghan state and 'softening' the Taliban by constructing a regional phalanx of countries are essential to avert New Delhi's worst nightmares in the coming decade.

Trump's demission from global governance is thus India's historic chance for resurrection as a net provider of security and stability. India would be committing a grave blunder if it remains complacent and content that Trump or his successors in the future would never fully abandon Afghanistan because of America's prioritisation of countering radical jihadists wherever they exist in the world. Trump's populism does have a strong component of Islamophobia and he has committed the US to crush remnants of ISIS and Al Qaeda. His blunt talk to Pakistan, cancellation of military aid to it, and warnings that it must end sponsorship of jihadist proxies lulled many in India to initially believe that Trump bodes well for Indian interests. His claim that the US and India will jointly 'destroy terrorist organisations and the radical ideology that drives them'[71] does hold out potential for deepening counter-terrorism and intelligence-sharing missions between New Delhi and Washington.

But, as Obama discovered during the course of his eight years in the White House, a narrow US focus on counterterrorism is not viable amid complex regional proxy wars where national interests of local players clash. Trump's anti-Muslim bias and bid to go down in history as the man who crushed Islamist extremism are politically appealing to his domestic far-right voter base, but he has no appetite for cultivating formal or informal alliances in Asia and the Middle East that would entail coalition maintenance costs. In July 2019, Trump caused a firestorm in India by falsely claiming in the presence of the Pakistani Prime Minister Imran Khan that Modi had asked the US president to mediate on the Kashmir dispute. It was a rhetorical giveaway to Pakistan, on whom Trump depended for extricating the US military out of Afghanistan. India's preference not to internationalise Kashmir by bringing in third parties was impaired by Trump's opportunistic pandering to Pakistan for fulfilling his domestic political objectives. It was a stark reminder to India that Trump did not respect any strategic partnership as sacrosanct. Destroying 'radical Islamic terrorism' is easier said than done and needs a strategy far bigger and broader than aerial bombardment of ISIS or Muslim visa bans to enter the US homeland. Trump, and globalism-weary average Americans, are unprepared for leading a global anti-jihadist coalition. So, it is up to capable rising powers like India to pick up the slack and stabilise South-Central Asia.

In 2016, Modi's Foreign Minister Sushma Swaraj commented on India's ethos of empowering its smaller neighbours in South Asia with a totally different philosophy from that of the West.

> The Hindi meaning of big brother is elder brother. But the construct of big brother is a Western one. Its Indian translation is elder brother. We view it from a different perspective. Big brother is egotist whereas elder brother shows concern. Elder brother tries to assist you in solving your problems. India is that elder brother who will never become the cause of your difficulties and will assist you. I welcome you as the elder sister of that elder brother.[72]

Trump has jolted India into playing this elder brother character not just in its immediate neighbourhood but across South-Central Asia. His exasperated question about Afghanistan, 'Why are we there, and we're 6,000 miles away?' when India, Russia and Pakistan were apparently not there,[73] is emblematic of how the US has lost interest and wants to shed the burden of running the show by transferring it to local actors. India's rise as a great power can only occur if it grasps this opportunity and helps construct an alternative regional order as per non-Western civilisational principles.

Indo-Pacific from Inside

The same eureka moment applies to the Indo-Pacific region, where Trump's ham-fisted policies emboldened China and scared off America's treaty allies and partners. India is too big and ambitious an emerging power to bandwagon with China as an escape from the dilemma posed by Trump's insouciance for the mantra of offshore balancing to limit Chinese expansionism. New Delhi's 'Act East' policy (a phrase uttered by Obama's Secretary of State Hillary Clinton in 2011, which was adopted as official Indian strategy in 2014) has to evolve into a long-term quest for endogenous collective security across Asia's littoral space.

Officials in the Trump administration often reiterate Obama-era language that the US wants India to be the 'leading power' in the Indo-Pacific.[74] But as I adumbrated in the Introduction, the liberal American strategic thrust to contain China through multilateral coalitions has gone abegging under the populist Trump. Instead of liberally putting backbone into US allies and partners in Asia, which have to contend with a sharply deteriorating balance of power as China grows in heft, Trump has spooked a whole range of them through insults and threats. South Korea, the essential actor for finding a solution to the nuclear and missile threat of North Korea and a key component in the US Pacific alliance to check China, was dealt an untimely confidence shock by Trump's aggressive renegotiation of the KORUS trade deal and his hardball bargaining to force Seoul to pay more for hosting American soldiers. The episodes confirmed the worst fears in East Asia that the US can no longer be relied upon as a magnanimous great power.

The mercantilist and economic nationalist America First ideology, which blames trading partners for the woes of the US working class, goes against the bedrock principle with which the US built its post-World War II alliances in the Pacific—generosity as a provider of security, market access and financing. Trump's insistence that South Korea should pay $1 billion for the THAAD anti-missile system[75] and his pre-presidential jab that South Korea and Japan should acquire their own nuclear weapons have sown massive doubts about the historic assumption that the US bears costs to defend its allies and thereby earns their gratitude and acceptance. As an unabashed salesman, Trump's mercenary offers to South Korea and Japan to buy 'highly sophisticated military equipment' to ward off the North Korean menace[76] reconfirmed how transactional his foreign policy is. Ally or foe, whoever shells out cash gets Trump's thumbs-up and anyone who seeks the old arrangements of taking shelter under a big American tent will be told to take a walk.

The patronage machine that was America and which attracted many due to its free public goods is being wound down. South Korean President Moon Jae-in realised this and announced a New Southern Policy in November 2017 to reduce dependence on traditional partners like the US and diversify Seoul's connections with ASEAN and India. As I mentioned in the Introduction, South Korea has also adjusted to Trump through economic bandwagoning with China and Moon has labelled his Southern Policy a mirror of his New Northern Policy to cooperate more deeply with China, Japan, Russia and Mongolia.[77] Anyone but the US is now valuable to a South Korea that feels spurned and humiliated by its historic ally.

Japanese Prime Minister Shinzo Abe was the only significant ally that Trump did not rub the wrong way, possibly due to the US president's personal quirks and Abe's assiduous personalised courting of Trump from the moment he won the election. But on the question that really matters to Japan—will America stand up for it against a progressively assertive China and a fiery North Korea—Abe got no unambiguous strategic assurance from the Trump administration. Tokyo watched with dismay as China's sphere of influence expanded to unprecedented levels in Asia and Trump blew hot and cold on Beijing with no doctrinal certainty. The revival of discourse within Japan about developing pre-emptive military capabilities to strike North Korea on its own[78] showed how low Trump was rated in Tokyo beyond polite niceties and invocations of the special alliance. Japan's stewarding of the TPP-11 without the US, which pulled out the moment Trump entered the White House, was an indicator that even obedient allies have limits to their patience and that multilateral processes for regional integration and stability will not wait for the US to exorcise Trump's ghost and revert to liberal internationalism.[79]

Following Trump's grumpy personal exchanges with then Australian Prime Minister Malcolm Turnbull in early 2017, Canberra has also mulled its traditional reliance on the American alliance and showed signals that it may have to acquiesce to China's inevitable supremacy. Australian scholar Hugh White's analysis that Trump was pushing Australia into China's lap because the US president 'believes that allies are dispensable',[80] and former diplomat Stephen FitzGerald's comment that Australia should adjust to 'living in a Chinese world'[81] were canaries in the coal mine. But like South Korea and Japan, Australia cannot entirely untie its entrenched security alliance network with the US because of its dependent situation and panic about Chinese intervention in its internal politics.[82] Cast away by Trump and coveted by Xi, these countries have to come up with new modes of survival and prosperity.

There is only one viable long-term strategy for smaller powers to maintain independence in the Indo-Pacific when the US has gone AWOL as the regional policeman and China is too overbearing and dangerous—forming non-American and non-Chinese groupings that ensure endogenous security and prosperity. India has the potential to step up and be a coordinator of these intra-Asian stabilising mechanisms. It has the goodwill and capabilities to overcome the imbalance in power in Asia by coordinating a new intra-Asian formation for stability. In 2014, with Obama seemingly indecisive to roll back Chinese hegemony, an Indian and an Australian scholar recommended a model of 'minilateral cooperation' among Asia's middle powers, India, Japan, South Korea, Australia, Indonesia, Vietnam and other ASEAN countries, so as to 'build regional resilience against the vagaries of the US–China relationship'.[83] With Trump's isolationist and opportunistic foreign policy, this idea carries greater merit and relevance.

Flexible coalitions of Asian middle powers cannot strictly counter China in the event of an armed conflict involving the latter and a smaller Asian power because 'the material capacities of a combination of regional powers minus the United States—say Japan and India plus several others—would not be a match for China'.[84] Moreover, China wields an advantage in Asia by virtue of internal divisions between Japan and South Korea, courtesy historical bad blood,[85] and Beijing's skill in sowing divisions within ASEAN into sub-blocs of pro-China and anti-China groupings.[86] Even in South Asia, where India hopes to unify the entire subregion under its leadership as a counterweight to China, Beijing has made crucial inroads and forged a set of nations who have sought participation in the BRI to attract Chinese financing.[87]

Nonetheless, among all these countries, there is trepidation about China trampling on their sovereignty or crushing them under a debt trap. All of them are looking for freedom of choices to avoid dictation by China. Security coordination among Asia's smaller players that do not include China or the US would signal to Beijing and Washington that the era of dependence on either of them is passé in the Asian century. Relatively weaker but upwardly mobile Asian states have to be proactive in their geostrategic approach in keeping with their rising power profiles or suffer the fate of becoming vassals or tribute-paying territories to an imperial Beijing, as was the case in East Asia before the advent of the Europeans and Americans.[88] In the case of the Philippines, as I mentioned in the Introduction, President Rodrigo Duterte rhetorically proclaimed a drastic policy shift of separation from the US and a new alliance with

China and Russia.[89] But there cannot be a partnership of equals between puny Philippines and mighty China. It would be wiser for the Philippines to join a non-Chinese, non-American constellation to protect its interests. Trump's illiberal reversal of Obama-era American criticism of Duterte's abusive war on drugs and his praise for the autocratic actions of the latter produced an improvement in ties between the Philippines and the US after 2017,[90] but Manila needs to look beyond oscillating between Washington and Beijing in the long run.

In the Trumped world order, leading Asian powers like India and Indonesia, which abhor being subordinated either under Chinese or American hegemony, have to assay central roles in strengthening the bonds among countries falling in the subregions of South Asia, Central Asia, Southeast Asia and Northeast Asia. New Delhi and Jakarta could come up with a novel diplomatic forum for Asian Alternative Security that explicitly keeps out the US and China and promotes intra-Asian conflict mitigation solutions and builds strategic trust in the entire continent. Neutrality from the US and China could be the cornerstone of this alternative institution, earning respect from both Washington and Beijing and hence safe from being sabotaged by either of them. Admittedly, there cannot be security in Asia without China's consent and willingness, but in the absence of a pan-Asian institution like the pan-European Organization for Security and Cooperation in Europe (OSCE), it would make sense for multipolar Asia to evolve new non-universal security coordination mechanisms that disallow China or the US to trample over or curtail the interests of rising powers.

More Asian countries are individually empowered today than they were at the turn of the twenty-first century. But for this individual growth and success to translate into collective security manned by a network of multiple power centres, institutional innovation is the need of the hour. The ideation and conceptualisation of cohabitation mechanisms must come from Asia's ascendant and independent power centres, like India and Indonesia, for wider acceptance and credibility. India and Indonesia once found common cause as the guiding stars of the Non-Aligned Movement during the Cold War era. Then, they were recently decolonised, poor and weak nations struggling to build viable nation-states and driven by anti-imperial ideals. Today, they are en route to the club of great powers in a multipolar order. If they fail to grasp the historical window of opportunity to act as leaders and anchors of multipolarity in Asia, they would be the ultimate losers of the deteriorating strategic milieu around them.

The agreement in May 2018 between New Delhi and Jakarta for India to develop its first overseas deep-sea port in Indonesia's Sabang is a landmark step in the right direction. Sabang would grant India greater access to ASEAN markets and give it a strategic hedge at a time China is increasing its presence in the Strait of Malacca (as also the larger Indian Ocean).[91] As an independent developing country with a sense of post-colonial grievance, India once abhorred power politics and rejected the quest for overseas military bases as imperialist. During the height of the Cold War, India vehemently opposed American, British and French militarisation of the Indian Ocean and sought to exclude these extra-regional powers from its maritime neighbourhood. Ideological objections to engage in geopolitics and use the Indian military to establish a sphere of influence continued to restrain New Delhi even after the Cold War. The port of Hambantota at the southern end of Sri Lanka, which was handed over to China on a 99-year lease in 2017, was first offered to India in 2003. Despite repeated invitations from the Sri Lankan government, Indian leaders hemmed and hawed, losing a chance to shape the central sector of the Indian Ocean region. The huge Chinese presence at Hambantota, close to the tip of southern India, has now become a strategic nightmare for New Delhi. In 2017, Modi extracted a commitment from Colombo for India to develop the Trincomalee port on Sri Lanka's east coast to counter the Chinese.[92] Still, Hambantota poses a risk to India that echoes the threat the US once faced from the Soviet Union's presence in Cuba, just 90 miles (about 145 kilometres) from Florida's beaches.

In 2011, Vietnam offered New Delhi exclusive naval access to the port of Nha Trang, overlooking China's key naval and cyberwarfare centre on Hainan Island. But India failed to move this proposition forward.[93] New Delhi has since struggled to find a permanent base in the South China Sea region due to its relatively limited naval might and angst amid Southeast Asian countries about upsetting China. The aggressive inroads that China has made in the Indian Ocean over the last decade and Beijing's assertion that it does not accept these seas as India's backyard pose an unprecedented challenge to New Delhi. Regular Chinese naval activity in Myanmar, Bangladesh, Sri Lanka, the Maldives and Djibouti has worried India and increased pressure on it for a firm response.

In March 2018, India signed a military agreement with France, which paved the way for Indian armed forces to use France's defence installations in Djibouti, Abu Dhabi and Reunion Island, all pivotal locations in the western Indian Ocean. Modi has also engaged in proactive defence diplomacy to gain entry to the port of Duqm through a military agreement with Oman in February 2018 that will allow Indian military vessels to dock for maintenance. Duqm will help India to buttress its most valuable asset in the Arabian Sea, the Iranian port of Chabahar, which is New Delhi's gateway to Afghanistan and Central Asia.[94] Further south off the east African coast, India is working to improve surveillance and defence infrastructure by developing Assumption Island with the Seychelles and Agalega Island with Mauritius.

Taken together, the French footholds and naval arrangements with Middle Eastern and African countries help advance India's claims to be a 'net security provider' in the Indian Ocean. Modi's naval strategy is a marked departure from the doubts that historically cost India heavily as it conceded geopolitical space to adversaries, notably China. The economic benefits China dangles to poor nations throughout the Indian Ocean region surpass whatever grants or loans India can afford to muster. Yet, paucity of funds has not dulled India's eagerness. Aware that India cannot win a one-to-one contest with a richer China, Modi is relying on partnerships with friendly countries across Asia, the Middle East and Africa, which is the ideal approach for an emerging power that lacks preponderant economic and military might of its own.

India could also enhance its international prestige by taking the lead in institutional innovation to solve the pressing global challenge of climate change, which Trump initially derided as a 'hoax' and later switched to denying it had man-made causes or any long-lasting harmful impact.[95] India was one of the key developing countries that reiterated its commitment to the Paris Climate accord after Trump pulled the US out of the Obama-supported multilateral environmental pact in June 2017. Modi's brainchild, the International Solar Alliance (ISA), which brings together 122 member countries around the shared interest of a post-fossil fuel future, has the potential to be a leading forum for ushering in a direly needed green energy transition. Modi envisages the 'ISA will play the role of OPEC [Organisation of the Petroleum Exporting Countries] in the future and will meet the energy requirements of the world in the years to come'.[96] As the US under Trump shifts to digging more coal and subverting the international structure for mitigating climate change, India is poised to fill the vacuum in partnership with developed and developing countries that care about the planet's welfare.[97]

On matters of economic connectivity and modernisation in Asia too, India will have to show acuity to correct the imbalance in favour of China's BRI, which has enveloped most of the region in its fold. China's rapid progress in connectivity diplomacy prompted India to pull up its socks and make haste with endeavours like the Chabahar port project with Iran. This scheme was originally mooted with Iran in 2002 but became a reality only under Modi in 2016. The BRI's advance into India's sphere of influence is a spur for New Delhi to speed up its own smaller multilateral connectivity arrangements like the Asia–Africa Growth Corridor (AAGC), in collaboration with Japan.[98] India's old reputation as a bureaucratically hampered slowcoach has been mitigated by Modi's urgent push to avoid geostrategic marginalisation. Japan's keenness to team up with India on AAGC as well as Chabahar shows that other Asian countries are also intent on catching up with China's advances by floating rival projects.

Competition with China is not unhealthy if it drives India and others to raise their game, to invest more in communications in Asia and project their own influence and ideas. The AAGC and Chabahar could be launch pads for an Indo-centric Indo-Pacific, whether or not the US wants to be involved. These international connectivity corridors could ultimately prove more fruitful than the Quad of India, Japan, Australia and the US—a joint security cooperation format devoted to a 'free and open Indo-Pacific', which has made fitful progress mainly due to Trump's blindness to geopolitical counterbalancing and antagonising attitude to Asian allies.[99] The US under Trump is the weakest link in the

Quad's chain. Waiting for it to revert to a liberal internationalist posture is a recipe for forfeiting valuable time and space as China extends its arc of influence.

Indian academic S.D. Muni stated even before Trump's isolationist reversal that India had cooperated with Obama's pivot to Asia only on its terms and not as an appendage of the US.[100] Asserting India's footprint in Asia instead of leaning on America's shoulders has become more imperative with the unpredictable and materially self-centric Trump in office. India does not presently have the wherewithal to replace the US or China as the pre-eminent actor in Asia, but it has the soft power and convening power attributes to construct a balanced region in concert with other middle powers. Ideationally, emerging powers like India and Turkey have their own sense of exceptionalism that is distinct from liberal American exceptionalism or Chinese civilisational exceptionalism.[101] Swaraj spelt this out in 2018 by narrating an exchange that occurred on the sidelines of the UN General Assembly.

> I was sad when President Trump, in the UN General Assembly, said his slogan was 'Me First'. There is a storm of protectionism at the global level, which is centred around the concept of 'Me and Myself' but India believes in the concept of 'We, Us and Ourselves'. If everyone views the other as equal, then there is no place for protectionism in it. A Foreign Minister of a small country spoke about President Trump's speech of 'Me First'. She said if everyone says (and follows the policy) of 'Me First' then how will my country sustain? I said India does not have the tradition of 'Me First'. I said my speech will have 'Om Sarve Bhavantu Sukhinah' (May everyone be happy). India believes in the policy of assisting other countries, especially those who require a helping hand. If we don't do this, then developed countries will continue to grow and underdeveloped countries will remain underdeveloped. So how will economic disparity reduce?[102]

Emergence is a condition and a process of rising from one level to a higher one. Under Modi, India embarked on this journey in 2014. It has miles to go. But when it does become a great power, historians will look back and judge how well it utilised the unprecedented opening offered by Trump's ceding of liberal American hegemony.

Endnotes

1. PTI, 'America a "Developing Nation", Can't Fund India, China Subsidies,' *The Times of India*, 9 September 2018, https://timesofindia.indiatimes.com/world/us/america-a-developing-nation-cant-fund-india-china-subsidies-trump/articleshow/65737758.cms.
2. AFP, 'India's Modi Defends Open Trade Despite Globalisation's Waning Allure,' *Gulf News*, 23 January 2018, https://gulfnews.com/business/indias-modi-defends-open-trade-despite-globalisations-waning-allure-1.2161905.
3. Yashwant Raj and Jayanth Jacob, 'Obama Accepts Modi's Invitation to be Chief Guest at Republic Day,' *Hindustan Times*, 22 November 2014, https://www.hindustantimes.com/india/obama-accepts-modi-s-invitation-to-be-chief-guest-at-republic-day/story-c3aaQCr7iieLWNQwJEy5aI.html.
4. Lalit Jha, 'Barack Obama Invite Idea Came from Narendra Modi,' *Mint*, 21 January 2015, https://www.livemint.com/Politics/bibEbK4ORYJc5irrGsazgJ/Barack-Obama-invite-idea-came-from-PM-Narendra-Modi.html.
5. Patrick Goodenough, 'India's Warm Ties with US Not Reflected in Its Voting at UN,' CNS News, 9 June 2016, https://www.cnsnews.com/news/article/patrick-goodenough/indias-warm-ties-us-not-reflected-its-voting-un.
6. Rama Lakshmi, 'US Firms Lose Out in India Fighter Jet Deal,' *The Washington Post*, 28 April 2011, https://www.washingtonpost.com/world/us-companies-bypassed-in-india-fighter-jet-deal/2011/04/28/AFPVwC5E_story.html?utm_term=.a0e593e9eddb.
7. Nayanima Basu, 'India Has Weak Intellectual Property Rules: Michael Froman,' *Business Standard*, 15 July 2013, https://www.business-standard.com/article/economy-policy/india-has-weak-intellectual-property-rules-michael-froman-113071500029_1.html.
8. 'Remarks by the President to the Indian Joint Session of Parliament', 22 March 2000, Parliament, New Delhi, https://clintonwhitehouse6.archives.gov/2000/03/2000-03-22-remarks-by-the-president-to-the-indian-parliament.html.
9. 'President Discusses Strong US–India Partnership in New Delhi, India,' 3 March 2006, Purana Qilla, New Delhi, https://georgewbush-whitehouse.archives.gov/news/releases/2006/03/20060303-5.html.
10. PTI, 'Obama Formally Invites Modi, Wants "Defining Partnership",' *The Hindu*, 11 July 2014, https://www.thehindu.com/news/national/obama-formally-invites-modi-wants-defining-partnership/article6200680.ece.
11. Dennis Kux, *India and the United States: Estranged Democracies* (Washington DC: National Defense University Press, 1992).
12. 'President Bush Goes to India,' *The New York Times*, 28 February 2006, https://www.nytimes.com/2006/02/28/opinion/president-bush-goes-to-india.html.
13. Gautam Datt, 'US Defence Secretary Leon Panetta Identifies India as "Linchpin" in US Game Plan to Counter China,' *India Today*, 7 June 2012, https://www.indiatoday.in/india/north/story/leon-panetta-identifies-india-as-linchpin-to-counter-china-104814-2012-06-07.
14. Ashley Tellis, 'Avoiding the Labors of Sisyphus: Strengthening US-India Relations in a Trump Administration,' *Asia Policy*, Vol. 23, Issue 1 (January 2017): 45–46.
15. 'Remarks by the President to the Joint Session of the Indian Parliament in New Delhi, India,' 8 November 2010, New Delhi, https://obamawhitehouse.archives.gov/the-press-office/2010/11/08/remarks-president-joint-session-indian-parliament-new-delhi-india.

16. PTI, 'John McCain Believed in the Future of Strong US–India Ties,' *The Economic Times*, 26 August 2018, https://economictimes.indiatimes.com/news/defence/john-mccain-believed-in-the-future-of-strong-us-india-ties/articleshow/65550508.cms.
17. 'Transcript: Donald Trump Expounds on His Foreign Policy Views,' *The New York Times*, 26 March 2016, https://www.nytimes.com/2016/03/27/us/politics/donald-trump-transcript.html.
18. David Jacoby, *Trump, Trade and the End of Globalization* (Santa Barbara: Praeger, 2018), 64.
19. 'United States Launches WTO Challenge to Indian Export Subsidy Programs,' 14 March 2018, Office of USTR, https://ustr.gov/about-us/policy-offices/press-office/press-releases/2018/march/united-states-launches-wto-challenge.
20. Ellen Sheng, 'Silicon Valley is Fighting a Brain-Drain War with Trump that it May Lose,' CNBC, 9 April 2018, https://www.cnbc.com/2018/04/09/trumps-war-on-immigration-causing-silicon-valley-brain-drain.html.
21. 'Donald Trump Does a Fake Accent and Mocks Indian Call Center Representatives,' *India Today*, 23 April 2016, https://www.indiatoday.in/world/story/donald-trump-does-an-indian-accent-and-mocks-call-center-representatives-319531-2016-04-23.
22. Neha Dasgupta and Sanjeev Miglani, 'India Seeks Waiver from US Steel and Aluminum Tariffs,' *Reuters*, 28 March 2018, https://in.reuters.com/article/us-usa-trade-india/india-seeks-waiver-from-u-s-steel-and-aluminum-tariffs-idINKBN1H41O8.
23. Ian Marlow, 'Why India Could Be the Winner of a US–China Trade War,' *Bloomberg*, 7 April 2017, https://www.bloomberg.com/news/articles/2017-04-06/india-could-win-from-a-u-s-china-trade-row-modi-s-party-says.
24. Chidanand Rajghatta, 'Narendra Modi Phones Donald Trump over Afghanistan, Receives Trade Deficit Advice,' *The Times of India*, 9 January 2019, https://timesofindia.indiatimes.com/india/modi-phones-trump-over-afghanistan-receives-trade-deficit-advice/articleshow/67443800.cms.
25. Siobhan Hughes, 'House Speaker Ryan Breaks with Trump Over Steel Tariffs,' *The Wall Street Journal*, 5 March 2018, https://www.wsj.com/articles/house-speaker-ryan-breaks-with-trump-over-steel-tariffs-1520275634.
26. PTI, 'Donald Trump Says India Wants Trade Deal with America Primarily to Keep Him Happy,' *The Economic Times*, 2 October 2018, https://economictimes.indiatimes.com/news/international/world-news/india-wants-to-start-trade-talks-with-us-immediately-trump/articleshow/66033280.cms.
27. Martin Farrer, 'Soaring US Dollar Threatens Trouble for Emerging Markets,' *The Guardian*, 4 October 2018, https://www.theguardian.com/business/2018/oct/04/soaring-us-dollar-threatens-trouble-for-emerging-markets.
28. Mohan Kumar, 'The US–China Trade War Will Impact Negotiation Dynamics of the WTO,' *Hindustan Times*, 10 December 2018, https://www.hindustantimes.com/analysis/the-us-china-trade-war-will-impact-negotiation-dynamics-of-the-wto/story-JIMQCcvM1lAQJcAs3QPg0O.html.
29. Elizabeth Roche, 'India Keeps Expectations Low on 2+2 Talks with US,' *Mint*, 4 September 2018, https://www.livemint.com/Politics/v57E4KhIN0qZkHg1JO8m9L/India-keeps-expectations-low-on-22-talks-with-US.html.
30. William Burns, *The Back Channel: A Memoir of American Diplomacy and the Case for its Renewal* (New York: Random House, 2019), 390.

31. Charlie Laderman and Brendan Simms, *Donald Trump: The Making of a Worldview* (London: I.B. Tauris, 2017), 38, 46.
32. Laderman and Simms, *Donald Trump: The Making*, 33.
33. Laderman and Simms, *Donald Trump: The Making*, 57.
34. Laderman and Simms, *Donald Trump: The Making*, 74.
35. PTI, 'India–US Defence Sales at All-Time High: Pentagon,' *Mint*, 13 February 2019, https://www.livemint.com/politics/news/india-us-defence-sales-at-all-time-high-pentagon-1550001486583.html.
36. Rahul Singh, 'India Still Largest Arms Importer, Spent More Than $100b in Last 10 Years: SIPRI,' *Hindustan Times*, 12 March 2018, https://www.hindustantimes.com/india-news/india-still-largest-arms-importer-sipri/story-w7R3VCsWxuelz97N2OsOqI.html.
37. Elizabeth Roche, 'James Mattis in India: US Commits to Transfer Advanced Defence Technology for Make in India,' *Mint*, 26 September 2017, https://www.livemint.com/Politics/07dee1V8WtcWlYPFcFeslM/US-commits-to-transfer-advanced-defence-technology-for-Make.html.
38. Dinaker Peri, 'Rafale, S-400 Deals are Like a Booster Dose to IAF: Air Chief Marshal Dhanoa,' *The Hindu*, 3 October 2018, https://www.thehindu.com/news/national/rafale-will-be-game-changer-for-subcontinent-iaf-chief/article25111152.ece.
39. 'Trump Hints at Punitive Action Against India for Buying S-400 from Russia,' *India Today*, 11 October 2018, https://www.indiatoday.in/india/story/donald-trump-india-russia-s-400-1366457-2018-10-11.
40. Sushant Singh, 'Washington Lets Delhi Know: Buy our F-16s, Can Give Russia Deal Waiver,' *The Indian Express*, 20 October 2018, https://indianexpress.com/article/india/washington-lets-delhi-know-buy-our-f-16s-can-give-russia-deal-waiver-5409894/.
41. Chidanand Rajghatta, 'US NSA to Visit China and India, Signalling Shift from G-2 to G-3,' *The Times of India*, 20 October 2011, https://timesofindia.indiatimes.com/world/us/US-NSA-to-visit-China-and-India-signaling-shift-from-G-2-to-G-3/articleshow/10421456.cms.
42. Bharat Karnad, 'America an Unreliable Partner,' *The New Indian Express*, 24 January 2014, http://www.newindianexpress.com/opinion/America-an-Unreliable-Partner/2014/01/24/article2016305.ece.
43. Brahma Chellaney, 'The Orient Express,' *India Today*, 29 May 2008, https://www.indiatoday.in/magazine/society-the-arts/story/20080609-the-orient-express-736462-2008-05-29.
44. 'Modi Mustn't Pull India into Reckless Conflict,' *Global Times*, 4 August 2017, http://www.globaltimes.cn/content/1059715.shtml.
45. IANS, 'India of 2017 Different from India of 1962: Jaitley Responds to China Threat,' *Hindustan Times*, 30 June 2017, https://www.hindustantimes.com/india-news/jaitley-responds-to-chinese-threat-india-of-2017-different-from-india-of-1962/story-zfR7xqJsphnowhcdqjeM4H.html.
46. PTI, 'Xi Jinping Sees PM Modi as a Leader Who is Willing to Stand Up for Indian Interests: US Expert,' *The Times of India*, 8 August 2017, https://timesofindia.indiatimes.com/india/xi-jinping-sees-pm-modi-as-a-leader-who-is-willing-to-stand-up-for-indian-interests-us-expert/articleshow/59964484.cms.
47. PTI, 'US Supports "Return of Status Quo" on Doklam Issue: Trump Official,' *Hindustan Times*, 27 August 2017, https://www.hindustantimes.com/india-news/us-supports-return-of-status-quo-on-doklam-issue-trump-official/story-DLHDAGQABurE0EwSDozKlI.html.

48. Sumit Ganguly, 'After All That Embracing, has US Left India Out in the Cold Over Standoff with China?' *South China Morning Post*, 31 July 2017, https://www.scmp.com/week-asia/politics/article/2104779/after-all-embracing-has-us-left-india-out-cold-over-standoff.
49. Robert Farley, 'Why Hasn't the United States Thrown its Support Behind India in the Doklam Standoff?' *The Diplomat*, 7 August 2017, https://thediplomat.com/2017/08/why-hasnt-the-united-states-thrown-its-support-behind-india-in-the-doklam-standoff/.
50. Sachin Parashar and Saibal Dasgupta, 'US, India's Asia-Pacific Vision Makes the Chinese Dragon Uneasy,' *The Times of India*, 27 January 2015, https://timesofindia.indiatimes.com/india/US-Indias-Asia-Pacific-vision-makes-the-Chinese-dragon-uneasy/articleshow/46024597.cms.
51. 'India, US Pledge to Maintain Peace Across Indo-Pacific Region,' *The Indian Express*, 15 August 2017, https://indianexpress.com/article/india/modi-trump-agree-to-enhance-peace-across-indo-pacific-region-4798156/.
52. Ronak Desai, 'Why the Mattis Resignation is a Loss for US–India Relations,' *Forbes*, 26 December 2018, https://www.forbes.com/sites/ronakdesai/2018/12/26/why-the-mattis-resignation-is-a-loss-for-u-s-india-relations/.
53. NYT, 'Read Jim Mattis' Letter to Trump: Full Text,' *The New York Times*, 20 December 2018, https://www.nytimes.com/2018/12/20/us/politics/letter-jim-mattis-trump.html.
54. Bob Woodward, *Fear: Trump in the White House* (New York: Simon & Schuster, 2018), 146.
55. PTI, 'Will Review Sino-Indian Ties from Strategic and Long-Term Perspective: PM Modi Ahead of Talks with Xi Jinping,' *Daily News & Analysis*, 26 April 2018, https://www.dnaindia.com/india/report-will-review-sino-indian-ties-from-strategic-and-long-term-perspective-pm-modi-ahead-of-talks-with-xi-jinping-2608902.
56. Sachin Parashar, 'Modi, Xi Issue "Strategic Guidance" to Militaries to Build Trust on Border Affairs,' *The Times of India*, 29 April 2018, https://timesofindia.indiatimes.com/india/modi-xi-issue-strategic-guidance-to-militaries-to-build-trust-on-border-affairs/articleshow/63956477.cms.
57. Sreeram Chaulia, 'New Delhi's Delicate Dance Over Tibet,' *Nikkei Asian Review*, 9 April 2018, https://asia.nikkei.com/Opinion/New-Delhi-s-delicate-dance-over-Tibet2.
58. Abhishek Bhaya, 'Uzbek-Afghan Railway to Put "China-India Plus" Plan on Track,' *China Global Television Network*, 10 October 2018, https://news.cgtn.com/news/3d3d774e7a597a4e7a457a6333566d54/share_p.html.
59. Dipanjan Chaudhury, 'PM Narendra Modi Calls for Early Conclusion of RCEP,' *The Economic Times*, 15 November 2018, https://economictimes.indiatimes.com/news/politics-and-nation/pm-narendra-modi-calls-for-early-conclusion-of-rcep/articleshow/66622263.cms.
60. Mao Keji, 'Hints of Major Shift in Sino-Indian Relations,' *Global Times*, 24 April 2018, http://www.globaltimes.cn/content/1099486.shtml.
61. Bruce Stokes et al., 'India and the World,' Pew Research Center, 15 November 2017, https://www.pewglobal.org/2017/11/15/india-and-the-world/.
62. Richard Fontaine and Daniel Kliman, 'India as a "Global Swing State"—A New Framework for US Engagement with India,' The National Bureau of Asian Research, 22 July 2013, https://www.nbr.org/publication/india-as-a-global-swing-state-a-new-framework-for-u-s-engagement-with-india/.
63. Chidanand Rajghatta, 'Blow to India as US to Recall 50% Troops in Afghanistan,' *The Times of India*, 22 December 2018, https://timesofindia.indiatimes.com/world/

us/trump-throws-kabul-new-delhi-under-the-bus-with-afghan-withdrawal-move/articleshow/67188406.cms.
64. 'Remarks by President Trump on the Strategy in Afghanistan and South Asia,' issued on 21 August 2017, Fort Myer, Arlington, https://www.whitehouse.gov/briefings-statements/remarks-president-trump-strategy-afghanistan-south-asia/.
65. Ayaz Gul, 'Ghani Concerned About Exclusion From US–Taliban Talks,' *Voice of America*, 25 January 2019, https://www.voanews.com/a/ghani-voices-concern-about-exclusion-from-us-taliban-talks/4758962.html.
66. PTI, 'Trump: Why Isn't India Fighting Taliban in Afghanistan, No Point Funding Libraries There,' *India Today*, 3 January 2019, https://www.indiatoday.in/world/story/donald-trump-why-is-india-not-fighting-taliban-in-afghanistan-1422419-2019-01-03.
67. Laderman and Simms, *Donald Trump: The Making*, 81.
68. Marvin Weinbaum, 'A Challenged Pakistan and its Afghan Policies,' *Bustan: The Middle East Book Review*, Vol. 4, Issue 1 (2013): 1–16.
69. Indrani Bagchi, 'Iran: Can Use "Influence" over Taliban for India,' *The Times of India*, 9 January 2019, timesofindia.indiatimes.com/india/iran-can-use-influence-over-taliban-for-india/articleshow/67446237.cms.
70. 'India Says is in Touch with Russia, Iran & Saudi on US–Taliban Talks,' *The Times of India*, 15 February 2019, https://timesofindia.indiatimes.com/india/india-says-is-in-touch-with-russia-iran-saudi-on-us-taliban-talks/articleshow/68001068.cms.
71. Varghese George, 'India, US Determined to Destroy Terrorist Organisations, Says Trump,' *The Hindu*, 27 June 2017, https://www.thehindu.com/news/national/modi-meets-trump/article19151643.ece.
72. PTI, 'India is Nepal's "Elder Brother", Not "Big Brother": Sushma Swaraj,' *The Economic Times*, 22 February 2016, https://economictimes.indiatimes.com/news/politics-and-nation/india-is-nepals-elder-brother-not-big-brother-sushma-swaraj/articleshow/51093851.cms.
73. 'Remarks by President Trump in Cabinet Meeting,' 2 January 2019, Cabinet Room, White House, https://www.whitehouse.gov/briefings-statements/remarks-president-trump-cabinet-meeting-12/.
74. Kenneth Juster and C. Raja Mohan, 'India–US Relations: Building a Durable Partnership for the 21st Century,' Carnegie India, 11 January 2018, https://carnegieindia.org/2018/01/11/india-u.s.-relations-building-durable-partnership-for-21st-century-event-5789.
75. Choe Sang-hun, 'Trump Rattles South Korea by Saying it Should Pay for Antimissile System,' *The New York Times*, 28 April 2017, https://www.nytimes.com/2017/04/28/world/asia/trump-south-korea-thaad-missile-defense-north-korea.html.
76. Julian Borger, 'Trump Offers to Sell '"Sophisticated" Military Gear to Japan and South Korea,' *The Guardian*, 7 September 2017, https://www.theguardian.com/world/2017/sep/06/donald-trump-north-korea-arms-deal-japan-south-korea.
77. Darren Whiteside, 'South Korea's Moon Unveils New Focus on Southeast Asia,' Reuters, 9 November 2017, https://in.reuters.com/article/indonesia-southkorea/update-1-south-koreas-moon-unveils-new-focus-on-southeast-asia-idINL3N1NF4D0.
78. Motoko Rich, 'North Korea's Threat Pushes Japan to Reassess Its Might and Rights,' *The New York Times*, 15 September 2017, https://www.nytimes.com/2017/09/15/world/asia/japan-north-korea-missile-defense.html.

79. Yoichi Funabashi, 'In America's Absence, Japan Takes the Lead on Asian Free Trade,' *The Washington Post*, 22 February 2019, https://www.washingtonpost.com/news/global-opinions/wp/2018/02/22/in-americas-absence-japan-takes-the-lead-on-asian-free-trade/.
80. Hugh White, 'Trump Pushes Australia Toward China,' *The New York Times*, 9 February 2017, https://www.nytimes.com/2017/02/09/opinion/trump-pushes-australia-toward-china.html.
81. Damien Cave, 'In Australia, a Call for Closer Ties to China Gains Support,' *The New York Times*, 16 March 2017, https://www.nytimes.com/2017/03/16/world/australia/trump-us-china-relations-fitzgerald.html.
82. Clive Hamilton, *Silent Invasion: China's Influence in Australia* (Richmond: Hardie Grant, 2018).
83. Rory Medcalf and C. Raja Mohan, 'Responding to Indo-Pacific Rivalry: Australia, India and Middle Power Coalitions,' Lowy Institute for International Policy (August 2014): 1.
84. Medcalf and Mohan, 'Responding,' 13.
85. Kim Youngho, 'Japan–South Korean Tensions Threaten Regional Security,' *Nikkei Asian Review*, 5 February 2019, https://asia.nikkei.com/Opinion/Japan-South-Korean-tensions-threaten-regional-security.
86. Daniel O'Neill, *Dividing ASEAN and Conquering the South China Sea: China's Financial Power Projection* (Hong Kong: Hong Kong University Press, 2018).
87. Sudha Ramachandran, 'The Belt and Road Initiative Still Afloat in South Asia,' *China Brief*, Vol. 19, Issue 1 (January 2019): 14–18.
88. John Fairbank, ed., *The Chinese World Order: Traditional China's Foreign Relations* (Harvard: Harvard University Press, 1968).
89. Ben Blanchard, 'Duterte Aligns Philippines with China, Says US Has Lost,' Reuters, 20 October 2016, https://www.reuters.com/article/us-china-philippines/duterte-aligns-philippines-with-china-says-u-s-has-lost-idUSKCN12K0AS.
90. PTI, 'Philippines' Rodrigo Duterte Apologises for Cursing Obama, Calls Trump "Good Friend",' *Hindustan Times*, 3 September 2018, https://www.hindustantimes.com/world-news/philippines-rodrigo-duterte-apologises-for-cursing-obama-calls-trump-good-friend/story-pctRzodbXBQPjlIUNHmMxN.html.
91. 'Why India is Developing its Maiden Deep-Sea Port in Indonesia,' *The Times of India*, 21 March 2019, https://timesofindia.indiatimes.com/india/why-india-is-developing-its-maiden-deep-sea-port-in-indonesia/articleshow/68511228.cms.
92. Sachin Parashar, 'Sri Lanka to Offer India Port Development to Balance Out China,' *The Economic Times*, 19 April 2017, https://economictimes.indiatimes.com/news/politics-and-nation/sri-lanka-to-offer-india-port-development-to-balance-out-china/articleshow/58253212.cms.
93. Bharat Karnad, 'Foreign Military Bases: How India Shoots Itself on the Foot,' *Swarajya*, 5 October 2015, https://swarajyamag.com/culture/foreign-military-bases-how-india-shoots-itself-on-the-foot.
94. Dipanjan Chaudhury, 'PM Modi's Oman Visit: Indian Navy Can Now Access Duqm Port,' *The Economic Times*, 13 February 2018, https://economictimes.indiatimes.com/news/defence/pm-modis-oman-visit-navy-can-now-access-duqm-port/articleshow/62894357.cms.
95. Emily Holden, '"It'll Change Back": Trump Says Climate Change Not a Hoax, But Denies Lasting Impact,' *The Guardian*, 15 October 2018, https://www.theguardian.com/us-news/2018/oct/15/itll-change-back-trump-says-climate-change-not-a-hoax-but-denies-lasting-impact.

96. 'Solar Alliance to play OPEC's role,' *The Hindu Business Line*, 2 October 2018, https://www.thehindubusinessline.com/economy/international-solar-alliance-will-take-over-from-opec-as-energy-policy-dictating-body-modi/article25105026.ece.
97. 'India at Davos: PM Modi Takes Leadership on Climate Change at his Maiden Plenary Address of WEF,' *The Financial Express*, 23 January 2018, https://www.financialexpress.com/economy/india-at-davos-pm-modi-takes-leadership-on-climate-change-at-his-maiden-plenary-address-of-wef/1026895/.
98. Dipanjan Chaudhury, 'India, Japan Come up with AAGC to Counter China's OBOR,' *The Economic Times*, 26 May 2017, https://economictimes.indiatimes.com/news/economy/policy/india-japan-come-up-with-aagc-to-counter-chinas-obor/articleshow/58846673.cms.
99. Mark Champion and Iain Marlow, 'India's Modi Threads Path between Rising China, Uncertain US,' *Bloomberg*, 1 June 2018, https://www.bloomberg.com/news/articles/2018-06-01/india-s-modi-threads-path-between-rising-china-uncertain-u-s.
100. S.D. Muni, 'Obama Administration's Pivot to Asia-Pacific and India's Role,' Institute of South Asian Studies, NUS, Working Paper 159 (August 2012).
101. Nicola Nymalm and Johannes Plagemann, 'Comparative Exceptionalism: Universality and Particularity in Foreign Policy Discourses,' *International Studies Review*, Vol. 21, Issue 1 (March 2019): 12–37.
102. PTI, 'India Does Not Believe in "Me First" Approach: Sushma Swaraj,' *The Economic Times*, 22 May 2018, https://economictimes.indiatimes.com/news/politics-and-nation/india-does-not-believe-in-me-first-approach-sushma-swaraj/articleshow/64262704.cms.

Map not to scale.

II
Turkey: Spurned Ally to Potential Alternative

I have just authorized a doubling of Tariffs on Steel and Aluminium with respect to Turkey as their currency, the Turkish Lira, slides rapidly downward against our very strong Dollar! Aluminium will now be 20% and Steel 50%. Our relations with Turkey are not good at this time!
—President Donald Trump, 10 August 2018[1]

Over the years, Turkey rushed to America's help whenever necessary. Yet the United States has repeatedly and consistently failed to understand and respect the Turkish people's concerns. Before it is too late, Washington must give up the misguided notion that our relationship can be asymmetrical and come to terms with the fact that Turkey has alternatives. Failure to reverse this trend of unilateralism and disrespect will require us to start looking for new friends and allies. You can never bring this nation in line with the language of threats.
—President Recep Tayyip Erdogan, 10 August 2018[2]

The Populist and the Sultan

Hours after President Recep Tayyip Erdogan narrowly won a controversial referendum in April 2017 to convert Turkey's parliamentary system into an executive presidency with sweeping powers vested in himself, he received a surprising congratulatory phone call. It came from the erstwhile capital of the free world, Washington DC. The heterodox occupant of the White House who unabashedly admired Erdogan's dictatorial power grab, was the first Western leader to pat him on the back for attaining the status of a modern-day sultan and surpassing the founder of the Turkish republic, Mustafa Kemal Ataturk, in concentration of authority. Call it an endorsement or encouragement, Trump reached out to Erdogan in spite of rampant criticism of the latter's authoritarianism by Western news media, America's European allies and liberals within the Trump administration.

On the same day Trump was toasting Erdogan and boosting his newly acquired power as the ultimate Middle Eastern illiberal strongman, the US State Department had called out Turkey's fatal referendum for 'irregularities' and 'an uneven playing field'.[3] The dichotomy between Trump the populist and a permanent American foreign policy bureaucracy on matters like democracy, human rights, free markets and the liberal international order as a whole could not have found a starker illustration. Only a month after Erdogan crowned himself with unparalleled power to rule Turkey, Trump hosted him in the White House for a summit. Erdogan returned Trump's compliments by hailing his 'legendary victory' in the 2016 US presidential election and dubbing it a watershed moment that 'has led to an awakening of new expectations for Turkey and the region it is in'.[4] The personal chemistry between the two persisted despite myriad bilateral disagreements and conflicts of interest, with Trump avowing 'he's become a friend of mine' and giving him 'very high marks for running a very difficult part of the world'. For effect, Trump added, 'We're, right now, as close as we have ever been. And a lot of that has to do with the personal relationship.'[5]

In the Introduction of this book, I analysed how Trump's far-right populist ideology led him to embrace Russian President Vladimir Putin. In Erdogan, Trump saw a similar kindred spirit, although the Turkish leader's right-wing populism was based on mobilisation of Islamist sentiment with strong anti-Western overtones. The commonality of the two was buttressed by the fact that the 'reactionary conservative populism' of Trump, Erdogan and other 'ring of autocrats' occurred in 'the same global context—a structural breakdown in the functioning of world capitalist system'.[6] Erdogan's rise to power as an outsider who stood for the poor Turkish masses against the established elites was the product of accumulated grievances from three economic crises in 1994, 2000 and 2001, the last of which was devastating and caused by excessive financial deregulation and the integration of Turkey into global capitalist markets.⁷ His Justice and Development Party (AKP) did not fully overturn the prescriptions and conditionalities of the International Monetary Fund (IMF) and the World Bank, but projected itself as an 'Islam-sensitive' and 'socially caring' force, winning elections on a trot through welfare policies.⁸

While Trump has been stymied in his bid to dismantle checks and balances in American politics, Erdogan succeeded to amass untrammelled power in Turkey, an achievement that Trump obviously envies. Trump's paeans to Egypt's military dictator, President Abdel-Fattah El-Sisi, as a 'fantastic guy' who 'took control of Egypt, he really took control of it',⁹ reveals his innermost wish to replicate dictators who trample over their national institutions in American politics. Erdogan, who uneasily coexisted with and outlived two liberal internationalist presidents—George W. Bush and Barack Obama—fathomed the core illiberal character of Trump from the very start and never let go of this golden talisman to advance Turkey's objectives.

In Chapter I, I showed how democratic India under Narendra Modi tried staying out of Trump's bad books and unobtrusively sustaining its strategic partnership with the US via liberal internationalist 'grown-ups' in the Trump administration. In the case of Erdogan, who has continuously been in power in Turkey since 2003 and grown progressively undemocratic, the process was reversed. He has placed tremendous faith in the non-judgemental populism of Trump and his select illiberal advisers, while staying wary of the deep state in the US national security and foreign policy apparatus, which is imbued with liberal bias against Turkey's human rights abuses and descent to one-man rule.

Like Putin, Erdogan has repeatedly alluded to the American government's permanent establishment as the sinister hurdle stymieing Trump from going the whole hog and reviving its alliance with Turkey. Erdogan's political legitimacy and appeal among Turkey's devout Muslim masses rest inter alia on his taming of Turkey's own elitist deep state or parallel state of unelected secular military officers, police, judges, news media, bureaucrats and capitalists, who had historically constituted the Kemalist ruling class in the country prior to his Islamist party's ascent.¹⁰ Transposing the Turkish deep state on to the US is a fallacy because Turkey's secular military establishment undertook multiple *coup d'états* to overthrow democratically elected leaders. Later in this chapter, I will elaborate how the failed putsch to overthrow Erdogan in 2016 coloured his outlook towards liberal internationalists in the US government. For now, it is enough to note that the internal resistance Trump faces within the American state structure is neither as capable nor as ruthless as the violent and shadowy influences behind the throne that Turkey endured since the days of the Ottoman Empire.[11]

Nonetheless, it is undeniable that Trump and Erdogan have an uncanny camaraderie owing to their shared contempt for liberal opponents of their respective agendas. In March 2019, as Trump appeared to have been persuaded by mainstream globalists in his administration to slow down and complicate his isolationist choice to withdraw all US troops stationed in Syria, Erdogan voiced his frustration at the delay and offered his interpretation of the 'two-track presidency' in America.

> Trump has shown a determined stance during this process. Of course, there's an established order in the United States we can call the 'Deep State', and they've obstructed this.[12]

Top Trump administration officials, who have earned Erdogan's ire for sticking to liberal internationalist views and attitudes include National Security Adviser (NSA) H.R. McMaster, his successor John Bolton, and Secretary of State Mike Pompeo. In December 2017, Ankara expressed outrage at McMaster's claim that Turkey and Qatar had become 'the main sponsors' of extremist Islamist ideologies targeting the West while Saudi Arabia had stopped doing so. These remarks were not entirely inaccurate but drew a sharp reprimand from the Turkish Foreign Ministry as 'non-factual, astonishing, baseless and unacceptable'.[13] Resentment against American humiliation and pressure are mainstays of Erdogan's populist foreign policy and these have grown more nuanced since Trump took over in Washington.

Bolton was snubbed in January 2019 when the NSA's request for meeting Erdogan during his Turkey visit was rebuffed. The president slammed Bolton's 'grave mistake' of asserting that the US would not pull out its troops from Syria unless Turkey protected Syrian Kurds, whose militants Ankara deems as terrorists, across its southern border. The AKP's mouthpiece, *Daily Sabah*, accused Bolton of belonging to a cabal in Washington that was carrying out 'a soft coup against Trump' and which wanted to 'go rogue and try to impose conditions on the United States' withdrawal from Syria'.[14] Pompeo has been scrutinised in Ankara for his past record of criticising Erdogan's project to turn Turkey into an 'Islamist totalitarian dictatorship' and his warnings that 'Turkey is a NATO ally and should behave as such'. Pompeo's evangelical Christian political base in the US and related closeness to Israel, whose Zionist enterprise Erdogan denounces as a 'crime against humanity', reinforced Ankara's conviction that some of Trump's team members are inherently biased against Turkey,[15] and that the US president should be directly engaged with Erdogan instead of going through regular institutional channels.

In the conspiratorial worldview of Erdogan and the AKP, the only hopeful person within the Trump administration who could have done miracles for Turkey was Michael Flynn, the ill-fated first NSA. He lasted only a few weeks before quitting over a scandal surrounding his secret dealings with Russia. But lesser-known were Flynn's extensive lobbying efforts on behalf of the Erdogan government in the US during Obama's administration. In December 2016, with Flynn working as a top aide in the Trump transition team, he is alleged to have discussed a plot with Turkish officials to bribe US authorities and get the Pennsylvania resident and anti-Erdogan cleric Fethullah Gulen kidnapped and transported on a private jet to a Turkish prison island.[16] In December 2018, two of Flynn's business aides were indicted for working as agents of Turkey and 'illegally lobbying in the US to discredit Gulen and have him extradited'.[17]

The expectation that Trump would overrule the American legal process and his liberal internationalist aides to deliver Gulen for facing trial in Turkey is embedded into Erdogan's mind. Gulen is the Turkish leader's bête noire. The two Islamists were once allies, carrying out sensational purges of the secularist military elites and establishing civilian supremacy in Turkey. But they later fell out and Gulen stands accused of capital crimes such as inciting terrorism and provoking the coup attempt of 2016. Having vanquished the secular Kemalists, Erdogan turned against Gulen and saw in his Hizmet movement a reincarnation of the parallel state that could undermine his power. Erdogan had no luck with the liberal Obama in getting Gulen extradited from his perch in Pennsylvania, but he hoped that the populist and transaction-focussed Trump would do it as part of a quid pro quo.

Asked in November 2018 if Trump would oblige Turkey's request to hand over Gulen, the US president was equivocal.

> I get along very, very well with the President (Erdogan). He's a friend of mine. He's a strong man, he's a tough man, and he's a smart man. But he's a friend of mine. And whatever we can do, we'll do. But—and that is something that we're always looking at. But at this point, no.[18]

In December 2018, Turkish Foreign Minister Mevlut Cavusoglu claimed that Trump had assured Erdogan he was working on Gulen's extradition,[19] an interpretation that the US government subsequently denied. Yet, the ambiguous and tantalising stand by Trump on Gulen has kept Erdogan interested. The Turkish president's personal vendetta against Gulen is an all-consuming affair and the scalp of this elderly Sufi cleric in exile is the ultimate prize or confidence-building measure as far as complex US–Turkey relations go.

Out of the Western Shadow

To better comprehend how the Trump whipsaw has both helped and hindered Turkey, one needs to revisit the rock-solid alliance of the Cold War and the nebulous post-Cold War era when the underlying rationale for the US–Turkey alliance went up in the air. Ankara and Washington had a fairly simple and straightforward embrace as long as the Soviet Union existed. Turkey was one of the linchpin states of the American-crafted liberal international order from the late 1940s. Bound to the US by mortal fear of Soviet encroachment and driven by the Kemalist elite's project to Europeanise and Westernise its society, Turkey contributed troops to the American side during the Korean War and strove to enter NATO in 1952. It participated in America's alliance system in the Middle East and served as an instrument for Washington to apply pressure on the southern flank of the Eastern Bloc and prevent Communist domination of the Mediterranean.[20]

Barring rows over Turkey's military intervention in Cyprus in 1974 and America's hesitation to back Turkey in its age-old conflict with NATO ally Greece, the Cold War provided a stable, mutually beneficial backdrop for Ankara and Washington to cooperate. Turkey hosted US troops and military bases on its soil and developed a deep-knit intelligence-sharing arrangement with the US. Turkish academic Ayse Atmaca argues that alliance with Turkey was 'an important part of US geopolitical discourse during the Cold War, [as] from the Truman Doctrine to the Carter and Reagan doctrines, Turkey was part of every strategic plan developed by Washington in that era'.[21] Dependence on America was ingrained in the Turkish foreign policy psyche of that time, even though episodes like the Cyprus invasion caused consternation and set off occasional outpourings of anti-Americanism, particularly from left-wing Turkish political parties.[22]

Once the Cold War ended, the foundation of the alliance was rendered moot. American scholar Stephen Larrabee says 'the disappearance of the Soviet threat reduced Ankara's dependence on Washington for its security' and rendered irrelevant the concept of Turkey as a 'flank state'.[23] If the main threat to Turkey's security had once come from the north, that is, the USSR, its locus shifted to its southern borders with Syria, Iran, Iraq and Lebanon. Ankara thus had to move its strategic gaze away from the West and towards the Middle East to face this transformed environment. Establishing cordiality with Arab and Persian neighbours, especially Syria and Iran, which were antagonistic to the US, became vital for Turkey to manage regional volatility at its southern doorstep. Larrabee notes, 'As a result, US and Turkish interests in and policies toward both countries— and the Middle East more broadly—have increasingly diverged in recent years.'[24]

The US invasion of Iraq in 2003 was a watershed moment in this denouement. Freshly in power and sporting a moderate and pragmatic image, Erdogan sounded sympathetic to Washington but deferred to the Turkish parliament and public opinion and did not concede to Washington's demands that Turkish military bases be available to open a northern front against Saddam Hussein. The foreboding that America would yet again use Turkey for its own selfish ends like in the 1990 Gulf War and then leave it with destabilising havoc in its backyard, especially by igniting Kurdish separatism, grew in Ankara as the Iraq war dragged on and Turkey's bid for EU membership got stalled.

President Bush's global war on terror (GWOT) and the neoconservative atmosphere of targeting Islam as a religion of hatred and terrorism was the red rag to the bull for AKP's Islamist ideology. Turkish writer Cengiz Gunay argues that Erdogan and the AKP skilfully exploited Turkish people's historical sense of victimhood, humiliation and solidarity with Muslim nations for gaining legitimacy at home. By presenting himself as 'the voice of a deprived global Muslim community against Western double standards' and defying American liberal hegemony in global affairs, Erdogan consolidated domestic political support and monopolised power.[25] Along the way, he also completed the post-Cold War evolution of Turkey's identity from a loyal Western nation into a defiant and proud country with an imperial past and a mind and will of its own in the present. Distancing Turkey from America and Europe while pivoting to the Muslim world was geopolitically as well as electorally an astute choice.

Erdogan's one-time Foreign Minister and Prime Minister, Ahmet Davutoglu, devised the blueprint for this pivot. His doctrine of 'zero problems with neighbours' was premised on the logic that Turkey could be powerful only if it utilised the full 'strategic depth' of its adjacent Arab and Persian lands by harnessing Islam as the cementing and unifying factor. Remaining stuck in the US fold and appearing to be coordinating regional strategy with Israel (secular Turkey was the first Muslim-majority country to legally recognise Israel and establish diplomatic relations with it in 1949) would prevent Ankara from realising said strategic depth and revive its historical influence in the Muslim world.[26] Erdogan's self-anointed role as the champion of Palestinian self-determination and his fervent advocacy for Muslim minorities suffering oppression in countries as far as China and Myanmar are part of this broader push to make Turkey count in the world. In December 2018, his crowning as the 'most influential Muslim' on earth by a Jordanian think-tank was accompanied by a citation that he had overseen Turkey's 're-emergence as a major global power'.[27]

Ankara's reorientation to the Islamic world under Erdogan has been described as a sign of a 'more independent-minded and assertive Turkey' and its emergence as 'an important diplomatic actor'.[28] For Turkey to rise as a regional power, it had to break out of the Western shadow and develop its own agenda that often clashed with that of

America. In 2005, Aylin Guney traced the step-by-step transition of Turkey's post-Cold War ties with the US from full-on 'alliance' to 'enhanced partnership' to 'strategic partnership' and to 'partnership for democracy' in the context of Ankara pursuing 'a more independent and multidimensional policy'.[29] By the time Trump took office in 2017, Erdogan's foreign policy had grown far more activist and he had pulled Turkey further apart from the West. In the words of Turkish journalist Burak Bekdil, Ankara and Washington became 'former strategic allies that are now only allies in theory or, in a more realistic lexicon, ideological adversaries'.[30]

The Kurdish Contradiction

The interests and statecraft of established powers are distinct from those of rising powers in every region of the world. The former are outsiders with a bird's-eye view and often try to balance out competing local actors to maintain their overall hegemony in a specific area. The latter are insiders who are directly part of the competition in their surroundings and often find great powers to be constraining and suffocating. The deep contradiction between Ankara and Washington on the issue of Kurdish secessionism fits this generalisation to a tee.

Since the 1980s, Turkey has faced a resilient armed insurgency by the Kurdistan Workers Party (PKK) and its offshoots, which fight on and off for an independent state on behalf of the 15 million or so discriminated and persecuted Kurdish minorities (nearly 20 per cent of the Turkish population). The presence of another 20-odd million Kurds in neighbouring Syria, Iraq and Iran, and linkages between the PKK and affiliated Kurdish militants in these countries, make this a broader regional problem for Turkey. Notwithstanding disputes and struggles over a gamut of issues, Ankara shares a common interest with Damascus, Baghdad and Tehran in wanting to squelch the movement for a greater Kurdistan that encompasses contiguous breakaway bordering territories of all four countries.

The Turkish goal of occluding a Kurdish state has been threatened by America's sponsorship and support for Kurdish guerrillas and autonomous entities across Turkey's borders in Iraq, Syria and Iran. Even though the US designated the PKK as a terrorist organisation in 1997, Washington abetted Kurdish separatists in Iraq as a means to weaken Saddam and carry out the GWOT against Sunni jihadist groups in the region like Al Qaeda and ISIS. If George H.W. Bush carved out a demilitarised no-fly zone for Iraqi Kurds in 1991, Bill Clinton expanded it. Bush Junior rewarded Iraqi Kurds for participation in the war to topple Saddam by granting them greater self-rule and unprecedented American investment and economic opportunities during the US occupation of Iraq (2003–11).[31] Obama relied on Syrian Kurdish militants known as the People's Protection Units (YPG) to counter ISIS from 2014, and it was under his watch that a de facto Kurdish self-governing 'federal region' in northern Syria, known as Rojava, which could be amalgamated with the Kurdistan Regional Government (KRG) of northern Iraq was set up.[32]

From the perspective of Erdogan and Turkish nationalism, the entire history of America's coddling of Kurdish separatists is a grand betrayal.[33] By boosting the morale of Syrian and Iraqi Kurds and fomenting unrest among Iranian Kurds against their central government in Tehran, Washington magnified Turkey's national security problem because Ankara saw all armed Kurds as offshoots of PKK or infectious militants whose interrelated dreams of independence stoke secessionism and civil war within Turkey. Erdogan's remark that Obama 'deceived us' by promoting and arming the YPG and 'we can't destroy one terrorist group (ISIS) with another one (Kurdish) when we are strategic partners with the US'[34] sums up Ankara's vexation with Washington's geopolitical games. Iraq has also protested against the way the US actively fomented Kurdish separatism in its north and abetted its fragmentation. On their part, US administrations tried to assuage Turkish and Arab anger by maintaining that they were walking a tightrope and restraining Kurdish allies from threatening these countries' sovereignty.[35]

Indeed, from the Kurdish point of view, America has terrible habits of not enabling them wholeheartedly or backstabbing them after they outlive their immediate utility of overthrowing anti-Western regimes or defeating jihadist terrorists.[36] It is true that liberal internationalists in the US have romanticised the Kurds as a reliable, modern, egalitarian, feminist and secular people who can blaze a new trail of democratic and moderate governance in a Middle East full of intolerant extremists and dictators.³⁷ But the opportunistic realpolitik calculus of a superpower has meant that America often dropped the Kurds like hot potatoes and left them high and dry. Still, the Turkish narrative is that if there is a fait accompli of emboldened and entrenched Kurdish separatists across the Middle East, Washington is the main culprit. Besides the US, Ankara blames Israel for stoking Kurdish aspirations for statehood. Erdogan has alleged that the KRG of northern Iraq is 'hand-in-hand together with Mossad' as per Israel's design to weaken Turkey and exclude it as 'a playmaker in the region'.³⁸

During its first year in office, the Trump administration seemed to dash Erdogan's initial hopes by doubling down on the standard American boilerplate of propping up the Kurds and imperilling Turkish security. Washington's decision to directly supply arms to Syrian Kurds in May 2017 to checkmate ISIS was met with outrage and invective in Ankara. By January 2018, as the ISIS Caliphate in Syria and Iraq was being decimated, the US military announced the launch of a 'border force' in northern Syria composed of 30,000 fighters drawn from Kurdish and Arab forces to 'prevent the resurgence of ISIS'.³⁹ It looked like the last straw on the camel's back for Turkey, which believed that Washington was hunkering down for a permanent occupation of parts of Syria, entrenching the YPG and formalising it as an official army just across its border. Erdogan lashed out, saying, 'A country we call an ally is insisting on forming a terror army on our borders,' and vowed, 'Our mission is to strangle it before it's even born.'⁴⁰ He intensified Turkey's entente with Russia and Iran (more about it later in this chapter) and engaged personally with Trump to whittle down the border force idea, which stemmed from the Pentagon and votaries of traditional American hegemony in the Middle East.

Eventually, it turned out that Erdogan's shrewd reading of Trump the isolationist and populist politician was not off the mark. By December 2018, the American president had tired of open-ended military commitments in the Middle East and was itching to withdraw US forces from Syria. Erdogan proclaimed that he got a 'positive response' from Trump to allow the Turkish military to carry out another incursion deep into YPG territory in northern Syria.⁴¹ Around that time, there was an extraordinary phone conversation between Trump and Erdogan, which deserves lengthy quotation.

'The talking points were very firm,' said one of the officials, explaining that Trump was advised to clearly oppose a Turkish incursion into northern Syria and suggest the US and Turkey work together to address security concerns. Erdogan, though, quickly put Trump on the defensive, reminding him that he had repeatedly said the only reason for US troops to be in Syria was to defeat the Islamic State and that the group had been 99 per cent defeated. 'Why are you still there?' the second official said Erdogan asked Trump, telling him that the Turks could deal with the remaining IS militants. With Erdogan on the line, Trump asked national security adviser John Bolton, who was listening in, Erdogan's point, Bolton was forced to admit, had been backed up by [James] Mattis, Pompeo, US special envoy for Syria Jim Jeffrey and special envoy for the anti-ISIS coalition Brett McGurk, who have said that IS retains only 1 per cent of its territory, the officials said. Bolton stressed, however, that the entire national security team agreed that victory over IS had to be enduring, which means more than taking away its territory. Trump was not dissuaded, according to the officials, who said the president quickly capitulated by pledging to withdraw, shocking both Bolton and Erdogan.[42]

In another reading of this historic exchange, Trump replied to Erdogan's queries as to why the US should retain troops in Syria after ISIS' rout with a stunning concession: 'OK, it's all yours. We are done.'[43] Mattis resigned as Defence Secretary immediately after this stunning reversal by Trump, having failed to convince the president that America should 'stand by' its Kurdish allies and stay put in Syria for long-term strategic purposes.[44] McGurk, Trump's envoy for the Global Coalition to Counter ISIS, also quit with the lament that the president erroneously 'bought Erdogan's proposal' even though Turkey is 'not a reliable partner'.[45] Trump's tweet, '[Erdogan] has very strongly informed me that he will eradicate whatever is left of ISIS in Syria… and he is a man who can do it plus, Turkey is right "next door". Our troops are coming home!'[46] left no doubt that the US president wanted to unburden America's liberal hegemonic mantle in the Middle East and hand over the reins to local powers like Turkey, even if this meant a repetition of American treachery against the Kurds in a long litany of such perfidies.[47] Trump had to keep promises to American voters to focus on domestic affairs and this populist need overrode all the geostrategic thought of liberal internationalist experts and advisers.

Erdogan latched on to Trump's withdrawal promise as a tacit permission for Turkey to attack the YPG the moment US forces left. He exulted at Trump's abandonment of Syria as the 'right call' and bragged that Turkey was the 'sole stakeholder that can work simultaneously with the United States and Russia' and 'get the job done in Syria'.[48] But as time passed, he found the delay in the US pull-out of its 2,000 troops frustrating. In Ankara's estimation, the globalists in the Trump administration and mainstream Republicans in Congress were the villains attempting to slow down the president's isolationist decision-making and somehow sustain an American foothold in Syria. By early 2019, Washington floated formation of a multinational Western monitoring and observer force in a buffer zone in northern Syria, including a token 400 American soldiers, to check ISIS' recrudescence and protect the YPG from a Turkish onslaught. It ran counter to Erdogan's assertions that Turkey can form the 'safe zone' in Syria by itself 'under our control because that is my border'.[49] The tussle between Erdogan's 'neo-Ottoman' urge to dominate Arab neighbours and the remnants of liberal internationalism in Washington is not over, even though Trump's domestic populism favours Ankara's objective of vanquishing the Kurds.

Intermestic Trouble

As I have explained in the Introduction, Trump's foreign policy is entirely derived from his domestic political need to keep his base of American voters happy. The meshing of his domestic and international policies has generated a confused intermestic approach to different regions of the world. In his outlook to the Middle East, one of the central domestic factors motivating Trump is the evangelical Christian vote bank, which is fanatically supportive of Israel and its policies. Evangelical myth espoused by Christian Zionists holds that Jesus Christ's second coming on earth requires Jewish control over greater Israel between the Mediterranean Sea and the Jordan River, that is, the whole of Jerusalem and occupied Palestinian territories. Trump's Vice-President Mike Pence and Pompeo wear their evangelical identities on their sleeves and the president has made retention of his vast voting constituency in the Christian right-wing a top priority. Fulfilling US evangelical expectations that Trump would be a 'modern Cyrus' who oversees the Jews' return to Jerusalem and rebuilds the temple is politically paramount for Trump.[50]

The Trump administration's unquestioning fealty to Israel (unlike Obama who was highly critical of Tel Aviv's illegal settlements on Palestinian land) is a direct consequence of evangelical pressure rather than lobbying by American Jewry, which is more liberal and often critical of Israel's right-wing policies under Prime Minister Benjamin Netanyahu. Trump's radical policy change of recognising Jerusalem as Israel's capital in December 2017, thereby shedding the pretence that Washington was a 'neutral broker' between Israel and Palestine, was a tectonic shift in the Middle East that played to US evangelical galleries. His proclamation in March 2019 that the Israeli-occupied Golan Heights, which used to belong to Syria, was sovereign Israeli territory was another crowd-pleasing alteration of US foreign policy. Trump made it plain that he did the unthinkable, unlike previous American presidents—by moving the US Embassy from Tel Aviv to Jerusalem—with an eye on evangelicals. His chat with Mike Huckabee, a Christian Zionist Republican, is revelatory.

> I tell you what, I get more calls of thank you from evangelicals, and I see it in the audiences and everything else, than I do from Jewish people. And the Jewish people appreciate it but the evangelicals appreciate it more than the Jews… it really affects Jewish people in theory more, but… people of the book, people of the Bible really appreciate it and that makes me feel good. It was a campaign promise, I was going to keep it.[51]

For Erdogan, who has made confrontation with Israel a byword of Turkey's Islamist national identity, Trump's electoral gimmick in Jerusalem stung. Erdogan's warning to Trump not to cross a 'red line for Muslims'[52] fell on deaf ears in the face of the US president's domestic preoccupation. The Turkish president ramped up criticism of Washington for its 'huge mistake' of bowing to Netanyahu's wishes and claimed that the Jerusalem move signalled America's 'new operations against the Islamic world'. His statement, 'The United States is not the part of solution in the Middle East today, it is part of the problem,'[53] was a classic refutation. To reinforce Erdogan's image as the defender of the Islamic Ummah or brotherhood, he led the campaign for a UN General Assembly resolution to render the status of Jerusalem as Israel's capital 'null and void', claiming credit for mobilising the international community against the unjust US.[54] Erdogan did not resort to extreme reactions like expulsion of US troops from Turkey's military bases, de-recognition of Israel or imposing economic sanctions. But the episode fed into the AKP's discourse that the West was the enemy of Islam and that the Middle East would be better off without America's neocolonial interference. We will see later in this chapter how Erdogan solidified his partnership with Iran as part of his distancing act from American Zionism.

If the evangelical fire lit a fuse in Turkey–US ties over Israel, then it set off an inferno in 2018 over Ankara's detention of an American pastor, Andrew Brunson. Turkey arrested Brunson in October 2016 and indicted him as an accomplice of the banned Gulenist movement and an American spy working with the PKK. He was swept up alongside hundreds of thousands of Turks of different hues in the post-coup political purges unleashed by Erdogan and his compliant law enforcement machinery. Unlike Obama, who did not escalate the Brunson affair with Erdogan, Trump amped up demands that he had to be released and returned to the US. Sensing Brunson's political value to Trump's evangelical base, Erdogan offered a brazen deal of trading him for Gulen's extradition to Turkey. 'You have a pastor too. Give him to us… Then we will try Brunson and give him to you.'[55]

But Trump, the guru of the *Art of the Deal*, had other ideas. He ratcheted up pressure by slapping trade tariffs on Turkey and complaining he felt personally let down and 'very disappointed in Erdogan'.[56] He threatened to 'impose large sanctions on Turkey for their long-time detainment of Pastor Andrew Brunson, a great Christian, family man and wonderful human being',[57] and followed up the hard-nosed rhetoric with a series of punitive economic measures that caused a sharp plunge in the Turkish lira, investor panic, credit rating downgrades and a nosedive for the Turkish economy. Erdogan fumed about America's 'economic war on Turkey' and vowed to resist it tooth and nail by retaliatory sanctions and boycotting iconic American brands like Apple and switching to South Korea's Samsung instead. He mobilised Turks by invoking the memory of 'the Turkish nation', which had 'many times shown that if its independence and its future was at risk, it would put forward its life, its property and all its wealth. We will stand against the dollar, currency rates, inflation, interest rates. I believe in my nation.'[58]

The 2018 currency and debt crisis in Turkey had other causes besides Trump's economic coercion, but the populist US president showed how far he was willing to go to appease his domestic evangelical base. His undiplomatic taunting of Turkey for acting 'very, very badly' and being 'a problem for a long time', which the US was 'not going to take it sitting down'[59] sent Ankara into a tizzy. Erdogan sardonically retorted, 'Shame, shame! You prefer a pastor over a strategic partner of yours in NATO',[60] but for Trump there was no shame in pressing all levers at his disposal to free Brunson. Disregarding traditional US foreign policy caution of avoiding humiliation of allies is the hallmark of Trump's America First, and Erdogan learnt this bitter lesson. In October 2018, as the economic noose tightened around Turkey, Erdogan bit the bullet and released Brunson to earn relief from America's financial chokehold.

But once the genie of US economic pressure was out of the bottle, it could not be put back. Having seen Erdogan capitulate despite his nationalistic bravado on Brunson, Trump raised this card on the YPG matter. In an unprecedented threat by one NATO member to another, Trump warned in January 2019 on Twitter that he would 'devastate Turkey economically if they hit Kurds'.[61] Erdogan was uncharacteristically mellowed in his riposte, saying he was 'saddened [by] messages from Trump's social media accounts'.[62] He decided that Turkey would any day take Trump and his maverick foreign policy based on populism and isolationism compared to the American globalists and liberal internationalists, who detested Erdogan's authoritarianism and wanted the US to check his neo-Ottoman agenda in the Middle East.

Ankara did not miss the fact that throughout Erdogan's continuing mass arrests, trials and sentences of thousands of Turks for involvement in the 2016 coup attempt, Trump did not utter a single word of condemnation. A Washington guided by America First would wage economic war for the life of a single American pastor, but it could care less about the lives of tonnes of Turkish citizens caught up in Erdogan's tyrannical crackdown. The way in which the Trump administration dropped criminal charges against Erdogan's bodyguards for physically assaulting Turkish democracy activists in broad daylight when he was visiting Washington confirmed there was no liberal hegemonic pressure on Turkey whatsoever.⁶³ The slide in democratic checks and balances within Turkey and worsening human rights conditions there have attracted plenty of Western liberal attention and prompted calls for it to be disciplined, isolated or expelled from NATO,⁶⁴ but Trump conveniently ignored these voices even as he weaponised the same human rights and democracy issues towards regime change in Iran.

The New Triad

Iran and Russia are the twin pillars of Turkey's illiberal anti-Western geopolitical axis in the Middle East. This coalition predates Trump's presidency but has gained traction since 2017. Its origins lie in Erdogan's failure to unseat President Bashar al-Assad in Syria since civil war broke out in 2011, as well as the 2016 coup attempt, which he blamed on the US. When the Arab Spring uprising against Assad quickly devolved into a multisided proxy war in Syria, Erdogan eschewed the AKP's 'zero problems with neighbours' doctrine and got entangled in promoting Sunni Arab jihadist rebel insurrections to overthrow the Iran-backed Alawite Shiite leader, Assad. Domestically, fuelling and facilitating Sunni Arab extremist groups in Syria like Ahrar al-Sham and possibly those allied to Al Qaeda and ISIS⁶⁵ shored up Erdogan's political legitimacy among religious Turks. He projected Turkey as the frontline state in aiding the democratic rights of Syria's majority Sunnis against Assad's repressive minority Shiite-dominated dictatorship and its benefactor Iran.

The sectarian motives behind Erdogan's fateful decision to intervene in Syria were obvious when he first demanded Assad's removal in 2011. He claimed that Ankara did not want to meddle in neighbouring countries, but 'while a nation—especially one that is our kin and relative—is being tormented, we have absolutely no intention to turn a blind eye, to turn our backs against Syria with a 910-kilometre-long borderline'.⁶⁶ The kin and relative reference was a dog whistle to Sunni Islamists within Turkey, who sympathise with Turkmen minorities in Syria, and also a way of mobilising majoritarian sentiment in Turkey against its own Alevi minorities (who bear similarities to Syria's Shiite Alawites). If it was crafty politics at home that raised Erdogan's stature as a defender of pious

Muslims against oppressive regimes, it turned into a disastrous foreign policy move.

As Erdogan waged proxy war on Assad by allowing thousands of Sunni jihadists funded by Persian Gulf monarchies to gather and pass through southern Turkey to attack the Syrian military, he came face to face with Iran, which fielded its proxy Shiite militias across Syria to defend Assad. By 2015, Russia directly entered the fight on the corner of Assad and Iran and tilted the scales against the Sunni coalition of Turkey and the Gulf states. With Obama reluctant to commit a large American military operation against Assad, Erdogan and the Gulf countries were outgunned by the Iran–Russia combine. Turkey was forced to reckon with ground reality as the Syrian war wound down, that Iran 'steadily gained ground as the balance of power between the two powers shifted, and ultimately increased Iranian influence in the region'. Even during the Iraq war, Turkey had contested Iranian dominance and sought to push back Tehran's influence in Iraq, but Erdogan had to reckon with a regional balance of power that advantaged Iran more and gave 'Iranian foreign policy precedence over Turkey'.[67] Erdogan's bitter lament to Obama in late 2011, 'You [US] left Iraq in the hands of Iran once you withdrew,'[68] was the Turkish leader's first comeuppance. Defeat at the hands of the Iran–Russia duo in the Syrian war compounded Erdogan's problem and drove him to do an about-turn on his previous inveterate opposition to Shiite Iran and overcome Turkey's historical wariness about befriending Russia.

The underlying factor in bringing about the Turkey–Iran–Russia axis has been the unreliability of America. Turkish scholar Gulden Ayman notes that Erdogan kept the option of repairing ties with Iran 'especially after having been frustrated with US policy in Iraq and its inaction in Syria'.[69] If Washington is unwilling to bolster Turkey's geopolitical position in the region, Ankara has to find other anchors to enhance its influence. Ofra Bengion, an Israeli strategist, aptly explains why Erdogan shed taboos and hitched Turkey's wagon to erstwhile opponents.

> The erstwhile unipolar world where the US was the only power in the Middle East has disappeared and the resulting vacuum enabled Russia to spread its influence in many countries in the region. This structural

shift has convinced Turkey's President Recep Tayyip Erdogan to follow the adage 'if you cannot beat your enemy, join him'.[70]

In December 2016, Turkey, Russia and Iran declared themselves as 'guarantor countries' and launched the Astana process for a negotiated settlement of the Syrian war, parallel to the US and Europe-initiated Geneva process. Tripartite diplomatic summits among Erdogan, Putin and Iranian President Hassan Rouhani began in earnest from 2017 and the three have stuck together in their common quest to ensure that US troops leave Syria as per Trump's diktat and 'reject all attempts to create new realities on the ground under the pretext of combating terrorism'. The language the trio has adopted in diplomatic communiques of 'standing against separatist agendas aimed at undermining the sovereignty and territorial integrity of Syria as well as the national security of neighbouring countries'[71] is unmistakably an indication that Ankara, Tehran and Moscow want to thwart the liberal internationalist American establishment's emphasis on sustaining Western assistance to the Kurds and setting up a permanent Kurdish bulwark in the region on behalf of Washington and Tel Aviv.

Sceptics have questioned how viable the Turkey–Iran–Russia axis is because of internecine conflicts of interest among the three partners. Anonymous Turkish officials have been quoted as saying that Ankara's military presence in enclaves of northern Syria will be 'temporary but indefinite' and that Turkey's approach to Iran is a mix of 'rivalry and cooperation' because Turkey is forever 'wary of Iran's expansionism and dominance in Damascus'.[72] Given that Turkey remains a NATO member and its Incirlik airbase continues to be accessed by the US military for aerial operations in the region, Iran does have reservations about how genuinely anti-Western Erdogan is. Utterances by American officials that Turkey and the US are working to contain Iran in the region do not lend much confidence to Tehran. US readouts of conversations between Trump and Erdogan 'to improve the strategic partnership between the United States and Turkey, particularly in fostering regional stability and combating terrorism in all its forms, including Iranian-sponsored terrorism',[73] have not gone down well in Tehran. Pompeo's expression of hope in November 2018 that 'President Erdogan will come to understand the US is a better partner than Iran',[74] and comments by lower-level American officials that 'Turkey has a vested strategic interest in checking the spread of Iranian influence'[75] convey to Iran that Erdogan is hedging and will not adopt an unequivocal anti-US position. Turkey's proxy fighting units in Syria like Ahrar and the Free Syrian Army (FSA) are hostile to Iranian militias and the sectarian Sunni-Shiite enmity will not vanish.

As to Turkey and Russia, their endearment has been cast as a marriage of convenience that masks divergences on Assad and the future of Syria, plus the geostrategic vulnerability of Ankara to Moscow. American scholar Henri Barkey argues that Turkey 'needs the protection' that NATO offers, as without it, 'the Russians would be able to intimidate Ankara at will'.[76] Jeffrey Mankoff of the Center for Strategic and International Studies in Washington likewise doubts the viability of the Turkey–Russia entente and labels it 'a highly unequal partnership' where Turkey is 'weaker and therefore more vulnerable to Russian coercion'.[77] As Erdogan had his back to the wall in Syria and therefore was compelled to make peace with Putin, the latter did hold more aces. As per Turkish historian Soner Cagaptay, Putin would offer ad hoc deals to Erdogan to curb the Kurds in Syria and, in return, get Erdogan to stay within NATO 'as a non-participating member, thereby undermining the organisation's effectiveness'.[78]

Erdogan has to manage tremendous pressure from NATO not to venture too far into Moscow's domain. As we saw in the Introduction, Trump has no qualms about Putin's expanding spheres of influence in Eastern Europe and the Middle East, but the deep state in the US wants Erdogan to avoid Putin like the plague as it would unravel NATO. In September 2017, Erdogan announced that Turkey had already paid Russia a deposit and signed an agreement for buying the S-400 anti-aircraft missile defence system for $2.5 billion. Despite internal disagreements and strains, no member state of NATO had until then broken the unwritten norm underpinning the alliance since 1949 of avoiding strategic defence cooperation with Russia. That Erdogan could contemplate such a bold démarche and undermine the existential anti-Russian logic of NATO says much about how dramatically the US has lost command over its ally.

While American allies have often cavilled about Washington's commitment to fulfilling its defence obligations to them after the Cold

War, the phenomenon of treaty-bound partners defiantly and openly deserting ship is a worrisome possibility staring at the US. And the credit for bringing the global American alliance system to a crisis point goes to the captain-in-charge, Trump, who has deconstructed a carefully erected liberal international structure of trust and faith since World War II. In Turkey's case, although Erdogan had been miffed by Obama for the latter's suspected abetment of the 2016 coup attempt,[79] his run-ins with Trump exacerbated matters and forced him into strategic somersaults. The S-400 purchase from Russia was a retort in the face of a US that was taking Turkey for granted. Trump's unpredictable policymaking and lack of a consistent approach to the Middle East are too unsettling for an Erdogan who at least knows exactly what Putin is after.

Trump's mercantilist economic nationalism is a confounding element in how deep Erdogan would go with Putin. The populist US president lives on an alternative planet from mainstream globalists who are enraged that Russia would get a Trojan Horse to detect vulnerabilities of American-supplied hardware and software once its S-400 missiles are incorporated into the Turkish arsenal.[80] Despite serious objections from the Pentagon and NATO commanders that Turkey must be punished for buying the Russian S-400 and denied purchase of American-made F-35 fighter jets and Patriot air defence systems, Washington announced in December 2018 that Ankara had been cleared to purchase Patriots worth $3.5 billion. This breakthrough (Turkey had sought Patriots with technology transfer for years but was rebuffed by the US) was described as 'an opening gambit by the Trump administration to get Turkey to halt its purchase of Russia's S-400'.[81]

But as we saw in Chapter I in the case of India's acquisition of the same S-400s from Russia, Trump might just be satisfied if Turkey buys more US weaponry and spare Ankara from sanctions. The Turkish government's insistence that it is not an either/or scenario as it wants the S-400 as well as Patriots and F-35s[82] will not cut ice with globalists in Washington, but it holds out prospects of billions of dollars of additional American defence sales to Turkey, which Trump would prefer not to pass up. The Pentagon had warned that 'if Turkey goes ahead with plans to purchase the $2.5-billion Russian system, the United States will withhold F-35 aircraft and Patriot Missile batteries earmarked for Turkey',[83] but

Washington ultimately did not come down like a tonne of bricks on India after delivering similar threats to New Delhi about its S-400 deal with Moscow.

Whether or not Trump is appeasing, accommodating and placating Erdogan through the US troop withdrawal from Syria and sale of Patriots,[84] the heterodox American president has opened vistas to Turkey that may let Erdogan have the Russia–Iran cake and eat the American pie too. The demarcation between the good Trump and the bad American deep state reached such a level in Ankara that by March 2019, the pro-AKP media claimed that the US president was eager to visit Turkey but was being prevented by spoiler 'subordinates' at the 'lower levels' of the US government who wanted to penalise Erdogan for buying the Russian S-400.[85] Erdogan also claimed that he got a personal telephonic concurrence from Trump that he had 'made the right decision' in buying the S-400 from Russia after he convinced the American president of Turkey's rationale that it faced a threat to its airspace from Syria.[86] If true, it was yet another instance of Trump undercutting his own liberal deep state establishment and other anti-Russia NATO allies so that Erdogan would cooperate on a US troop withdrawal from Syria.

Like Trump, Erdogan is a right-wing populist and there is also domestic political arithmetic behind his courtship of Russia. Erdogan critic and former Turkish parliamentarian Aykan Erdemir believes that 'Erdogan's heart is with Russia [as] radical changes in the (Turkish) military since the 2016 coup attempt—with Eurasianists on the ascent and Transatlanticists marginalized—may have sealed Turkey's turn away from the West.' Erdemir's prediction, 'NATO military culture could be gradually replaced by a Russian military culture,' in Turkey[87] is futuristic, but Erdogan has tried to escape the conundrum of dependency on Western and Eastern powers for defence by fast-forwarding Turkey's indigenous defence manufacturing base. The Turkish president's claim that his country was meeting '65 per cent of its defence needs' through indigenous manufactured products, and his reminder that 'as long as we remain only a user of technology, we cannot guarantee our freedom in any area'[88] are indicative of long-term planning to liberate Ankara from the US–Russia dichotomy.

But where Russia has a leg up over America is in Putin's strong endorsement of Erdogan's authoritarian rule and his validation of the concept of regional stakeholders taking the lead in stabilising their environs. Italian analyst Carlo Frappi argues that Turkey and Russia are welded by their

> joint proposition of a 'regional ownership' principle, whereby countries belonging to the same area are—borrowing words from then Foreign Minister Davutoglu—'to find regional solutions to their regional problems, rather than waiting for other actors from outside the region to impose their own solutions.'[89]

If this principle had brought Ankara and Moscow together sometimes in earlier periods in the Black Sea and Central Asia, it has now been extended to the Middle East 'and widened through the inclusion of Iran, as epitomised by the so-called Astana Process'.[90]

Under Trump, who is captive to domestic evangelical interests in America in favouring Israel and toeing the Israeli line in the Middle East, Iran has been demonised as an evil state and 'the world's leading sponsor of terror'.[91] Pompeo's comment, 'As a Christian, I certainly believe [that Trump is like the Biblical Queen Esther who has been sent by God to] help save the Jewish people from the Iranian menace,'[92] reveals the predominantly domestic populist lens through which Tehran has been appraised by Trump's core team. The Trump administration's hard line on Iran by exiting Obama's 2015 nuclear deal and ratcheting up pressure for regime change through reimposition of sanctions, deployment of additional military assets and selective usage of human rights promotion, has exacerbated the fundamental problem of the Middle East's regional security architecture, that is, deliberate exclusion of Iran from governance. Iranian-origin thinker Mehran Kamrava writes that the US, Saudi Arabia and Israel's exclusion of Iran from collective decision-making has triggered a 'region-wide security dilemma' and aggravated 'pervasive insecurity' to keep the Middle East perpetually on the boil.[93] Erdogan's Turkey had joined the anti-Iran club during the Syrian war and learnt a costly lesson by burning its fingers. It has no reason to yet again work with the US and Saudi Arabia to repeat the same mistake. From Ankara's chastened lens, cooperating with Russia and Iran offers better guarantees to check Kurdish separatism and have a say in the Syrian endgame than by loyally following the US, which has been a source of endless disappointment to Erdogan.

The shriller the admonitions from Washington to desist from Iran and Russia, the more determined Erdogan has become in pivoting towards them. Trump and Pence's loud and explicit warnings via Twitter and speeches that Erdogan is erring have made standing up to the West an existential political necessity for the Turkish leader. His retort to persistent American blackmail on the S-400 deal has been a firm assertion, 'We're not a slave, we're independent.' On the US cancelling GSP trade benefits to Turkey, he shot back with 'no one should attempt to tame Turkey' and that it would retaliate in kind.[94] Therefore, forming the triad with Iran and Russia is, on a broader level, an extension of Turkey's long-sought autonomy and freedom of choices that were denied by a stifling US alliance. This does not mean Ankara is severing relations with Washington. It is only readjusting them through its own transactionalism, which matches Trump's.

Beyond Neo-Ottomanism

Under Erdogan's prolonged tenure, Turkey has undergone multiple foreign policy pivots to the West (he tried earnestly for EU membership and enhancing the US alliance in his early years as Prime Minister), the South (Davutoglu's zero problems doctrine with Arab neighbours) and the East (the recent axis with Russia and Iran). In terms of yield, none of these paradigms has generated the ideal net returns that Turkey expected. Erdogan's 2023 Vision, unveiled in 2011, outlined a set of goals for Turkey to attain by the centenary year of the Turkish Republic. It included objectives of playing 'a much bigger role' in international institutions, becoming an 'even bigger contributor [in] re-establishing global order, restructuring regional and subregional orders', and turning into a 'global power [that's] one of the first ten big economic powers' in the world.[95] After almost two decades in the saddle, it is hard to see how Erdogan can reify such lofty ambitions.

A prime difficulty Turkey is facing today is that despite its tactical pivots hither and thither, it has alienated all potent actors of varied leanings in the Middle East and earned a reputation as strategically untrustworthy. Cagaptay holds that Erdogan has 'thus far failed in his quest to earn Turkey great power status' and his foreign policy 'has left Turkey weak and isolated, friendless with the exception of Qatar and increasingly on its own in the global arena'.[96] But Cagaptay also acknowledges that the lack of Western sensitivity and solicitousness to Turkey's independence and preferences has been a recurrent theme, which is as responsible for the impasse it finds itself in as Erdogan's follies. Trump has, in particular, rubbed Erdogan the wrong way owing to his intermestic policymaking and unheralded bullying of a fellow NATO member through trade war and economic sanctions. The US president's unapologetic lack of concern for liberal internationalist causes like democracy and human rights does give the authoritarian Erdogan relief from Western values-based criticism, but it has also generated dismay in Ankara, which still considers itself a rare democracy in a sea of dictatorships in the Middle East, and hence expects Western deference and respect.

The global scandal around the gory assassination of Erdogan's personal friend Jamal Khashoggi, the Saudi dissident journalist, in the Saudi Consulate in Istanbul in October 2018, brought home Trump's ruthless domestically focussed populism to a Turkey that hoped otherwise. Since the murder was committed on Turkish soil by hitmen dispatched by the highest echelons of the Saudi Arabian monarchy, Erdogan seized the opportunity to embarrass Crown Prince Mohammed bin Salman (known as MBS) and feverishly lobbied with the US to put Riyadh in the dock. Erdogan's assiduous cultivation of friendship with Qatar and his support for Doha when the state was subjected to an embargo by Saudi Arabia, his pivot to Iran, which is aligned with Qatar and a sworn enemy of Saudi Arabia, and his co-sponsorship with Qatar of radical non-state actors like the Palestinian Hamas and the Egyptian Muslim Brotherhood, greatly angered the conservative Saudi royalty. His posturing as the leader of the Sunni world never stopped irking the House of Saud, which deems itself numero uno by virtue of the country being home to Islam's two holiest shrines in Mecca and Medina.

The Khashoggi killing and the evidence Erdogan assembled around the case through Turkish intelligence agencies were acutely damaging to the crown prince's image as a reformer, presenting the ideal opportunity for Ankara to cut Riyadh down to size and unseat MBS. Erdogan loyalist and mouthpiece Abdulkadir Selvi gave a glimpse into official Turkey's paranoid purpose.

> The Saudi Crown Prince was caught red-handed in Jamal Khashoggi's murder. The US is playing both sides. On one hand, it is cornering the Crown Prince by using the murder, but on the other, it is trying to save him. This is because Crown Prince Mohammad bin Salman, Emirates' Crown Prince Mohammad bin Zayed, and Trump's son-in-law Jared Kushner make up the 'devil's triangle'. This trio's main goal is to topple President Erdogan. We should not close this file before the Crown Prince is held accountable and is removed from office. Otherwise, we cannot live with a Crown Prince who is Turkey's enemy for another 50 years.[97]

But no matter how many sensational intelligence leaks and disclosures Erdogan released in drips to excite international media about the Saudi act of state to brutally kill and dismember its own citizen, Trump was unmoved and refused to take Riyadh to task through sanctions or ultimatums. The populist American president chose to ignore the US intelligence community's conclusion that MBS ordered Khashoggi's murder and kept up one refrain throughout the furore—Saudi Arabia was sustaining American jobs and American corporate profits and these gains could not be jeopardised. Trump's America First consistency in this sordid drama was unmissable. His initial take when the Khashoggi murder surfaced on why the US was not halting arms sales to Saudi Arabia was, 'I don't like stopping massive amounts of money that's being poured into our country—they are spending $110 billion on military equipment and on things that create jobs for this country.'[98] He added, for effect, 'I would not be in favour of stopping a country from spending $110 billion—which is an all-time record—and letting Russia have that money and letting China have that money.'[99]

Weeks later, with US inaction and winking at Saudi Arabia continuing, Trump reiterated the populist line that provided a translucent insight into his ideology.

> After my heavily negotiated trip to Saudi Arabia last year, the Kingdom agreed to spend and invest $450 billion in the United States. This is a record amount of money. It will create hundreds of thousands of jobs, tremendous economic development, and much additional wealth for the United States. Of the $450 billion, $110 billion will be spent on the purchase of military equipment from Boeing, Lockheed Martin, Raytheon and many other great US defense contractors. If we foolishly

cancel these contracts, Russia and China would be the enormous beneficiaries—and very happy to acquire all of this new-found business. It would be a wonderful gift to them directly from the United States!

Adding that the Saudis were bosom allies of the US in countering Iran and controlling global oil prices, Trump ended his quintessentially illiberal statement with a flourish, 'Very simply it is called America First!'[100]

For Erdogan, *l'affaire* Khashoggi was a painful reminder that relying on Trump's US to advance Turkish interests in the Middle East was a chimera. Saudi Arabia was the largest buyer of American weaponry as of 2017, while Israel and the UAE were the fourth- and sixth-largest on the list.[101] For the mercantilist Trump who prizes customers of US exports the most, Turkey is small fry. Relatively speaking, Turkey is politically freer than Saudi Arabia in spite of Erdogan's absolutism.[102] Geopolitically, Turkey has relevance to the US even though it is no longer as salient as during the Cold War as a buffer against the Soviet Union. To Erdogan's chagrin, the populist Trump does not valorise Turkey the way a liberal internationalist like Obama or Bush might. Turkish scholar Kemal Kirisci demonstrates how Turkey had, for long, been an integral cog in the wheel in America's liberal international order, but Trump challenged this trajectory by placing 'more emphasis on realpolitik and transactional relations', leaving a 'question mark over the United States' continuing commitment to anchoring Turkey in this liberal order'.[103]

Back in 2009, when Turkey was yet to descend into an illiberal autocracy and the US was in liberal internationalist hands, Obama touted bilateral relations as a 'model partnership', which had the capacity to 'create a modern international community'.[104] So taken in was Obama by Erdogan's apparent genius in merging Islam and democracy that he named the Turkish leader among five international counterparts with whom he could forge 'bonds of trust'.[105] Today, not only have times changed but so have the leaders. Trump is neither fixedly optimistic nor pessimistic about Turkey. He blows hot and cold à la carte, depending on whether or not America is winning or losing monetarily from Turkey, or if he is gaining politically from snubbing or massaging it. Until Trump's advent, Turkey stared at a fork in the road where one track implied staying tethered to the liberal West and the other track entailed moving in an illiberal anti-Western direction.

Trump has undone this duality and left no West to speak of, with only a few European liberals like German Chancellor Angela Merkel and French President Emmanuel Macron holding aloft the liberal banner. On the anti-Western side, Turkey has found receptivity in Iran, Russia and China, but there are limits to it being accepted and assimilated into their ranks as long as it retains a seat at the NATO table. Admittedly, Erdogan has steered Turkey away from the Atlantic and towards Eurasia. Today's Turkey is not the stereotypical country that had one foot in the Occident and one in the Orient, but it has not severed itself from all Western institutions and linkages.

With no ideal options abroad, the quandary of how Turkey can actualise its worth and obtain the status of a global power can be resolved only through a two-step transformation of its domestic politics and an accompanying re-examination of its national identity. Unlike Modi in India, who completed five years in office in 2019 and still has the freshness and creative energy to pilot his country into the great power league, Erdogan has ruled way too long and locked Turkey into a jaded cul-de-sac. In theory, the 2017 referendum win permits Erdogan to cling to power until 2034 (ceteris paribus, he would be 80 years old then). The prospects of Turkey leaping ahead from its present seventeenth place in the list of the world's largest economies (India is sixth and Brazil is eighth)[106] and entering the top 10, as envisaged in its Vision 2023, are dim as Erdogan has installed his own Islamist capitalist cronyism; his brand of politics does not free the entrepreneurial energies of the country's youth. As a former governor of the Turkish Central Bank puts it, 'At every level of society, loyalty has replaced merit as the sole criterion. Corruption and cronyism are eating the country away like cancer. A culture of impunity pervades the government: Nothing is ever wrong, and no one is ever responsible.'[107] The insolence with which Erdogan pressured Turkish courts to annul a mayoral election in Istanbul in May 2019 simply because the AKP's candidate lost provided a clear view of how much patron–client politics determine all outcomes. The key to Istanbul's vast municipal budgets is such that Erdogan does not want to ever let go of it, meaning that democracy with sound economic management is impossible.

The manner in which the lira was battered when Trump slapped sanctions over the Brunson detention in 2018 showed how economically brittle Turkey was and how this weakness obliged Erdogan to swallow his pride and concede to the US. For all his nationalistic huffing and puffing, Erdogan has not been able to reduce Turkey's dependence on the West in economic and financial matters. By 2016, 85 per cent of Turkey's foreign direct investment (FDI) and 68 per cent of its foreign loans were still sourced from the EU and the US.[108] Bailouts from Qatar and capital inflows from China have mitigated Western market pressure on Turkey only slightly. Unlike India and Brazil, which have more diversified FDI and GDP profiles and were counted as the eleventh- and twenty-fifth most favoured investment destinations in the world by 2018,[109] Turkey is over-reliant on the West and no longer a happening emerging market economy (EME). If Erdogan, who has prioritised personal survival in power over economic reforms, hangs on and on, there is little hope of Turkey breaking back into the elite tier of EMEs. In 2011, Turkey was named by the financial consultancy Fidelity Investments as belonging to a promising new bunch of EMEs—Mexico, Indonesia, Nigeria and Turkey (MINT)—which were supposed to follow BRICS and churn out spectacular economic growth. But it has underperformed as Erdogan grew more autocratic and was unable to live up to that billing.

Erdogan's style of polarising politics has also limited Turkey's freedom to hold its own in foreign policy. He relaunched war in southern Turkey against the PKK in 2015 to consolidate his majoritarian appeal in elections. Resumption of fighting in Turkey's south embroiled Ankara in more disastrous military operations in Syria and Iraq, which ended in defeat. Unless Turkey settles the decades-long conflict with its own Kurdish citizens, it cannot breathe easily and chart a cooperative foreign policy course with its Arab and Persian neighbours. As Cagaptay has aptly written, 'to secure influence and stability in Syria and Iraq, Ankara has to make peace with its Kurdish community' through policies that grant cultural rights to Kurds and civil liberties for all Turkish citizens.[110]

The zero problems idea was a brilliant one, but its execution faltered due to Erdogan's politicisation of terrorism and temperamental handling of Turkey's Kurdish problem. His premise that present-day Turkey is an inheritor of the Ottoman empire and that its greatness can be restored through neo-Ottoman domination over Kurds and Arabs has backfired. Erdogan's neo-Ottomanism has been adumbrated by Turkish scholar Hakan Yavuz as pitting East against West, placing Islam at the core of national identity, acting upon an expanded concept of responsibility towards Muslims of former Ottoman territories (especially Arab Palestinians), pursuing 'Muslim hegemony and geopolitical power', and redefining the 'Islamic homeland [as] far greater than Turkey's geographical boundaries, encompassing those lands yearning to return to the Ottoman'.[111] Irredentism and aggrandisement abroad have been the flip sides of Erdogan's sultan-style despotism at home in a two-way mirroring process, and one cannot foresee normalisation of Turkey's ties with all Middle Eastern powers until a post-Erdogan dispensation arrives.

Lebanese-origin researcher Hussein Ibish has argued that Erdogan has carved out a 'distinctive third bloc' in the Middle East, separate from the pro-Iran coalition, which has Russia, and the anti-Iran group that includes Saudi Arabia, Israel and the US. This third bloc has 'a Sunni Islamist orientation' with Turkey in the lead and Qatar as the financial sponsor, and an array of non-state actors like the Muslim Brotherhood and Hamas as their proxies. Ibish claims that Turkey is 'turning into a major regional player with its own agenda, ambitions, ideology and allies', and that this third bloc could convert Turkey into 'a regional hegemon as ambitious as Iran and more effective'.[112] Such readings miss the point that an alliance of merely two countries, Turkey and Qatar, cannot by itself engineer a paradigm shift or tilt the regional balance of power in Ankara's favour. Nor is the radical Sunni Islamism espoused by Ankara and Doha the solution to ending the bitter enmity and endemic violence in the Middle East. For Arabs and Persians, Erdogan's neo-Ottomanism has weaved itself into the tapestry of problems they are facing and vitiated the regional atmosphere.

With neo-Ottomanism as its banner, Turkey has slim chances of being accepted as a leader in the Middle East. In Chapter I, I pointed to India inheriting a strong post-colonial identity that infused its foreign policy with anti-hegemonic tropes and character. Opposing imperialism, be it American or Chinese, is ingrained in the Indian psyche and that attribute serves it well in the journey to become a leading power. But Turkey's exceptionalism under the AKP has rested on recalling its imperial past, equating 'Ottoman conquests with Ottoman globalization', and positing a 'pax-Ottomana' in which the Turkish state is an inspirational alternative to Western globalisation for Muslim countries.[113] The first basic lacuna of neo-Ottomanism is that it invokes fear of Turkey among formerly colonised Arabs and antagonistic Persians. Early proponents of neo-Ottomanism denied it was a cover for imperial expansionism and stressed the 'soft power' dimensions of Turkey's pitch for international influence.[114] But Erdogan's praxis of neo-Ottomanism has included military misadventures and promotion of jihadist terrorists, which sowed mistrust and chaos in the Middle East. Even the softer Islamic, humanitarian and educational aid through Turkish state-run charities and foundations to succour Muslim communities has triggered a backlash, as Arab countries are uneasy about 'an imperial agenda behind Turkey's religious diplomacy'.[115] Consider how the rousing language of Turkey's Interior Minister Suleyman Soylu during an AKP election rally raised the hackles of Arab countries. His assertion, 'We are not only just Turkey, but also Damascus, Aleppo, Kirkuk, Jerusalem, Palestine, Mecca, and Medina. We are the grandchildren of a great civilization,'[116] drew flak for its 'grand hegemonistic ambition' from Riyadh[117] and portended more fragmentation and violence in the Middle East.

The second flaw of neo-Ottomanism is that it constricts Turkey's ambit of influence to Islamic nations and Muslims. Erdogan has not been able to transcend his Islamist identity to cast Turkey as a benefactor and leader of the wider Global South. In Africa, where Turkey has presented itself as a 'virtuous power' compared to the neocolonial EU, Ankara has been most active in Islamic countries like Somalia. It has been accused of fuelling Islamist insurgents in Muslim-majority countries such as Nigeria, Chad and Mali. In non-Islamic parts of sub-Saharan Africa, 'rather than depart from the machinations of an "imperial" EU (or of rival BRIC nations), Turkey is instead seen as yet one more player in the new scramble for African markets'.[118] Economic fragility and downturns (Turkey's GDP shrank from $851 billion in 2017 to $784 billion in 2018)[119] and costly foreign military interventions in Syria and Iraq have not helped. Turkey's construct of an Ankara consensus of developmental assistance in Africa, distinct from the exploitative Washington Consensus and the Beijing Consensus, suffers from a paucity of resources. Until Erdogan was allied with Gulen in domestic politics, the latter's educational movement was the main carrier of Turkish cultural diplomacy in Africa. After the two Islamists fell out, Turkey has not found effective vehicles to walk the talk on South-South Cooperation and 'Third Worldism' in Africa and Asia.[120] In Chapter III, I will demonstrate how Brazil has fared a lot better through its developmental diplomacy in the Global South, thanks to a national identity that is not religious, sectarian or neo-imperialist like Erdogan's Turkey. What Erdogan considers to be Turkey's greatest civilisational calling card in world affairs—the Ottoman past—is actually a shackle that has not allowed Ankara to rise beyond a point as a shaper of regional and international orders.

To be fair, Erdogan has pulled up Turkey from a weaker and lesser state of existence around the turn of the millennium to a stronger and higher one over the last nearly two decades. He must be credited for his historical contribution of fundamentally elevating Turkey from its Cold War subservience to the US to a new assertive post-Cold War foreign policy player. Turkish scholar Sinan Ulgen has correctly noted, 'Ankara has begun defining national interests around strengthening its role as a regional power broker. That's an about-turn from the Cold War, when Turkey's foreign policy was focused on cementing its place within NATO—the ultimate defense against the powerful Soviet threat.'[121] But we are now knocking on the doors of the third decade of the twenty-first century. Trump has dealt the post-Cold War liberal international order a hard kick in the solar plexus. Erdogan's tack of juxtaposing Islamist and neo-Ottoman Turkey from the liberal capitalist West and stoking anti-Americanism in Turkish public opinion worked for a while, but that binary no longer holds in the wake of Trump and a wave of European right-wing populism.

Waiting for Trump the populist to turn saviour of Turkey's strategic interests while warding off America's liberal internationalist deep state is no deus ex machina. Trump's riddance of the globalist foreign policy mantle of controlling the Middle East and his unwillingness to commit US military and diplomatic resources to maintain the regional balance of power are not going to automatically give Turkey the advantage to shape and lead a new Middle East. Dubai-based defence analyst Riad Kahwaji posits that Putin's Russia is 'seen as the go-to power for a region consumed by crises and unsure of Washington's reliability'.[122] Assessments that Putin has become the new master of the Middle East thanks to Obama's detachment and 'total chaos under Trump'[123] do contain some validity. They suggest that America's pullback could set off a bandwagoning process, wherein weak states like Egypt, Syria, Libya and Iraq will gravitate to Russia for protection, rather than knock on Turkey's doors. Erdogan could score a win over the Kurds with Trump's tacit cooperation, but Turkey is presently neither welcomed nor acceptable in the Middle East to be an alternative provider of regional public goods to the US or Russia.

In the Introduction of this book, I stressed that emerging powers aiming to be great powers have an independent gene and do not bandwagon with pre-existing or new hegemons. Turkey's axis with Russia and Iran is not tantamount to bandwagoning, but a readjustment in light of Obama's non-commitment and Trump's isolationism. Turkey is too proud a neo-Ottoman state to kowtow to Russia or the US. Erdogan's message to Washington in November 2018, 'Turkey is not a country which can be used as pawn in the game of power played in any country [and] not a country to be caught in the crossfire of inconsistent policies pursued by the US in our region,'[124] underscores that Turkey has come a long way since it was firmly ensconced in the NATO alliance. Ankara is aiming to be an alternative to Washington or Moscow and looking for followers in the region to come under its umbrella. Fragile states in the Middle East are, by design, looking to bandwagon with whoever can assure their survival. But Turkey is a long way from fulfilling its potential to be a substitute to the US or Russia that can secure the weak countries of the Middle East and cement them into a dynamic force.

In Chapter I, we noted that India too lacks the means to replace the US or China as the pre-eminent actor in Asia. But what India has going for it is its ability to build endogenous plurilateral coalitions within Asia to put up a third show apart the US and China. Turkey's only salvation lies in convening and forging a similar broad intra-Middle Eastern coalition. For this sort of formation to emerge, though, Erdogan is not the suitable vector since he perceives Turkey to be in competition for one-upmanship with Saudi Arabia and Iran, and derives his foreign policy from narrow identity politics in Turkish society. To elevate itself as a leader, Turkey needs a revamped national identity that has to synthesise the liberal Kemalist and conservative Islamist elements, as well as the peripheral identities of the Kurds and the Alevi minorities. Once Turkey is whole and united around a non-polarising form of nationalism and a non-imperialistic and non-religious form of international engagement, it can resume its stalled march to great power status by building a broad coalition of Arab and Persian forces that would terminate wars and usher in regional peace and stability.

Political personalities of elites are understated but essential components in the emergence of rising powers to their due places in the international order. This book is showing how Trump's personality and politics are unwitting enablers of emerging powers. But to make the most of the opportunity presented by the isolationist and populist Trump, emerging powers must have their own visionary political personalities who realise that they are at an inflection point and craft new domestic and foreign policies to grasp the opening. Until Erdogan departs, Turkey's trek to the haloed global power status will be slow and stuttering.

Endnotes

1. Jim Tankersley et al., 'Trump Hits Turkey When It's Down, Doubling Tariffs,' *The New York Times*, 10 August 2018, https://www.nytimes.com/2018/08/10/us/politics/trump-turkey-tariffs-currency.html.
2. Recep Erdogan, 'How Turkey Sees the Crisis with the US,' *The New York Times*, 10 August 2018, https://www.nytimes.com/2018/08/10/opinion/turkey-erdogan-trump-crisis-sanctions.html.
3. Samuel Osborne, 'Donald Trump Criticised for Congratulating Recep Tayyip Erdogan on Winning Turkish Referendum,' *The Independent*, 18 April 2017, https://www.independent.co.uk/news/world/americas/us-politics/donald-trump-recep-tayyip-erdogan-congratulate-turkey-referendum-president-powers-increase-reaction-a7688171.html.
4. AFP, 'Trump and Turkey's President Show Strained Unity at White House Meeting,' *The Guardian*, 16 May 2017, https://www.theguardian.com/us-news/2017/may/16/trump-turkey-president-erdogan-white-house-meeting-isis.
5. 'Remarks by President Trump and President Erdogan of Turkey Before Bilateral Meeting,' 21 September 2017, Lotte New York Palace Hotel, New York, https://www.whitehouse.gov/briefings-statements/remarks-president-trump-president-erdogan-turkey-bilateral-meeting/.
6. 'The Rise of "Authoritarian Populism" in the 21st Century: From Erdoğan's Turkey to Trump's America,' *Journal of Global Faultlines*, Vol. 4, Issue 1 (January–May 2017): 3.
7. Umit Cizre and Erinc Yeldan, 'The Turkish Encounter with Neo-Liberalism: Economics and Politics in the 2000/2001 Crisis,' *Review of International Political Economy*, Vol. 12, Issue 3 (August 2005): 387–408.

8. Marcie Patton, 'The Economic Policies of Turkey's AKP Government: Rabbits from a Hat?' *Middle East Journal*, Vol. 60, Issue 3 (Summer 2006): 515–16.
9. Harriet Alexander et al., 'Donald Trump Welcomes Egypt's President and Says He Has "Been Close to Him Ever Since the First Time We Met",' *The Telegraph*, 3 April 2017, https://www.telegraph.co.uk/news/2017/04/03/donald-trump-welcomes-egypts-president-says-has-close-ever-since/.
10. Mehtap Soyler, *The Turkish Deep State: State Consolidation, Civil-Military Relations and Democracy* (London: Routledge, 2015).
11. Dov Zakheim, 'Think There's a Deep State? Take a Look at Turkey,' *The National Interest*, 18 February 2018, https://nationalinterest.org/feature/think-theres-deep-state-take-look-turkey-24553.
12. '"Deep State" Preventing Trump's Syria Withdrawal—Erdogan,' Ahval News, 6 March 2019, https://ahvalnews.com/us-withdrawal/deep-state-preventing-trumps-syria-withdrawal-erdogan.
13. 'Turkey Slams Trump's National Security Advisor McMaster Over "Islamic Extremism" Remarks,' *Hurriyet Daily News*, 13 December 2017, http://www.hurriyetdailynews.com/turkey-slams-trumps-national-security-advisor-mcmaster-over-islamic-extremism-remarks-124065.
14. Carlotta Gall and Mark Landler, 'Turkish President Snubs Bolton Over Comments that Turkey Must Protect Kurds,' *The New York Times*, 8 January 2019, https://www.nytimes.com/2019/01/08/world/middleeast/erdogan-bolton-turkey-syria-kurds.html.
15. Ilhan Tanir, 'Pompeo Becoming US Secretary of State Alarming for Turkey,' Ahval News, 20 April 2018, https://ahvalnews.com/mike-pompeo/pompeo-becoming-us-secretary-state-alarming-turkey.
16. James Grimaldi et al., 'Mueller Probes Flynn's Role in Alleged Plan to Deliver Cleric to Turkey,' *The Wall Street Journal*, 10 November 2017, https://www.wsj.com/articles/mueller-probes-flynns-role-in-alleged-plan-to-deliver-cleric-to-turkey-1510309982.
17. Kevin Johnson, 'Michael Flynn's Ex-Business Associate Charged in Illegal Lobbying Effort to Extradite Turkish Cleric,' *USA Today*, 17 December 2018, https://www.usatoday.com/story/news/politics/2018/12/17/michael-flynn-bijan-rafiekian-business-partner/2335768002/.
18. 'Remarks by President Trump Before Marine One Departure,' 17 November 2018, https://www.whitehouse.gov/briefings-statements/remarks-president-trump-marine-one-departure-24/.
19. 'Trump Told Erdogan He's Working to Extradite Gulen, FM Çavuşoglu Says,' *Daily Sabah*, 16 December 2018, https://www.dailysabah.com/diplomacy/2018/12/16/trump-told-erdogan-hes-working-to-exradite-gulen-fm-cavusoglu-says.
20. Ihsan Gurkan, *NATO, Turkey and the Southern Flank* (New York: National Strategy Information Center, 1980).
21. Ayse Atmaca, 'The Geopolitical Origins of Turkish–American Relations: Revisiting the Cold War Years,' *All Azimuth*, Vol. 3, Issue 1 (January 2014): 26.
22. Aylin Guney, 'Anti-Americanism in Turkey: Past and Present,' *Middle Eastern Studies*, Vol. 44, Issue 3 (May 2008): 471–87.
23. Stephen Larrabee, *Troubled Partnership: US–Turkish Relations in an Era of Global Political Change* (Washington DC: RAND Corporation, 2010), 6.
24. Larrabee, *Troubled Partnership*, 7.
25. Cengiz Gunay, 'Foreign Policy as a Source of Legitimation for "Competitive Authoritarian Regimes": The Case of Turkey's AKP,' *Georgetown Journal of International Affairs*, Vol. 17, Issue 2 (Summer/Fall 2016): 43.

26. Ahmet Davutogu, *Stratejik Derinlik: Turkiye'nin Uluslararasi Konumu* (Istanbul: Kure Yayinlari, 2001).
27. Anadolu, 'Erdogan Named World's Most Influential Muslim by Jordan-Based Center,' *Daily Sabah*, 22 October 2018, https://www.dailysabah.com/politics/2018/10/22/erdogan-named-worlds-most-influential-muslim-by-jordan-based-center.
28. Stephen Larrabee, 'Turkey Rediscovers the Middle East,' *Foreign Affairs*, Vol. 86, Issue 4 (July 2007): 103, 111.
29. Aylin Guney, 'An Anatomy of the Transformation of the US–Turkish Alliance: From "Cold War" to "War on Iraq",' *Turkish Studies*, Vol. 6, Issue 3 (September 2005): 341.
30. Burak Bekdil, '"Make Turkey Great Again" Collides with the US,' Gatestone Institute, 22 February 2019, https://www.gatestoneinstitute.org/13788/make-turkey-great-again.
31. Rand Khalid, 'No Longer Forgotten: A Kurdish View of the Iraq War,' *The Guardian*, 11 March 2013, https://www.theguardian.com/world/2013/mar/11/not-forgotten-kurd-perspective-on-iraq-war.
32. Roy Gutman, 'America's Favorite Syrian Militia Rules with an Iron Fist,' *The Nation*, 13 February 2017, https://www.thenation.com/article/americas-favorite-syrian-militia-rules-with-an-iron-fist/.
33. Barcin Yinanc, 'From Father Bush to Trump, the Continuing Kurdish Legacy,' *Hurriyet Daily News*, 4 December 2018, http://www.hurriyetdailynews.com/opinion/barcin-yinanc/from-father-bush-to-trump-the-continuing-kurdish-legacy-139411.
34. 'Turkey's Erdogan: Barack Obama Deceived Us Over PKK,' Al Jazeera, 19 April 2017, https://www.aljazeera.com/news/2017/04/turkey-erdogan-barack-obama-deceived-pkk-170419165646123.html.
35. Karen DeYoung, 'Biden Warns Kurds Not to Seek Separate Enclave on Turkish–Syrian Border,' *The Washington Post*, 24 August 2016, https://www.washingtonpost.com/world/biden-visits-turkey-on-mission-to-repair-strained-relations/2016/08/24/bc684904-6a04-11e6-99bf-f0cf3a6449a6_story.html; Rhys Dubin and Emily Tamkin, 'Iraqi Kurds Vote for Independence Over US Objections,' *Foreign Policy*, 25 September 2017, https://foreignpolicy.com/2017/09/25/iraqi-kurds-vote-for-independence-over-u-s-objections/.
36. Terry Glavin, 'No Friends but the Mountains: The Fate of the Kurds,' *World Affairs*, Vol. 177, Issue 6 (March/April 2015): 57–66.
37. Sherko Kirmanj, '8 Reasons Why America Supports the Syrian Kurds,' *The National Interest*, 13 September 2017, https://nationalinterest.org/feature/8-reasons-why-america-supports-the-syrian-kurds-22290.
38. Fulya Ozerkan, 'Erdogan Claims Mossad Played a Role in Iraqi Kurdistan's Independence Vote,' *The Times of Israel*, 30 September 2017, https://www.timesofisrael.com/erdogan-claims-mossad-played-a-role-in-iraqi-kurdistans-independence-vote/.
39. AFP, 'US Coalition to Build 30,000-Strong Syrian Border Force; Turkey Cries Foul,' *Business Standard*, 15 January 2018, https://www.business-standard.com/article/international/us-coalition-to-build-30-000-strong-syrian-border-force-turkey-cries-foul-118011500027_1.html.
40. Patrick Wintour, 'Erdogan Accuses US of Planning to Form "Terror Army" in Syria,' *The Guardian*, 15 January 2018, https://www.theguardian.com/world/2018/jan/15/turkey-condemns-us-plan-for-syrian-border-security-force.
41. Daren Butler and Phil Stewart, 'Erdogan Says Trump Positive on Turkish Military Plan to Push East in Syria,' Reuters, 17 December 2018, https://www.reuters.com/

article/us-mideast-crisis-syria-turkey/erdogan-says-trump-positive-on-turkish-military-plan-to-push-east-in-syria-idUSKBN1OG16T.
42. Matthew Lee and Susannah George, 'Trump Call with Turkish Leader Led to US Pullout from Syria,' Associated Press, 21 December 2018, https://www.apnews.com/ec2ed217357048ff998225a31534df12.
43. 'Trump Said to Have Told Erdogan that Syria is "All Yours. We Are Done",' *The Times of Israel*, 24 December 2018, https://www.timesofisrael.com/trump-said-to-have-told-erdogan-that-syria-is-all-yours-we-are-done/.
44. Julian Borger, 'Mattis Resignation Triggered by Phone Call between Trump and Erdogan,' *The Guardian*, 21 December 2018, https://www.theguardian.com/us-news/2018/dec/21/james-mattis-resignation-trump-erdogan-phone-call.
45. Brett McGurk, 'Trump Said He Beat ISIS. Instead, He's Giving It New Life,' *The Washington Post*, 18 January 2019, https://www.washingtonpost.com/outlook/trump-said-hed-stay-in-syria-to-beat-isis-instead-hes-giving-it-new-life/2019/01/17/a25a00cc-19cd-11e9-8813-cb9dec761e73_story.html.
46. 'Trump Says Erdogan Will "Eradicate" ISIL in Syria,' Al Jazeera, 24 December 2018, https://www.aljazeera.com/news/2018/12/trump-erdogan-eradicate-isil-syria-181224060230929.html.
47. David Phillips, *The Great Betrayal: How America Abandoned the Kurds and Lost the Middle East* (London: I.B. Tauris, 2018).
48. Recep Erdogan, 'Trump Is Right on Syria. Turkey Can Get the Job Done,' *The New York Times*, 7 January 2019, https://www.nytimes.com/2019/01/07/opinion/erdogan-turkey-syria.html.
49. 'Turkey Must Control Safe Zone in Northern Syria, Says Erdogan,' Ahval News, 24 February 2019, https://ahvalnews.com/safe-zone/turkey-must-control-safe-zone-northern-syria-says-erdogan.
50. Julian Borger, '"Brought to Jesus": The Evangelical Grip on the Trump Administration,' *The Guardian*, 11 January 2019, https://www.theguardian.com/us-news/2019/jan/11/trump-administration-evangelical-influence-support.
51. JTA, 'Evangelicals Appreciate US Embassy Move More than Jews, Trump Says,' *The Times of Israel*, 24 June 2018, https://www.timesofisrael.com/evangelicals-appreciate-us-embassy-move-more-than-jews-trump-says/.
52. 'Jerusalem "Red Line" for All Muslims, President Erdogan Says,' *Daily Sabah*, 5 December 2017, https://www.dailysabah.com/diplomacy/2017/12/06/jerusalem-red-line-for-all-muslims-president-erdogan-says.
53. Ilhan Tanir, 'Jerusalem Move Signals New US Operations Against Islamic World—Erdogan,' Ahval News, 18 May 2018, https://ahvalnews.com/oic/jerusalem-move-signals-new-us-operations-against-islamic-world-erdogan.
54. 'Turkey Hails UN Vote Against Trump's Jerusalem Move,' *Hurriyet Daily News*, 22 December 2017, http://www.hurriyetdailynews.com/turkey-welcomes-un-resolution-on-jerusalem-124568.
55. Bill Chappell, 'Turkey's Erdogan Suggests Swap: Jailed U.S. Pastor for Turkish Cleric,' NPR, 29 September 2017, https://www.npr.org/sections/thetwo-way/2017/09/29/554451339/turkeys-erdogan-suggests-swap-jailed-u-s-pastor-for-turkish-cleric.
56. 'Trump Says He is "Very Disappointed in Erdogan" Over Pastor Brunson,' *Hurriyet Daily News*, 31 August 2018, http://www.hurriyetdailynews.com/trump-says-he-is-very-disappointed-in-erdogan-over-pastor-brunson-136336.

57. 'Trump Threatens "Large" Sanctions on Turkey Unless US Pastor Released,' *The Guardian*, 26 July 2018, https://www.theguardian.com/us-news/2018/jul/26/andrew-brunson-trump-turkey-threaten-sanctions.
58. Prashant Rao, 'Turkish President Calls for Boycott of US Electronics Including the iPhone,' *The New York Times*, 14 August 2018, https://www.nytimes.com/2018/08/14/business/turkey-erdogan-apple-iphone.html.
59. 'Remarks by President Trump Before Marine One Departure,' 17 August 2018, South Lawn, White House, https://www.whitehouse.gov/briefings-statements/remarks-president-trump-marine-one-departure-10/.
60. DPA, 'US Prefers Pastor Over NATO Partner: Erdogan,' *Gulf Times*, 12 August 2018, https://www.gulf-times.com/story/602566/US-prefers-pastor-over-Nato-partner-Erdogan.
61. Thomas Gibbons-Neff, 'Trump Threatens to "Devastate Turkey Economically" if It Attacks Kurds,' *The New York Times*, 13 January 2019, https://www.nytimes.com/2019/01/13/us/politics/trump-turkey-kurds.html.
62. Onur Ant and Justin Sink, 'Trump and Turkey's Erdogan Ease Rhetoric After Threat of Ruin,' *Bloomberg*, 14 January 2019, https://www.bloomberg.com/news/articles/2019-01-14/turkey-s-erdogan-calls-trump-to-ease-syria-tensions.
63. Dion Nissenbaum, 'Dismissal of Charges Against Erdogan Bodyguards Draws Criticism,' *The Wall Street Journal*, 22 March 2018, https://www.wsj.com/articles/dismissal-of-charges-against-erdogan-bodyguards-draws-criticism-1521758981.
64. David Welch, 'It's Time to Drum Increasingly Authoritarian Turkey Out of NATO,' *The Globe and Mail*, 22 April 2018, https://www.theglobeandmail.com/opinion/article-its-time-to-drum-increasingly-authoritarian-turkey-out-of-nato/.
65. Humeyra Pamuk and Nick Tattersall, 'Exclusive: Turkish Intelligence Helped Ship Arms to Syrian Islamist Rebel Areas,' Reuters, 21 May 2015, https://www.reuters.com/article/us-mideast-crisis-turkey-arms/exclusive-turkish-intelligence-helped-ship-arms-to-syrian-islamist-rebel-areas-idUSKBN0O61L220150521.
66. Sebnem Arsu, 'Turkish Premier Urges Assad to Quit in Syria,' *The New York Times*, 22 November 2011, https://www.nytimes.com/2011/11/23/world/middleeast/turkish-leader-says-syrian-president-should-quit.html.
67. Marianna Charountaki, *Iran and Turkey: International and Regional Engagement in the Middle East* (London: I.B. Tauris, 2018), 18, 200.
68. Lale Kemal, 'Erdogan to Obama: You Left Iraq in Iran's Hands,' *Today's Zaman*, 21 March 2012.
69. Gulden Ayman, 'Turkey and Iran: Between Friendly Cooperation and Fierce Rivalry,' *Arab Studies Quarterly*, Vol. 36, Issue 1 (Winter 2014): 23.
70. Ofra Bengio, 'Strange Bedfellows: The Russian–Turkish–Iranian Axis,' *The Jerusalem Post*, 25 January 2017, https://www.jpost.com/Opinion/The-Russian-Turkish-Iranian-axis-Strange-bedfellows-479495.
71. 'Joint Statement by the President of the Islamic Republic of Iran, the President of the Russian Federation and the President of the Republic of Turkey,' 14 February 2019, http://en.kremlin.ru/supplement/5388.
72. Kyle Orton, 'Turkey Keeps an Eye on Assad's Fate with No Intention to Leave,' *The Arab Weekly*, 10 March 2019, https://thearabweekly.com/turkey-keeps-eye-assads-fate-no-intention-leave.
73. 'Readout of President Donald J. Trump's Call with President Recep Tayyip Erdogan of Turkey,' issued on 24 January 2018, https://www.whitehouse.gov/briefings-statements/readout-president-donald-j-trumps-call-president-recep-tayyip-erdogan-turkey-4/.

74. Michael Pompeo, 'Interview With Tony Katz of Tony Katz Today,' 1 November 2018, https://www.state.gov/interview-with-tony-katz-of-tony-katz-today/.
75. 'US Policy Toward a Turbulent Middle East' (Washington: US Government Publishing Office, 2018), https://docs.house.gov/meetings/FA/FA00/20180418/108182/HHRG-115-FA00-Transcript-20180418.pdf.
76. Henri Barkey, 'Putin and Erdogan's Marriage of Convenience,' *Foreign Policy*, 11 January 2017, https://foreignpolicy.com/2017/01/11/putin-and-erdogans-marriage-of-convenience/.
77. Jeffrey Mankoff, 'Russia and Turkey's Rapprochement: Don't Expect an Equal Partnership,' *Foreign Affairs*, 20 July 2016, https://www.foreignaffairs.com/articles/turkey/2016-07-20/russia-and-turkeys-rapprochement.
78. Soner Cagaptay, 'Turkish–Russian–Iranian Summit: Limits to a Tripartite Entente,' *The Globalist*, 5 April 2018, https://www.theglobalist.com/turkey-iran-russia-putin-erdogan-rouhani-syria/.
79. Tim Arango and Ceylan Yeginsu, 'Turks Can Agree on One Thing: US Was Behind Failed Coup,' *The New York Times*, 2 August 2016, https://www.nytimes.com/2016/08/03/world/europe/turkey-coup-erdogan-fethullah-gulen-united-states.html.
80. Anadolu, 'US Warns of "Grave Consequences" if Turkey Buys S-400s,' *Hurriyet Daily News*, 9 March 2019, http://www.hurriyetdailynews.com/us-warns-of-grave-consequences-if-turkey-buys-s-400s-141774.
81. Anthony Capaccio and Nick Wadhams, 'US Backs Patriot Missile Sale to Turkey in Breakthrough,' *Bloomberg*, 19 December 2018, https://www.bloomberg.com/news/articles/2018-12-19/state-department-backs-missile-sale-to-turkey-in-breakthrough.
82. 'US Delegation, Turkish Officials Discuss Compatibility of S-400 Systems, F-35 Jets,' *Daily Sabah*, 15 February 2019, https://www.dailysabah.com/diplomacy/2019/01/18/us-delegation-turkish-officials-discuss-compatibility-of-s-400-systems-f-35-jets.
83. 'Pentagon Spokesman Discusses Variety of Topics with Reporters,' 8 March 2019, Washington, https://dod.defense.gov/News/Article/Article/1780584/pentagon-spokesman-discusses-variety-of-topics-with-reporters/.
84. Aykan Erdemir and John Lechner, 'Trump's Gifts to Turkey Repeat Mistakes and Set Bad Precedents,' Defense One, 20 December 2018, https://www.defenseone.com/ideas/2018/12/trumps-gifts-turkey-repeat-old-mistakes-and-set-bad-precedents/153712/.
85. Ilhan Tanir, 'Is It a Good Idea for Erdogan to Visit Washington?' Ahval News, 9 March 2019, https://ahvalnews.com/us-turkey/it-good-idea-erdogan-visit-washington.
86. Ilhan Tanir, 'Trump Agrees with Turkey's S-400 Purchase, Says Erdogan,' Ahval News, 14 March 2019, https://ahvalnews.com/turkey-us/trump-agrees-turkeys-s-400-purchase-says-erdogan.
87. Endy Zemenides, 'Will the US and Turkey Break Up Over Russian S-400?' *Kathimerini*, 9 March 2019, http://www.ekathimerini.com/238410/opinion/ekathimerini/comment/will-the-us-and-turkey-break-up-over-russian-s-400.
88. 'Turkey Using 65 Percent Indigenous Defense Industry Products: Erdogan,' *Hurriyet Daily News*, 22 September 2018, http://www.hurriyetdailynews.com/turkey-using-65-indigenous-defense-industry-products-erdogan-137117.
89. Carlo Frappi, 'The Russo-Turkish Entente: A Tactical Embrace Along Strategic and Geopolitical Convergences,' in *Turkey: Towards a Eurasian Shift?* ed. Valeria Talbot (Milan: Istituto Per Gli Studi Di Politica Internazionale, 2018), 59.
90. Frappi, 'The Russo-Turkish Entente,' 66.

91. 'Trump: Iran Used Nuclear Deal Funds to Become "World's Leading Terror Sponsor",' *The Times of Israel*, 26 September 2018, https://www.timesofisrael.com/trump-iran-used-nuclear-deal-funds-to-become-worlds-leading-terror-sponsor/.
92. Sarah Bailey, 'Pompeo: Perhaps Trump is, Like the Bible's Esther, Meant to Save the Jewish People from Iran,' *The Washington Post*, 22 March 2019, https://www.washingtonpost.com/religion/2019/03/22/pompeo-perhaps-trump-is-like-bibles-esther-meant-save-jewish-people-iran/.
93. Mehran Kamrava, *Troubled Waters: Insecurity in the Persian Gulf* (Ithaca: Cornell University Press, 2018), 7–8.
94. Selcan Hacaoglu, 'Erdogan Breaks Silence on US to Stand by Russian Missile Deal,' *Bloomberg*, 7 March 2019, https://www.bloomberg.com/news/articles/2019-03-07/erdogan-breaks-silence-on-u-s-to-stand-by-russian-missile-deal.
95. H.E. Ahmet Davutoglu, Minister of Foreign Affairs of the Republic of Turkey, 'Speech Entitled "Vision 2023: Turkey's Foreign Policy Objectives",' 22 November 2011, Turkey Investor Conference, London, http://www.mfa.gov.tr/speech-entitled-_vision-2023_-turkey_s-foreign-policy-objectives__-delivered-by-h_e_-ahmet-davutoglu_-minister-of-foreign-af.en.mfa.
96. Soner Cagaptay, 'Making Turkey Great Again,' *The Fletcher Forum of World Affairs*, Vol. 43, Issue I (Winter 2019): 175, 177.
97. 'From Today's Turkish Press,' *Mideast Mirror*, 22 October 2018, http://www.mideast-mirror.com/index.php?option=com_content&view=article&id=5419:22-10-18-turkey-and-iran&catid=40:archived-mirror-issues&Itemid=67.
98. Julian Borger et al., 'Trump Announces Jamal Khashoggi Investigation but Says He Won't Halt Saudi Arms Sales,' *The Guardian*, 11 October 2018, https://www.theguardian.com/world/2018/oct/11/jamal-khashoggi-saudi-arabia-under-pressure-from-trump-administration.
99. Edward Wong et al., 'Trump Calls Relations with Saudi Arabia "Excellent," While Congress is Incensed,' *The New York Times*, 11 October 2018, https://www.nytimes.com/2018/10/11/us/politics/trump-jamal-khashoggi-turkey-saudi.html.
100. 'Statement from President Donald J. Trump on Standing with Saudi Arabia,' 20 November 2018, White House, https://www.whitehouse.gov/briefings-statements/statement-president-donald-j-trump-standing-saudi-arabia/.
101. Martin Armstrong, 'The USA's Biggest Arms Export Partners,' Statista, 12 October 2018, https://www.statista.com/chart/12205/the-usas-biggest-arms-export-partners/.
102. 'Freedom in the World 2018: Table of Country Scores,' Freedom House, 16 January 2018, https://freedomhouse.org/report/freedom-world-2018-table-country-scores.
103. Kemal Kirisci, *Turkey and the West: Fault Lines in a Troubled Alliance* (Washington DC: Brookings Institution Press, 2017), 20.
104. Ivan Watson, 'Obama Says US, Turkey Can Be Model for World,' CNN, 6 April 2009, http://www.cnn.com/2009/POLITICS/04/06/obama.turkey/index.html.
105. 'Obama Names Turkish PM Erdogan Among Trusted Friends,' *Hurriyet Daily News*, 20 January 2012, http://www.hurriyetdailynews.com/obama-names-turkish-pm-erdogan-among-trusted-friends-11897.
106. 'World Economic Outlook Database,' International Monetary Fund, April 2018, https://www.imf.org/external/pubs/ft/weo/2018/01/weodata/index.aspx.
107. Durmus Yilmaz and Selim Sazak, 'How Turkey Dumbed Itself Down,' *Foreign Policy*, 22 August 2018, https://foreignpolicy.com/2018/08/22/how-turkey-dumbed-itself-down/.

108. Mustafa Sonmez, '85 Percent of Turkey's Foreign Investors Still from West,' *Hurriyet Daily News*, 4 January 2016, http://www.hurriyetdailynews.com/85-percent-of-turkeys-foreign-investors-still-from-west-93356.
109. Paul Laudicina et al., 'Investing in a Localized World,' *The 2018 A.T. Kearney Foreign Direct Investment Confidence Index*, https://www.atkearney.com/foreign-direct-investment-confidence-index/2018-full-report.
110. Soner Cagaptay, *The New Sultan: Erdogan and the Crisis of Modern Turkey* (London: I.B. Tauris, 2017), 153–55.
111. Hakan Yavuz, 'Erdogan's Ottomania,' *Boston Review*, 8 August 2018, http://bostonreview.net/politics/m-hakan-yavuz-erdogan-ottomanophilia.
112. Hussein Ibish, 'Turkey Is Changing the Middle East. The US Doesn't Get It,' *Bloomberg*, 14 March 2019, https://www.bloomberg.com/opinion/articles/2019-03-14/turkey-is-changing-the-middle-east-the-u-s-doesn-t-get-it.
113. Nicola Nymalm and Johannes Plagemann, 'Comparative Exceptionalism: Universality and Particularity in Foreign Policy Discourses,' *International Studies Review*, Vol. 21, Issue 1 (March 2019): 28.
114. Omer Taspinar, 'Turkey's Middle East Policies: Between Neo-Ottomanism and Kemalism,' Carnegie Middle East Center, Carnegie Endowment for International Peace, No. 10 (September 2008): 1.
115. Gonul Tol, 'Turkey's Bid for Religious Leadership: How the AKP Uses Islamic Soft Power,' *Foreign Affairs*, 10 January 2019, https://www.foreignaffairs.com/articles/turkey/2019-01-10/turkeys-bid-religious-leadership.
116. 'Turkish Interior Minister Says Turkey Spans from Damascus to Medina,' *Al Arabiya*, 3 March 2019, http://english.alarabiya.net/en/News/middle-east/2019/03/03/Turkish-interior-minister-says-Turkey-spans-from-Damascus-to-Medina.html.
117. 'Turkish Minister Reveals Ambition to Usurp Makkah and Madinah,' *Saudi Gazette*, 3 March 2019, http://saudigazette.com.sa/article/560353.
118. Mark Langan, 'Virtuous Power Turkey in Sub-Saharan Africa: The "Neo-Ottoman" Challenge to the European Union,' *Third World Quarterly*, Vol. 38, Issue 6 (2017): 1409.
119. 'Turkey's Economy Slides into Recession Before Key Election,' Ahval News, 11 March 2019, https://ahvalnews.com/turkey-economy/turkeys-economy-slides-recession-key-election.
120. Federico Donelli, 'The Ankara Consensus: The Significance of Turkey's Engagement in Sub-Saharan Africa,' *Global Change, Peace & Security*, Vol. 30, Issue 1 (2018): 74–75.
121. Selcan Hacaoglu, 'Trump's Syrian Detente with Erdogan Masks Rot that Runs Deep,' *Bloomberg*, 16 January 2019, https://www.bloomberg.com/news/articles/2019-01-16/trump-s-syrian-detente-with-erdogan-masks-a-rot-that-runs-deep.
122. Liz Sly, 'Why Russia is Back in the Middle East,' *Gulf News*, 1 January 2019, https://gulfnews.com/world/mena/why-russia-is-back-in-the-middle-east-1.60837087.
123. Chuck Freilich, 'Trump's Mayhem Allows Putin's Russia to Take Over the Middle East, One Country at a Time,' *Haaretz*, 19 July 2018, https://www.haaretz.com/us-news/.premium-how-putin-s-russia-is-taking-over-the-middle-east-one-country-at-a-time-1.6290146.
124. 'We Have the Power and the Will to Expand the Step We Took with the Operation Euphrates Shield All Along Our Borders,' 1 November 2018, 43rd Mukhtars Meeting, Presidential Complex, https://www.tccb.gov.tr/en/news/542/89060/firat-kalkani-harektiyla-attigimiz-adimi-sinirlarimiz-boyunca-genisletecek-guce-ve-iradeye-sahibiz.

Map not to scale.

III
Brazil: Wary Rival to Willing Partner

Trump serves as an example for me. I realize that there is a great distance between myself and Trump, but I plan to get closer to him for the good of both Brazil and the United States. We can take his examples from here back to Brazil.

—Congressman and Presidential Pre-Candidate Jair Bolsonaro, 9 October 2017[1]

... we're going to have a fantastic working relationship. We have many views that are similar. And we certainly feel very, very true to each other on trade. I think Brazil's relationship with the United States, because of our friendship, is probably better than it's ever been by far. You're doing a fantastic job. You've brought the country together. And I look forward to working with you in a very close relationship for many years to come.

—President Donald Trump, 19 March 2019[2]

Convergence of Miracles

Of all the emerging powers compelled to adjust to the vicissitudes of the Trump effect, Brazil is the one country that has swivelled with certainty from a wary rivalry to a close partnership with the US. This 360-degree volte-face came about due to a Black Swan event in Brazil in October 2018, when the far-right anti-establishment populist Jair Bolsonaro won the presidential election and ushered Latin America's powerhouse into uncharted territory. Until a few weeks before voting day, seven-time federal deputy legislator and firebrand militarist Bolsonaro was running a distant second behind the leftist former President Lula da Silva in opinion polls. But Lula's disqualification by the Brazilian judiciary from the contest owing to his criminal conviction over corruption charges suddenly pitchforked Bolsonaro from a pretender to the top of the ballot and carried him to the highest office. It was no less a miracle than Trump's shock success in the 2016 US presidential election.

The similarities between President Bolsonaro and his American counterpart are extraordinary. The Brazilian leader revels in the moniker Trump of the Tropics and Trump's National Security Adviser John Bolton has returned the compliment with the quip, 'Up here, maybe we'll call President Trump the Bolsonaro of North America.'[3] Many observers have drawn parallels between Trump and the values he espouses to right-wing populist leaders and movements in developed countries of Europe. But few foresaw that his near-perfect clone would arise on the soil of a leading developing nation in Latin America. Like his idol Trump, Bolsonaro overcame the centrist political mainstream and surged to power by exploiting a crisis of democracy and capitalism that pushed Brazilian voters to embrace his extremism and anti-elitist radicalism. With almost all right-of-centre and left-of-centre politicians smeared in cascading corruption scandals, the Brazilian economy tanking under years of mismanagement, and crime at record levels amid high inequality in income and wealth, Bolsonaro crossed the frontier from a controversy-courting fringe lawmaker into president of the republic. In the words of Brian Winter, populist Bolsonaro's rise to the pinnacle was a product of Brazil's 'severe economic, institutional and criminal crises since 2014' and a manifestation of 'system failure'.[4] Trump's ideologue and former White House Chief Strategist Steven Bannon observed on the eve of Bolsonaro's presidential election triumph, 'It was the 2008 financial crisis that lit the fuse that exploded with Donald Trump's candidacy and his presidency. Brazil is going through that type of crisis now.'[5]

Bolsonaro has likened himself to Trump as an outsider fighting a corrupt secular liberal establishment to save his country from moral and multicultural degeneration. His remarks, 'Trump faced the same attacks I am facing—that he was a homophobe, a fascist, a racist, a Nazi. But the people believed in his platform. I was rooting for him. Just like he wants to make America great, I want to make Brazil great,'[6] leave no doubt that Trump is his role model and inspiration. A leading Brazilian newspaper has listed a plethora of domestic and international issues on which Bolsonaro and Trump are almost identical in their approaches thanks to their shared populist ideological belief systems. These grounds of convergence include anti-establishment attitudes, contempt for political correctness and etiquette, dismissal of critical news media as 'enemies of the people', using social media to attack foes and declare policies, treatment of government as a family business with relatives in key positions, scandals over personal finances and criminal links during presidential transitions, zealous support for gun ownership, scepticism about climate change, support for Israel without qualifications, disdain for multilateral institutions, and hatred of liberal causes célèbres like immigration and rights of ethnic and religious minorities.[7]

The camaraderie between Trump and Bolsonaro has deeper roots at the level of populist intellectuals who have articulated the two leaders' visions to the American and Brazilian publics. Bannon has a close relationship with Bolsonaro's guru, the Brazilian far-right philosopher Olavo de Carvalho, whom Trump's erstwhile ideological guru hailed as his 'hero'. Like Bannon in the US, Carvalho has an agenda of eviscerating globalists, Marxists and feminists from Brazil and Latin America. His claims that communism 'was not destroyed, it only changed its strategic framework' and that there is still a 'global communist conspiracy' to weaken the moral fibre of Brazil, echo Bannon and Trump's ultra-conservative thoughts.[8] Bolsonaro's son, Eduardo, has been named by Bannon as the Latin American representative of an international consortium of populist nationalist politicians known as The Movement, with the goal of networking and coordinating to 'reclaim sovereignty from progressive globalist elitist forces and expand common sense nationalism for all citizens of Latin America'.[9] The vision of an alternative nationalist world order that buries the liberal international order is a cementing factor whose value cannot be underestimated in the new direction that US–Brazil relations is taking.

In the Introduction of this book, I demonstrated how domestic political calculations are foremost in the minds of right-wing populists when they approach international relations. Since anti-establishment populists like Trump and Bolsonaro chafe at what they deem biased and fake liberal news media coverage in their countries to tarnish their reputations, they band together for mutual legitimation across national boundaries. Bolsonaro chose Trump's US as the destination of his first foreign visit as president in March 2019 to prove a point at home in Brazil that he has powerful friends abroad and that the ideology he stands for is not a marginal one in the world. Bolsonaro began his tour of Washington by meeting Bannon and Carvalho at the residence of Brazil's Ambassador to the US, where the Brazilian president decried communism as an evil. Bannon intoned that the links between pro-Bolsonaro populists and pro-Trump conservatives in America were 'going to be very powerful'.[10] Bolsonaro's comment on the occasion, 'I have always dreamed of freeing Brazil from the dirty ideology of the Left,' and his vow 'to deconstruct, undo many things before we can even start. I'm happy to be the turning point,'[11] borrowed from Bannon's textbook and demonstrated the depth of their ideological connection. Trump reinforced the message that because America was no longer under liberal internationalist control, Bolsonaro could count on a solid new basis for bilateral relations. 'I think there was a lot of hostility with other (mainstream US) presidents. There's zero hostility with me.'[12]

The value of Trump's robust friendship and personal chemistry with Bolsonaro is all the more reinforced by intra-Brazilian political divisions. According to Brazilian academic Oliver Stuenkel, the Bolsonaro administration is not a homogenous entity but a patchwork of three allied but disagreeing segments, wherein

> the anti-globalist, pro-Trump faction of the Bolsonaro administration, which includes his foreign minister, will clash with the more prudent generals, led by Vice-President Hamilton Mourao, and the technocrats, represented by the Economy Minister Paulo Guedes and Justice Minister Sérgio Moro.[13]

Carvalho has clashed with the pragmatist Mourao and openly dissed him as an 'idiot'. Carvalho's declaration, 'I love this guy Bolsonaro, but he's surrounded by traitors,'[14] offers a glimpse into the struggle for control inside the Brazilian state. Like in America, Brazil has a long state tradition with set patterns and ideas of governance that cannot be summarily dispensed by radical populists.

Emerging powers like India and Turkey have tried to leverage the Trump administration's 'two-track presidency' while dealing with America. But in the case of Brazil, it is a strange situation of a possible 'three-track presidency' in Brasilia, where pro-Trump elements are eager to combine forces with their American counterparts and strengthen their internal bargaining position within the Brazilian polity. The alliance between the pro-Trump faction in Brasilia and the pro-Bolsonaro anti-globalists around Trump thus has a symbiotic political quality to it, which cannot be comprehended through the traditional foreign policy lenses of material economic interests and geostrategic needs that drive bilateral relations between countries. It is not so much a full alignment of two countries or governments but subunits of one country finding succour and affirmation in subunits of another and harnessing these transnational connections to their advantage to gain power in their domestic arenas.

South-South to North-South

The salience of Brazilian and American far-right birds of a feather flocking together lies in the paradigmatic overturning that Bolsonaro is attempting in Brazil's foreign policy. The legacy that Bolsonaro inherited from his predecessors and which he is out to deconstruct is premised on rejecting American hegemony in the Western Hemisphere and positioning Brazil as a leader of Latin America and the wider Global South. Since the restoration of civilian rule in Brazil in 1985, resentment of American domination had risen progressively under presidents of varied hues. Memories of the CIA-backed *coup d'état* of 1964, which overthrew the popular democratically elected President Joao Goulart, and of the Washington-allied harsh right-wing military dictatorships, which abused human rights in Brazil and across Latin America in the name of countering communism, generated unease once democracy took root. Jose Sarney, a centrist Brazilian president who anchored the new republic from 1985 to 1990, lambasted the great 'historical error' of the US of according 'third-class treatment' to South America as a 'backyard, or a vacant lot' where American multinational corporations could scramble for turf and profit and the US military could intervene at will. Sarney's message to Washington in 1986, 'Latin America, in part as a reaction to

US policy itself, is beginning to nurture anti-American feelings where they had not existed before,'[15] reflected the popular mood. His assertion that democratic Brazil had a 'different vision of ourselves' and that the US should not 'expect Brazil, with its riches, with its potential, with its determination, to be a second-rate country'[16] proved prescient.

In the post-Cold War era, President Fernando Cardoso (1995–2002) of the Social Democratic Party (PSDP) ushered in a policy of 'autonomy through integration' to adjust and accommodate unipolar American liberal hegemony while simultaneously forging closer ties with neighbouring countries to build a leadership profile for Brazil. Cardoso invested diplomatic energies into consolidating the Mercosur (Southern Common Market) trade block comprising Brazil, Argentina, Paraguay and Uruguay, and asserted that South America was 'our historical-geographical space' where Brasilia had the means to assert autonomous leadership and resist Washington-proposed models for integrating the entire Western Hemisphere under American diktat.[17] As a neo-Marxist sociologist before making it big in politics, Cardoso was a pioneer of 'dependency theory' that looked at the world as an unequal zero-sum-game between 'core' advanced capitalist countries and developing countries on the 'periphery' whose natural riches are exploited for enriching the former.[18] In office, Cardoso moderated his academic radicalism and pragmatically looked to avoid conflict with the US. At the same time, he was absolutely clear that Brazil's salvation lay in carving a system of regional economic and political cooperation that does not allow the US to call the shots.

Brazilian politicians viewed the concept of Free Trade Area of the Americas (FTAA), championed by the Bill Clinton administration, as a dangerous southward extension of NAFTA, which would swallow Mercosur, relegate Brasilia to second-class status and hand over economic control to the liberal internationalist hegemony of the US. To the Cardoso administration, Mercosur was the 'hub from which Brazil would build an alternative pole of attraction in the hemisphere, and as a result would attempt to create obstacles for greater US penetration in the South American subsystem'.[19] In fact, it was Cardoso who made a more-than-semantic distinction between Latin America and South America. Argentinian writer Bruno Binetti has written, '[South America is] a Brazilian idea and was designed to project Brasilia's influence over its immediate vicinity without interference from Mexico or the United States.'[20] Given the historical economic and military domination of the region by the US since the Monroe Doctrine of the nineteenth century, Brazil knew it could not displace the US or eject it outright. But constructing a parallel mechanism for South America that would be under Brazilian leadership, while North America including Mexico would continue to be in the US sphere, has been a byword of Brasilia's strategy.

The presidency of the charismatic socialist Lula (2003–10) not only redoubled Brazil's quest for endogenous consensus formation in South America but stepped out of the shadows of the US-style market-driven 'open regionalism' model in favour of a more radical 'post-hegemonic regionalism' where neoliberal capitalistic principles and rules were no longer the decisive factors but had to coexist with non-commercial and political forms of solidarity. Lula spearheaded the launch of Union of South American Nations (UNASUR) in 2008 by merging Mercosur member states with the Andean community countries (Bolivia, Colombia, Ecuador and Peru) and achieving something closest to the EU in terms of uniting the entire South American continent. UNASUR was a post-hegemonic construct as it allowed plurality and differences in economic strategies of members by accepting pro-free trade as well as protectionist outlooks, while prioritising cooperation in infrastructure, social development, energy and a common defence posture for the whole continent. Brazil's vision of UNASUR was to develop a 'space for the discussion and consolidation of consensus in the political and security areas and a minimum common denominator in the economic area'.[21]

The George W. Bush administration's reactivation of the US military's Fourth Fleet in 2008 and Washington's agreement with Bogota to deploy American troops and surveillance equipment in Colombia perturbed Brasilia, spurring Lula's brainchild of a South American Defense Council (SADC) under the aegis of UNASUR to handle security crises, develop regional military capabilities and collectively solve political problems of the continent by excluding the neocolonial and meddlesome US. SADC's purpose was to 'not only help to limit external intervention, but also to manage regional turmoil, which can be a pull factor for foreign powers'.²² UNASUR and SADC reified Henry Kissinger's reading at the turn of the millennium that Brazilian leaders are 'attracted by the prospect of a politically unified Latin America confronting the United States and NAFTA', and that 'Brazil and the United States find themselves in tacit competition'.²³ With Lula in charge in Brasilia, and a wave of elected left-wing regimes led by Venezuela's Hugo Chavez in power across the region, the tacit competition had moved into explicit territory.

Lula was never as stridently anti-American as Chavez and the Castro brothers of Cuba, who were at the forefront of a revolutionary institution devoted to countering Western neo-imperialism known as the Bolivarian Alliance for the Peoples of Our America (ALBA). Brazil was too moderate to formally join the radical Venezuela, but there was some overlap of membership between UNASUR and ALBA. Lula and Chavez cooperated to found a pan-regional bloc, Community of Latin American and Caribbean States (CELAC), in 2011 to counter the US-motored Organization of American States (OAS) that had ostracised Cuba. In the words of Argentina-based scholar Khatchik Der Ghougassian, UNASUR and ALBA shared 'a common post-Washington Consensus character of regional integration foreseen beyond free trade, and a renewed role for the state (in the market)'. But they were also different inasmuch as 'UNASUR is an attempt to modify the declining liberal order; ALBA reflects an overall rejection of the same'.²⁴ Venezuela's steep economic and political decline after Chavez's death in 2013 and the steady erosion of the leftist trend in Latin America have, over time, rendered ALBA irrelevant.

Even UNASUR and Mercosur did not manage to satisfy all stakeholders because of their reluctance to commit to trade liberalisation and democratisation, generating alternative pro-US groupings reclaiming the old 'open regionalism' like the Pacific Alliance formed by Chile, Colombia, Peru and Mexico in 2011. Lula and his successor from the Brazilian Workers Party (PT), President Dilma Rousseff (2011–16), eyed the Pacific Alliance with suspicion as liberal internationalist Washington's ploy to again divide the region and conquer it. The split between Atlantic-facing protectionist countries led by Brazil and Pacific-facing open economies close to the US was deep and caused observers to note there were practically 'two Latin Americas'.²⁵ This situation of Brasilia attempting to wean its neighbours away from Washington but not succeeding fully due to ideological limitations lasted as long as Brazil was ruled by Cardoso's PSDP and Lula's PT, which tried to weld the region around Brazil's 'consensual hegemony'.

By eschewing coercive and domineering forms of military and economic leadership and instead relying on consultative and inclusive multilateralism that gave weak countries voice and participation, Brazil counterpoised itself to the bullying and bossy US. The intent was 'not to subsume other regional states to Brazilian will, but instead to cycle the region-forming process through Brazil and position the country's propositions and prerogatives as the central unifying factor of a potential South American region'.[26] Italian scholar Gian Luca Gardini has argued that Brazil was not a typical great power that relied on hard military and economic advantages to gain influence in its surrounding areas. Rather, it was akin to an 'international manager' of regional and global affairs, which convened partners on the premises of solidarity and non-intervention in their internal matters, while avoiding the 'rhetoric and use of power and imposition over someone'.[27] It was meant to be a contrasting model from the other large power in the Western Hemisphere, the US, which used trade, aid and covert and overt military instruments to fragment and bend Latin America to its will. Lula avowed in 2009 that Brazil was consciously disabusing South American nations of America's propaganda and misinformation about its motives.

> I always say that Brazil should not work towards hegemony but just towards building partnerships, because during the 20th century, or at least two thirds of the 20th century, the state policy from the US was in the sense of convincing South American countries that the major empire was Brazil... under my government, we started to rebuild confidence in South America, because you can't develop politics without confidence.[28]

The two buzzwords of Brazilian diplomacy in the PSDP and PT eras were institutionalism and multilateralism. Lula's hyperactive diplomacy transcended Brazil's natural domain in South America and extended its reach to developing countries in Africa, the Middle East and Asia as part of a broader push for South-South cooperation. His goal was to 'mainly employ institutional strategies [and] political dialogue with a number of entities' to enhance Brazil's soft power and 'constrain the influence of the established great powers'.[29] Brazil's role in strengthening the fundamentals of the Global South was remarkable; we would not see the level of self-confidence in emerging and developing countries to deal with their own problems today without depending on superpowers had it not been for Brazil's stitching together of myriad cross-regional groupings across the world.

An interesting transcontinental South-South institution that Brazil cofounded in 2003 in Brasilia and has strived to sustain since is the India-Brazil-South Africa (IBSA) trilateral. It is officially described as a 'unique Forum which brings together… three large democracies and major economies from three different continents, facing similar challenges.' Further, 'all three partners are developing, pluralistic, multi-cultural, multi-ethnic, multi-lingual and multi-religious nations' which uphold 'participatory democracy, respect for human rights, the Rule of Law and the strengthening of multilateralism.'[30] These liberal precepts ruled out entry of China and Russia and conveyed a moderate and benign image to the West. Roberto Unger, Lula's Minister for Long-Term Strategic Planning, said in 2007 that IBSA had a 'shared geopolitical vision [of] a plurality of power', wherein the goal was to move away from

> a world that is organised either around duopoly of power of the US and China or a state of latent belligerence between the US and China. [Instead], our basic stake is to make the world situation more complicated and richer in sources of thought, of capability, of power.[31]

In other words, the objective was to promote a multipolar world where emerging powers of similar political orientation could transform the international order without having to bandwagon with the two existing great powers.

Lula's Foreign Minister Celso Amorim was asked in 2011 about the difference between IBSA and the much more prominent BRICS, which includes IBSA members. His reply confirmed the Brazilian strategic thought that emerging powers had to create pathways independent of the two great powers, China and the US.

> The commonalities of the IBSA countries are more evident than for the BRICS countries. For a start, two are permanent members of the UN Security Council and thus less interested in reform of global governance in security and peace... as a major developing country, China would make a major contribution towards strengthening its cooperation with the IBSA Forum if it took a more positive attitude towards UN Security Council reform... Russia is not a member of the WTO. On the other hand, the competitiveness of China given the currency and labour standards imbalance, among other factors, triggers a defensiveness that does not exist, at least to the same degree, among the IBSA countries.[32]

Cognisance of China and its enormous heft has kept IBSA alive despite BRICS. Beijing's repeated attempts to absorb IBSA into BRICS were rebuffed by the three developing democracies, which wished to carve out a deliberative and actionable policy space distinct from the Beijing Consensus and the Washington Consensus. Stuenkel has aptly argued,

> China's absence is precisely what makes IBSA an interesting platform for debating global challenges in a different context, and also speaks frankly about challenges that cannot be addressed at BRICS summits, including the question of how to deal with the rise of China.[33]

Although IBSA's achievements have been modest, its unity on reforming the UN Security Council (all three members have been chasing the holy grail of a permanent seat for decades), forming a developing country bloc in WTO negotiations, and engaging in trilateral joint military exercises demonstrated that Brazil under the PT took the institution seriously even as it parallelly advanced ties with China.

BRIC, founded in 2006 and expanded to BRICS with South Africa's inclusion in 2011, was a bigger vehicle than IBSA for Brazil's socialist internationalism and multilateralism under presidents Lula and Rousseff. With China and Russia integral to this larger grouping, BRICS had a harder edge as an alternative to the US-led liberal international order. The colossal failure of the Anglo-Saxon laissez-faire capitalist system during the global economic crisis, which began in 2008, and the contagious impact it had on other rich countries in Europe and Asia, convinced BRICS members that their statist developmental models were wiser and that the moment for them to remake the international economic architecture had arrived. Lula's chief diplomat Amorim heralded the 'exemplary ability of "non-rich" countries to mitigate possible effects of a crisis that originates mainly in the developed world', and declared BRICS' motto to 'strengthen themselves politically as a bloc that helps to balance and democratize the international order'.[34] Brazil had a pivotal hand in the institutional consolidation and innovation of BRICS, including the launch of the New Development Bank in 2014, the 2015 Contingency Reserve Arrangement, and the negotiations for a delayed Credit Rating Agency. The aim of these alternative economic initiatives was to democratise the unfair US-dominated liberal international order that proffered secondary status to rising powers like Brazil.

Stuenkel listed numerous strategic advantages accruing to Brazil from being a driving force in BRICS, including proving its 'convocatory power and regional leadership ambition', prodding the US to take it more seriously amid fears in Washington that BRICS could become a vehicle for Chinese expansion, and gaining knowledge and insight about Brazil's largest trading partner, China's global strategy by working intimately with Chinese officialdom in a multilateral setting.[35] Above all, Brazil gained international recognition and respect as a builder of a new multipolar world order via BRICS and could spread its reputation as a pillar of global governance. Amorim recalled that the US grew more receptive to involving Brazil in Middle East peace processes from 2007 after noticing and appreciating its role in convening IBSA and BRICS.[36] The facilitation role the administrations of Lula and Rousseff took up with regard to the Iran nuclear weapons crisis and the Syrian war were instances of the sheen of IBSA and BRICS enabling Brasilia to venture into fresh terrain as a global problem solver. In Africa, although Brazilian companies competed with Chinese rivals for natural resource contracts, Brasilia could reach beyond the Lusophone countries tied to it through shared Portuguese colonialism and diversify partnerships via IBSA and BRICS. As Ian Taylor noted, 'That the creation of IBSA coincided with Lula's African emphasis, ties in with the obvious desire to assert political influence in the international arena through such alliances.'[37]

Yet, despite the benefits of the South-South engagement policy for Brazil, doubts crept in about its long-term viability the moment

Rousseff was impeached in August 2016 and succeeded by a weak and corruption-riddled right-of-centre president, Michel Temer (2016–18). His interim government talked up realigning with the US, cutting down on the costs incurred by Brazil in providing public goods in Africa and the Caribbean, and shifting to a bilateral approach over the multilateral networking strategy of the PT governments.[38] Ideological repudiation of socialist internationalism as well as economic crisis and restructuring away from the welfare schemes of the PT at home contributed to Temer's watering down of South-South cooperation as a talisman of Brazilian foreign policy. Temer's Foreign Minister Jose Serra's call for a 'pragmatic solidarity towards countries of the Global South' to replace the previous strategy that brought 'low economic benefits and high diplomatic investments'[39] marked a shift that would become much more pronounced once the far-right populist Bolsonaro came to power.

If the transitional Temer administration mooted a modified, transactional South-South strategy, Bolsonaro's aides are ready to throw the baby out with the bathwater and switch to 'nothing less than a new North-South axis' with Trump's America.[40] Like Trump abandoning the liberal internationalist credo of his predecessors in US foreign policy, Bolsonaro seeks to eschew Brazil's erstwhile 'soft balancing' to constrain the power of the US through regional integration and coalitions with developing nations, a strategy which had been designed to rev up Brazil's ascent to great power status in the medium-term.[41] To Bolsonaro, the path to make Brazil great does not lie in making common cause with neighbours in South America or banding together with emerging powers across the world, but in allying with Trump's US in a crusade against the remnants of leftist regimes in Latin America. The Brazilian's president's tweet before landing on his first official visit to Washington was telling.

> Brazil and the USA together pose a threat to those who defend tyranny and other backwards ideologies across the globe. So only those who support those regimes would ever fear this cooperation.[42]

Bolsonaro's visceral hatred for communism and socialism and his instinctive opposition to left-wing politics goes back decades to the time he served in the Brazilian army in the 1970s and 1980s. Since the Brazilian military dictatorships of that era were allied to the US and worked in tandem with the Central Intelligence Agency (CIA) against leftist opponents within Brazil and across Latin America, his outlook towards the US had always remained rosy and positive. American journalist Vincent Bevins observes that 'what Bolsonaro offers is an explicit return to the values that underpinned Brazil's brutal dictatorship', including violent anti-leftist counter-revolutionary campaigns like Operation Condor devised by the Brazilian military and CIA during the Cold War. To Bevins, 'Bolsonaro's ideology is best understood as Operation Condor plus the Internet.'[43] Shedding post-dictatorship Brazil's reluctance to interfere in internal affairs of neighbouring countries, the populist Bolsonaro has declared that he's working with the US to force regime change in Venezuela, 'part of a broader international coalition, known as the "Sao Paulo Forum," which nearly conquered power throughout Latin America in recent times, [and which] by democratic means, we were able to rid ourselves from that project in Brazil'.[44] Later in this chapter, I will analyse the intricacies and pitfalls of Bolsonaro's Brazil and Trump's America forming a far-right entente to counter leftist governments in the region. Here, the point to be noted is that Brazil's conversion from South-South solidarity to a North-South axis is driven by the ideological polarisation between right and left that Bolsonaro has promoted domestically and also externalised in his foreign policy.

The déjà vu feeling that Bolsonaro has invoked by bringing back Cold War themes into Brazil's pro-US foreign policy also has an important racial dimension. Bolsonaro's voting base in Brazil includes middle class white Brazilians (especially men) fed up with redistributive welfare policies of the PT, religiously conservative Catholic and evangelical Christians opposed to feminism and homosexuality, and economic elites from landowning, mining and manufacturing sectors who resented the regulations of the socialist era. Many poor Brazilians of colour who were vexed by soaring crime and corruption also voted for Bolsonaro, but this was in spite of his overt racism and prioritisation of interests of white Brazilians of European ancestry.[45] The white nationalism Bolsonaro represents is a seminal factor in his foreign policy revolution of cosying up to Washington. His right-wing Christian vision for foreign policy is a product of the domestic 'Bible, Bullet and Beef' coalition (religious right, arms industry, agribusiness and mining lobbies), which underpins Brazil's shift towards the US.

Lula had conceptualised Brazil's Global South-oriented internationalism in a way that resonated with the socialist project of uplifting downtrodden Afro-Brazilians and mixed races at home. Ending racial discrimination of Brazilians of African and mixed origins (more than 50 per cent of the population as per the 2010 census)[46] was a hallmark of PT rule. To Lula and his successor, reversing centuries of racial injustice in Brazil had a corollary foreign policy goal to make the international order fairer, democratic and accountable to downtrodden developing countries of the Global South. Lula enlarged Brazil's presence in Africa thanks to the strength of Afro-descendant coalitions in domestic Brazilian affairs and the revival of a 'culturalist discourse [stressing] not only the relevance of African culture to Brazilian society but also the country's debt to Africa because of its history of slavery'.[47] The Brazilian left's apologies to Africa for the transatlantic slave trade and identification of Africa as one of the cradles of Brazilian civilisation laid a social identity basis for South-South foreign policy. As Amorim put it in 2003, 'With 76 million Afro-descendants (black- and brown-skinned people) [Brazil is] the biggest *black* nation in the world after Nigeria… and [consequently] the government is committed to reflect this reality in its foreign politics.'[48] Lula hinted at a profound internal transformation as a motivation for Brazil's South-South cooperation when he said in 2006 at an IBSA summit, 'We are overcoming historical, geographic, cultural and mental barriers that have always made us look to the North rather than the South.'[49]

Bolsonaro is the antithesis of the Brazilian left. He wants to return to looking to the North as his definition of Brazil's national identity is tethered to Portuguese colonisers and the white Western and Christian civilisation. Brazilian historian Paulo Pacha has shown how the Brazilian far-right idolises Europe and casts white Brazilians as the inheritors of a glorious Western classical past.

> By stressing the relationship between Brazil and Portugal, the far right erases the importance of indigenous and African peoples in the history of Brazil and ignores their social, cultural, and economic contributions. In this imaginary past, Portugal is not framed as a distant colonial power, but as the 'motherland' that gave Brazilians a European language and culture.[50]

Bolsonaro's Foreign Minister Ernesto Araujo is the most vocal proponent of Brazil having a Western identity and hence natural affinities with Europe and the US. His glorification of Trump and advocacy for a greater US role in Latin America are revelatory.

> President Trump proposes a vision of the West not based on capitalism and liberal democracy, but on the recovery of the symbolic past, history and culture of Western nations. Trump seems to have today a vision of the world that surpasses in many leagues, in depth and extension, the visions of the hyper-intellectualized and politicized elite that despises it… the West has opened the door for millions of immigrants because it denies itself, because it is psychically ill. Trump wants to stop this self-destructive advance… There is no 'us-versus-them logic' here, contrary to what Trump's detractors are fond of saying. There is instead an 'us seeking to reclaim ourselves' logic. The Brazilian people seem to be authentic and profoundly nationalistic, so Brazil would not have to feel uncomfortable about a project to recover the soul of the West from national sentiment. Brazil—even if it does not want to—is part of the West, and this West is—even if it does not see it—in a conflict of gigantic proportions for its own survival.[51]

In January 2019, Araujo stood beside Pompeo in Brasilia and explicitly linked the Bolsonaro administration's domestic racial politics with the move towards a North-South axis with the US.

> … with regards to alignment, I'd like to say that, in fact, Brazil is realigning itself. Brazil is just coming back to its own values and with its own ideals, and Itamaraty (Ministry of Foreign Affairs of Brazil) is actually realigning with the Brazilian people in our foreign policy, and the reflex of this is that we would get closer to those countries which have these same values. So in our relationship with the US is a consequence of this internal realignment in Brazil, and with other countries the same way.[52]

As a symbolic affirmation of Brazil's white Western and right-wing identity, Bolsonaro sought and got Trump's nod for initiating the accession procedure for Brazil's admission into the Organisation for Economic Cooperation and Development (OECD), the club of primarily rich Western, industrialised free market nations. President Temer had also sought entry into the OECD, but the USTR had objected on grounds of 'anachronistic positions that Brazilian governments have taken in trade negotiation organizations',[53] that is, the protectionist and anti-Western stances that Brasilia is known for in the WTO along with emerging powers like India. Bolsonaro's confidence that directly appealing to Trump would help overcome this barrier and his Economy Minister Guedes' hope that 'this issue will be resolved thanks to the personal harmony between Bolsonaro and Trump'[54] showed how Brazil aimed to convert the 'two-track presidency' in America to its advantage. Although the US enjoyed a $27-billion trade surplus with Brazil in goods and services by 2017, Trump had bracketed it along with India as a protectionist threat that was not being fair to US companies. In October 2018, Trump vented:

> Brazil's another one. That's a beauty. They charge us whatever they want. If you ask some of the companies, they say Brazil is among the toughest in the world—maybe the toughest in the world.[55]

But after Bolsonaro took office and signalled that Brazil would cease challenging the US in multilateral trade forums on behalf of the Global South and conduct 'bilateral trade with the entire world without an ideological bias',[56] Trump appreciated and changed tack. Asked in March 2019 if Trump could shepherd Brazil into the OECD by overriding the USTR's concerns, he replied:

> We will be supporting—we're going to have a great relationship in so many different ways. That's just a—just something that we're going to be doing in honor of the President and in honor of Brazil. We will be asking for things (trade concessions) but not necessarily having to do with that. I think we're just going to have a very fair relationship.[57]

Bolsonaro's decision to accede to a new US-encouraged pro-free trade agreement in South America called PROSUR, which the conservative president of Chile, Sebastian Pinera, declaimed as a forum 'without ideology and bureaucracy, but with a total commitment to freedom, democracy and human rights',[58] is another sharp departure in Brazilian foreign policy in line with Trump's preference for opening previously protected large markets like Brazil and Argentina in Latin America to American exports. PROSUR has merged members of the hitherto rival blocs Mercosur and the Pacific Alliance and is committed to reducing tariff barriers, making it a right-wing substitute to the earlier left-leaning UNASUR. Bolsonaro has ploughed ahead with PROSUR, undeterred by criticism within Brazil and from progressives around Latin America that joining it risks forfeiting Brazil's leadership in regional integration and handing the keys to the US to reinsert itself as an economic hegemon.[59]

On national security matters, Bolsonaro has also irked Brazil's left and dissenters in his own administration by plunging into an unprecedented alliance-like relationship with the US that was last witnessed during the Cold War. His high-profile visit to the CIA headquarters in March 2019, with his son Eduardo tweeting it was an honour for the Brazilian president and him to go to 'one of the most respected intelligence agencies in the world' where they would get 'an excellent opportunity to talk about international themes of the region with top-level experts and technicians',[60] was a stunning slap in the face to the Brazilian left's long-held conviction that the CIA was devil incarnate and should be warded off to save Latin America from repeating the destabilisation of a bygone era. The expose by Edward Snowden in 2013 that the US' National Security Agency was wiretapping Rousseff's communications had caused an uproar in Brazil and kept aloft the fear of American interventionism and sabotage in the region.

But as a far-right politician, Bolsonaro has chosen to rub it in for his political rivals by embracing the US like no democratically elected leader ever has. Trump's eagerness to grant Brazil the status of Major Non-NATO Ally, another trophy that Bolsonaro has lobbied for as part of his Northern turn, and the US president's tantalising comment that he would 'have to talk to a lot of people' but could eventually make Brazil 'maybe a NATO ally',[61] were shots in the arm for Bolsonaro's rightist manifesto of upturning Brazil's socialist international legacy. Amorim's horrified reaction to Bolsonaro's CIA visit, that it was 'an explicitly submissive position [and] nothing compares to this'[62] was catnip to the Brazilian far-right because such denunciations appeal to them as vindication of Bolsonaro's ideological revolution. Throughout the astonishing new foreign policy voyage that Bolsonaro has embarked on, he has projected a will to overcome past reservations and fears and claimed he is pursuing Brazil's national interests with a practical bent of mind. His son Eduardo has described Brazil and the US as 'two friendly nations that drifted apart in recent years for ideological reasons'.[63] But as I explained earlier, the North-South axis is absolutely ideological in nature. It would have been unthinkable had the US been led by a liberal internationalist president like Barack Obama or if the socialist Lula had returned as Brazil's president. Whether it is an uncanny conjuncture or a by-product of a global capitalist crisis affecting both countries, the fact that Bolsonaro and Trump find each other as counterparts at the same time is the chief reason why Brazil has gyrated so starkly in its foreign policy.

Populist Interventionism

As we saw in the Introduction of this book, Trump is a populist and isolationist with a narrow focus on domestic American interests. His renunciation of globalist diplomatic tenets like promotion of democracy and human rights abroad is well established and proven. Yet, in an oxymoronic twist, Trump has donned the mantle of a messiah who would cleanse Latin America of socialist and communist authoritarianism and usher in a new era of capitalist democracy in the region. His rousing speech in February 2019 before an audience of Venezuelan-American exiles in Florida was uncharacteristic. It sounded a clarion call that would make mainstream liberal internationalist Americans proud.

> We're here to proclaim a new day is coming in Latin America. It's coming. In Venezuela and across the Western Hemisphere, socialism is dying, and liberty, prosperity, and democracy are being reborn. The people of Venezuela are standing for freedom and democracy, and the United States of America is standing right by their side… as the United States stands up for democracy in Venezuela, we reaffirm the solidarity with the long-suffering people of Cuba and Nicaragua and people everywhere living under socialist and communist regimes. And one day soon, with God's help, we are going to see what the people will do in Caracas and Managua and Havana. And when Venezuela is free, and Cuba is free, and Nicaragua is free, this will become the first free hemisphere in all of human history.[64]

Trump's NSA Bolton has conceived of a 'Troika of Tyranny' consisting of Venezuela, Cuba and Nicaragua in what sounds like a Latin American variant of the neoconservative Bush's 2002 formulation of an Axis of Evil (Iran, Iraq and North Korea). Bolton vowed in November 2018 that the Trump administration 'will no longer appease dictators and despots near our shores... will not reward firing squads, torturers, and murderers... will champion the independence and liberty of our neighbours... will stand with the freedom fighters', and warned, 'The Troika of Tyranny in this hemisphere—Cuba, Venezuela, and Nicaragua—has finally met its match.' He added, 'Recent elections of like-minded leaders in key countries, including Ivan Duque in Colombia, and last weekend Jair Bolsonaro in Brazil, are positive signs for the future of the region,'[65] thereby mooting a right-wing alliance to uproot the remaining few leftist holdouts.

Among the sizeable bunch of rightist leaders of Latin America, Bolsonaro has been the most unabashed in wanting to associate with this renewed American Cold War-style counter-revolutionary interventionism. Asked by a reporter in the Rose Garden of the White House what Brazil's position would be if the US plans a military incursion into Venezuela to overthrow the authoritarian Nicolas Maduro's regime, Bolsonaro did not balk and dropped hints that these were 'reserved issues', which cannot be revealed. He called the military option 'a matter of strategy' and insinuated, 'Certain pieces of information, if are to come to the table, may not be debated publicly.'[66] When the president of Brazil used such language while standing beside his American counterpart, it conveyed intense behind-the-scenes intelligence and military cooperation between Brasilia and Washington for interfering in Venezuela. What was unthinkable under previous Brazilian and American administrations, which hewed to a cautious, non-interventionist foreign policy in the region, became possible with Bolsonaro and Trump in concord.

At first glance, Trump's aggressive drive for regime change in Latin America's left-ruled countries through economic sanctions, weaponisation of humanitarian aid and threats to unleash the 'military option'[67] appears to contradict his isolationist populism. Why is a president who prizes a non-judgemental foreign policy making pointed value judgements about types of regimes in Latin America and mustering a multilateral alliance of rightists to apply pressure on leftist governments? The answer lies in unpacking America's 'two-track presidency'. Trump's own motivation for declaring virtual war on Venezuela, Cuba and Nicaragua has less to do with any closet attachment to liberal ideals or a grand vision for transforming Latin America, and a lot to do with domestic electoral politicking in the US. Trump is bidding for the hearts and minds of close to half a million anti-Chavez and anti-Maduro Venezuelan-Americans, many of whom are settled in the swing state of Florida and who traditionally lean towards the Democratic party.

Trump's re-election campaign staff sense a 'golden opportunity' in trumpeting democratisation of Venezuela. 'If they succeed in driving Mr. Maduro from office, they believe, they may turn Venezuelan-Americans into Republican voters, much like Cuban-Americans before them.'[68] The outsized influence of the Cuban-American conservative Senator Marco Rubio, who has informally fronted the Trump administration's Venezuela offensive, is totally political. According to Latin America scholar William LeoGrande, 'Trump doesn't care about Latin America. It's all about domestic politics. Trump thinks he won Florida because of the Cuban-American vote. Rubio convinced him that that's what made the big difference in Florida.'[69] Another US academician, Paul Musgrave, argues that by conflating the Democratic party with Maduro's socialists and painting Democrats as apologists for Latin American tyranny, 'the "Venezuela" the Trump administration is dealing with is not a real country so much as it's an ideological construct designed to have maximum domestic impact'.[70]

To Bolsonaro too, countering long-standing leftist regimes in Venezuela, Cuba and Nicaragua, which were considered friendly by PT administrations, is an externality of his domestic struggle against progressive political tendencies. During his presidential election campaign in 2018, Bolsonaro popularised the slogan question, 'Is Brazil free from becoming the Venezuela of tomorrow?' and alleged that the PT's socialism would make Brazil a failed impoverished society like Venezuela and Cuba. He found an unsurprising echo in Trump, who ranted, 'The new Democrats are radical socialists who want to model America's economy after Venezuela,'[71] In both countries, the comparisons are exaggerated. Brazil's socialists are mild moderates vis-à-vis Chavistas and America's centrist Democratic party has a history of battling communism worldwide. But far-right populist presidents and their propagandists are immune to nuances about rivals who fall to their left on the ideological spectrum. They are all 'traitors' and 'cultural Marxists'.

For the pure populist factions in Trump's two-track and Bolsonaro's three-track presidencies, the anti-communist tirade is hardly a mammoth Cold War-like geostrategic commitment to spread liberal hegemony in Latin America. In Chapter II, I demonstrated how Trump's selective promotion of democracy in Iran is a derivative of his evangelical Christian voting base in America. The same analogy holds for Latin America. Trump and his populist aides have no genuine long-term plan or dedication to advancing liberty in the Western Hemisphere's few remaining left-ruled countries. His populist isolationist vision can countenance low-cost coups or regionally-led regime change missions in Venezuela, Cuba or Nicaragua, but not costly foreign entanglements that would necessitate deployment of American ground forces and detract from his domestic priorities. The only security crisis Trump sees as urgent and requiring action by the US military is at the border with Mexico to defend the homeland from the 'invasion' of immigrants. As of February 2019, Trump had dispatched 4,350 soldiers to the southern border with Mexico, while there was no sign of any menacing American military presence in Colombia and Brazil, which border Venezuela.

Bolton's inadvertent or deliberate display of a notepad with the words '5,000 troops to Colombia' handwritten on it during a press conference in January 2019 stirred up a hornet's nest in Latin America, with the US-allied right-wing Colombian government denying there was any mission to militarily depose the Venezuelan regime.[72] But this leak did prove that internationalists and hawkish neoconservatives in the Trump administration want to use Venezuela, Cuba and Nicaragua as justifications for reimposing American liberal hegemony in the Western Hemisphere. Bolton was the figure in the Bush administration who had added Fidel Castro's Cuba to the 'Axis of Evil' list in 2002 by branding it a state sponsor of terrorism. Globalists who served in the Trump administration, like Rex Tillerson, openly asserted that the US neglected and allowed relationships in Latin America to atrophy, '[Because] we have forgotten about the importance of the Monroe Doctrine and what it meant to this Hemisphere and maintaining those shared values. So I think it's as relevant today as it was the day it was written.'[73] This contrasted with the Obama era, when the US introduced a thaw with Cuba and

Venezuela and Secretary of State John Kerry had assured that 'the era of the Monroe Doctrine is over'.[74]

Reversing Obama's non-interventionist foreign policy and flexing muscle in America's historic backyard is very much on the agenda of the 'steady state' inside the Trump administration. The broader geostrategic concern propelling the globalist faction in the US government is China's penetration of Latin America and the perceived threat it poses to the US in its natural sphere of influence. Tillerson's warning, 'China is gaining a foothold in Latin America [and] Russia's growing presence in the region is alarming as well,' and his dictum, 'Latin America does not need new imperial powers that seek only to benefit their own people,'[75] was a throwback to the Cold War-era thinking of Washington preventing strategically valuable regions from falling under illiberal rivals of the US. But it is far from guaranteed that Trump the populist and isolationist will go along with a costly containment or counterbalancing programme against China in Latin America. For Trump, North Korea or Venezuela are sought-after targets not with an intent to challenge Chinese hegemony in Asia or Latin America, but narrowly conceived globally highlighted political crises he wants to milk for electoral gains. In this sense, the role of Bolsonaro's Brazil as a US ally in the region is not long-term strategic but tactical in outlook.

Thomas Shannon, former American Ambassador to Brazil, has correctly observed, 'What worries me, quite frankly, is that we won't do things in a big strategic way. Instead, the United States could just try to get them (Brazil) to help us on Venezuela or Nicaragua and then walk away.'[76] Unreliability is a built-in feature of Trump's populism and Brazil cannot assume that Washington would commit to a sustained involvement in Latin America with the larger goal of limiting Chinese power. The so-called 'prudent' faction in the Bolsonaro administration, led by Vice-President General Mourao, appears to have understood the transactional nature of Trump and hence not approved of the Brazilian president's wish for uninhibited military interoperability and cooperation with the US to unseat Maduro. Mourao's call for Brazil to avoid 'any extreme measure (regarding Venezuela) that confuses us with those nations that will be judged by history as aggressors, invaders and violators of national sovereignties',[77] uncovered the reluctance in Brazil's military establishment to enter a no-holds-barred regime change alliance with American liberal internationalists. The Brazilian army's appointment in February 2019 of a general to the US Southern Command 'for facilitating communication between armed forces in the region'[78] is not a portent of full-scale anti-leftist war in Latin America under US leadership, but instead a stratagem for the Brazilian military to avert what Mourao derides as 'adventures' in the region that could boomerang.[79]

The schisms in the divided Bolsonaro administration are evident when it comes to the controversy about Brazil hosting US military bases. Bolsonaro heartily approved the US request for commercial use of Brazil's Alcantara airbase on the Atlantic coast for rocket launching, which could improve business prospects of American space companies seeking an ideal location near the Equator. But on the geopolitical issue of stationing American troops on Brazilian bases, Mourao and the Brazilian army have balked despite Bolsonaro's enthusiasm for it as a means 'to counter Russian influence in Venezuela'. Bolsonaro was apparently persuaded to drop the offer to the US 'due to opposition from the armed forces, who see a foreign presence as a transgression of national sovereignty'.[80]

Senior cabinet ministers who belong to the Brazilian military were also peeved at their president for according Juan Guaido, the US-backed opposition politician who declared himself alternative president of Venezuela, treatment equivalent to a head of state when he visited Brasilia in February 2019. The army's preference was for Bolsonaro to meet Guaido discreetly without press conferences and public speeches so as not to worsen frictions with the Maduro regime when border tensions with Venezuela were simmering.[81] If the Trump administration is beset by internal incoherence over foreign policy, the Bolsonaro government is a veritable Tower of Babel with a far-from-united vision of Brazil's appropriate international relations. A hyperactive regional interventionist Brazil–US combo in Latin America is thus not destined to reach the level of a tight-knit alliance.

Ousting or Boosting China?

In earlier chapters, I have explained why emerging powers with ambitions to become great powers are loath to exchange Western masters for Asian ones. The decline and withdrawal of the US from various international institutions and regions of the world under Trump do not automatically translate into an expansionist China taking over the reins since emerging powers stand in the way and will pursue their own dreams of regional and global leadership. Trump's renewed interest in Latin America and Bolsonaro's advent have opened up a crucial debate in Brazil about whether it had been bandwagoning with China and if this process must be arrested to preserve Brazil's strategic autonomy. As a far-right politician who, like Trump, detests communist regimes, Bolsonaro has taken potshots at China for violating Brazil's sovereignty. As a presidential candidate, he visited Taiwan and famously quipped, 'The Chinese are not buying in Brazil. They are buying Brazil.' He opposed the sale of Brazilian state-owned energy corporations as such strategic acquisitions might 'put Brazil in the hands of China', whose cumulative investment in Brazil has been a staggering $124 billion since 2003.[82]

Like Bannon who guided Trump's worldview, Bolsonaro's guru Carvalho has outlined a demonology of China as part of a global Marxist cabal out to undermine Brazil's independence. He berated legislators from Bolsonaro's ultra-conservative Social Liberal Party (PSL) for seeking Chinese cooperation in surveillance techniques. 'You are handing Brazil over to China. Are you going to let these guys hand Brazil over to the Chinese system in this way?'[83] Carvalho's stated desire, 'The US should help Brazil so it is not sold off to China,'[84] reflects the deep unease among the white Christian far-right in Brazil about the PT-era South-South cooperation formula, which enabled China to displace the US and EU and rise to the status of the country's largest trading partner and investor.

As we saw earlier in this chapter, Bolsonaro's socialist predecessors preserved IBSA as a separate democratic grouping and were conscious not to place all their eggs in the Chinese basket. Yet, it is undeniable that Brazil's economic dependence on China has multiplied over the years. Bolsonaro inherited a 'concentrated export relationship' with China, which buys almost half of Brazil's commodities, while the US under the protectionist Trump has been raising tariff walls on Brazilian soybeans and metals.[85] With China alone accounting for one-third of total foreign sales of the Brazilian mining giant Vale, the economic fundamentals of Sino-Brazil relations are deeply entrenched. For all the racialised affinity for the West Bolsonaro's core populists nurture, Brazil's agribusinesses and mining megaliths cannot envisage how a protectionist Trump can substitute for a China whose insatiable appetite for Brazilian raw materials has been exceptional. Chinese state-owned media confidently quoted former Brazilian officials to remind Bolsonaro's radicals, 'There is not one economy in the world that can occupy the space China occupies [in Brazil].'[86] The technocratic camp in the Bolsonaro administration, represented by Economy Minister Guedes, echoed these fundamental realities. He asked in March 2019, 'Do you know who has the most direct investment here in the US? The Chinese. So why cannot we (Brazil) trade with China and let them invest in Brazil, on railroads to transport our soybeans?'[87]

Given that Trump's populist America is ill-equipped to replace China as a customer for Brazilian goods, the expectation that shifting to a pro-Western foreign policy will fulfil Brazil's need to diversify away from China is misplaced. The only diversification Guedes is looking for is to change the mix of products that Brazil sells to China so as to increase 'sales of products with more added value to the Chinese market and lowering the sale of commodities'.[88] The problem of 'reprimarisation' of Brazil, which exports soybeans, oil and iron ore to China while the latter pumps in manufactured goods into Brazil, is worrisome for Brazil in the long run as this hampers its industrialisation. The political economists Kevin Gallagher and Roberto Porzecanski wrote in 2006 that China had already out-competed Latin American manufacturers, including Brazilian firms, in world markets, as 91 per cent of Brazil's industrial exports were threatened by Chinese competition.[89] In the framework of Cardoso's 'dependency theory', China is the core that can be viewed as exploiting the natural wealth of Brazil even as it fired up Brazil's GDP to grow during the period of the global commodities super-cycle (2000–14).

Chinese foreign direct investment (FDI) in Brazil has been dominated by mergers and acquisitions, that is, takeovers of Brazilian firms, which frighten Brazilian ultra-nationalists like Bolsonaro, rather than greenfield projects that add fresh value to Brazil's economy.[90] The right-wing Brazilian government's plan to privatise state assets and develop 'pro-business' market conditions could invite extra Chinese interest and magnify dependence. Bolsonaro will look to American or European bidders to balance out the Chinese juggernaut, especially in deep sea oil contracts, using the OECD membership as a platform. Trump has praised Bolsonaro's 'vision for freeing the private sector and opening the economy', but inserted a caveat: 'Our great companies are ready to go when that table is flat and free,'[91] that is, only if Brazil's milieu for FDI is freer. Chinese corporations enjoy a lead in this race as they are state-owned and heavily subsidised by the Chinese government and hence less insistent on level playing fields as preconditions to invest in Brazil. Moreover, Trump's economic nationalism demands American companies to invest at home rather than in Mexico, Argentina or Brazil.

The Quest for Greatness

If predatory China is inescapably entwined with Brazil's destiny, and Trump's US or the inward-looking EU are not the panaceas, the strategic challenge facing Brazil is how it can avoid letting China determine its future. The economic recession Brazil suffered from 2014 to 2017 was a direct outcome of China's own slowdown,[92] showcasing the perils of coupling Brazil's fate with a China whose new normal is predicted to be tepid growth as its economy adjusts and matures. To avoid a 'lost decade' or worse, Brazil has to relook at its own neighbours in Latin America, other (emerging market economies) EMEs and developing countries seriously, that is, go back to the South-South cooperation model with a new emphasis on lessening China's shadow over it. When Lula's 'autonomy through diversification' policy was at its peak in the early 2000s, China was considered part of a wave of 'non-traditional markets' (alongside Africa, the Middle East, Eastern Europe and other countries of the Asia-Pacific) that would help Brazil attain 'more balanced relations with rich countries'.[93] Today, Brazil must accept a changed global configuration where China is an advanced power, and approach the remaining non-traditional countries to forge political, trade and investment coalitions to keep Chinese hegemony under check. Brazil has to come up with an 'IBSA Plus' network that will ultimately lift it to higher international power status.

Bolsonaro's rhetoric that Brazil cannot be yoked and sold to China is a correct diagnosis of the predicament his country is staring at. But his populist West-centric foreign policy is the wrong prescription for Brazil's quest to become a global power. Betting on the US to rebalance

Brazil's relations with China is a strategy that might have worked had a liberal internationalist and interventionist president been in charge in Washington. While Bolsonaro's own far-right credentials and anti-minority invective rile Western liberals, he could have played on the democracy and human rights agenda in Latin America and presented Brazil as a foil to illiberal China to ingratiate himself had there been a liberal establishment in the US willing to commit resources to push back against Chinese influence. With Trump, as I have analysed in this chapter, the rhetoric of the two largest democracies of the Western Hemisphere teaming up to vanquish communism in Latin America and eject China from the region is shallow and unlikely to elevate Brazil's stature as a leading power from a long-term perspective.

British journalist Michael Reid aptly noted that when Brazil was under the PT and America was ruled by the liberal internationalist Obama, there was a mismatch of expectations and interests between the two countries.

> The big misunderstanding in the relationship was that the two countries wanted different things out of it. The US was interested in trade, investment and energy, and in coordinating policy with Brazil in Latin America. Brazil wanted the US to treat it as a global power, rather than as a Latin American one. And it strongly resisted any suggestion that it might act as a South American sheriff on behalf of Washington. Yet the US did not see Brazil as being in the same league as China, Russia and India.[94]

With Trump, Bolsonaro can bridge some of these gaps but there are zero chances of the populist US leader actively promoting Brazil's rise through economic, military and institutional support. Trump's lack of a geopolitical compass and fleeting interest in expending American treasure to counterbalance China leaves Brazil's utility dubious. In Chapter I, I presented how India has learnt the hard way not to rely on Trump to contain China. But at least India's location as an immediate neighbour of China and a country with accumulating military hard power in the Indian Ocean region gives it certain purchase in Washington, if not for Trump himself then to elements in the permanent American deep state. Brazil's lack of comparable long-range military capabilities confines its international imprint to economic and institutional domains. It is ahead of other Latin American nations but ranks only thirteenth in an index of global military strength, behind Russia (second), China (third), India (fourth), Turkey (ninth) and Egypt (twelfth).[95]

Brazilian scholars Matias Spektor and Guilherme Fasolin have speculated that Bolsonaro would have no choice but to bandwagon with the US for domestic political survival, provided the US gives him 'side payments [like] military equipment transfers, facilitated sales to assist in the modernization of Brazil's armed forces, and well-funded training programs in the fields of anti-narcotics and antiterrorism'.[96] Be that as it may, it is difficult to visualise Brazil climbing the ladder of global hard power by clinging to Trump's US, which has a plainly utilitarian and transactional interest in cooperating with any country. If trade disputes or differences that impact domestic American politics arise, Trump can be nasty with foreign partners and totally blind to their strategic potential. The Bolsonaro camp's belief that reverting to the fold of the West will make Brazil great is a chimera that reflects the lack of independent thinking in the Brazilian far-right. In Chapter I, I demonstrated how Narendra Modi overcame the straitjacket of a 'swing state' and set forth on a bold journey to make India a leading power in world affairs. For all his ultra-nationalism, Bolsonaro is so enmeshed in the ideology of white identity that he is unable to transcend the swing-state logic and forge a path for Brazil's ascendance as an independent third force in Latin America and beyond, which is impervious to American or Chinese hegemony.

For sure, there are factions in his three-track presidency who have a vision for Brazil to escape the China–US duopoly. Bolsonaro's headlong rush to imitate Trump and satiate Brazil's evangelical right-wing Christians by recognising Jerusalem as Israel's capital was opposed by military officers in his cabinet. Mourao objected 'that moving the embassy was a bad idea because it would hurt Brazil's exports to Arab countries'.[97] Brazilian journalist Gustavo Ribeiro noted,

> Mr. Bolsonaro's moves pander to one of his bases, evangelicals, but go against the interest of another: big agro. Muslim-majority countries account for 6% of Brazilian exports and 10% of agricultural exports—a scenario which took over 40 years of effort to establish.[98]

Plus, the peacemaker and problem-solver role Brazil tried to assay during PT rule on burning issues in the Middle East like Iran's nuclear weapons and the Syrian war would disappear from the horizon if Bolsonaro had his way. His obvious racially motivated disinterest, if not contempt, for Africa, is another factor that does not bode well for Brazil's foreign policy renaissance. The technocrat faction in his government has to rein in Bolsonaro's instinct of frittering away Brazil's hard-earned influence in the developing world.

The far-right populist president's vow to do a Trump and pull Brazil out of the Paris Climate Accord is believed to have been stayed by the military.[99] Threats by France to stall a trade deal between the EU and Mercosur if Brazil departed from the Paris agreement[100] possibly added to the pressure on Bolsonaro to backtrack on quitting the multilateral environmental framework. In the Introduction of this book, I elaborated how neither domestic dissent nor international outrage could fully contain Trump's radical populist foreign policy. The same applies to Bolsonaro, although Brazil is relatively weaker than the US and cannot afford to be unbendingly unilateral in all foreign policy domains. Domestic and foreign constraints on an emerging power like Brazil could ultimately prove beneficial to it since Bolsonaro will not be able to walk the talk on each and every far-right foreign policy plank he brandished for electoral gains during the 2018 presidential race.

Crafting a calibrated new policy towards the Global South, including Africa and the Middle East, is a dire need for Brazil to find other legs to stand on besides China. Emerging powers that relinquish multilateralism will get no respite from the pull of bandwagoning to great powers. During the Lula era, Brazil had opted for 'institutionalised multilateralism as a means of increasing its bargaining capacity and hindering the unilateralism of major powers, without being antagonistic to them'.[101] It was an insurance policy against succumbing to great powers. Some form of multilateralism must be continued if Brazil is to keep alive hopes of rising to global prominence. Consolidating PROSUR for unleashing long-bottled-up intraregional trade in South America is one method by which Brazil can diversify its export destinations and retain autonomy from Chinese tutelage. With less than 17 per cent of Brazil's exports going to neighbours in South America and the Caribbean, contrasted to a whopping 44 per cent being delivered to Asian countries (China getting the lion's share), there is a vast integration deficit in trade that needs to be filled in Brazil's neighbourhood. Bolsonaro's free market and free trade policies may negatively impact the vast income inequalities within Brazilian society and exacerbate environmental degradation in the Amazon rainforest, but they do contain commercial seeds of what the American analyst Shannon O'Neill labels 'real integration' of the region that had been stalled by the right-left divide.[102]

Diplomatically, Brazil has to lean in and take the lead of the 14-nation Lima Group, which is devoted to a peaceful transition in Venezuela. Resolving the Venezuela crisis and stabilising its neighbour is the acid test for Brazil to reaffirm its leadership image. In the long run, it is less crucial as to who replaces Maduro in Caracas and more important as to how the South American region as a whole finds a pathway to integration, social peace and prosperity. In my discussions with Brazilian diplomats based in New Delhi, I inferred a feeling of resignation that they had little leverage over Venezuela, partly because of the linguistic divide in South America between the only Portuguese-speaking country, Brazil, and the rest that are Spanish-speaking. As the odd one out with economic and military superiority over neighbours, Brazil has the hard power to possibly shape the region, but the lack of ideational and cultural influence due to the language barrier is a lingering obstacle. The ambivalence and reluctance in Spanish-speaking countries to accept Brazil as a hemispheric leader was evident even during the heydays of Lula's activist region-building foreign policy, when Argentina, Mexico, Venezuela, Bolivia and Ecuador resisted Brazil's will.[103] Under the bilateral-oriented Bolsonaro, it will be an even tougher grind for Brazil to unify the region behind it.

Maintaining salience within IBSA and BRICS is an imperative if Brazil is to contribute to global governance and graduate into a rule-maker instead of rule-taker in the international system. During the PT period, Brazil fought pragmatically for its domestic economic interests at the WTO, but to a lesser extent also followed 'political ideas' of reforming Western-dominated multilateral institutions to make them fairer and responsive to developing countries as a whole.[104] That approach spoke of a selfless leadership gene in Brazil, a trait Bolsonaro appears to be squandering. The ideal foreign policy scenario that can revive Brazil's damaged soft power and spur its prestige in the world has been articulated by Stanford University's Harold Trinkunas.

> A Brazil that became moderately closer to the United States, set greater boundaries on China's influence, tuned up a long-stalled Mercosur, worked to bring the Lima Group and the United States together on a shared (and firmer) Venezuela policy, and doubled down on diplomacy and the international order could do much good for Brazil's influence abroad.[105]

But the dysfunctional and contradictory foreign policy emanating from Brasilia is a result of the disruptive nature of Bolsonaro's populism, which like Trump's anti-establishment ideology, has stripped Brazil of any inspiring international orientation. Since the 2014 economic recession and simultaneous corruption scandals pulled Brazil into a downward spiral, the uppermost question has been whether it is internally too contorted to drop out of contention to be a great power. One of the leitmotifs of this book is that political leadership is a central variable that can make or mar emerging powers on their sojourn to enhanced status in international affairs. In 2018, with the feckless Temer muddling through a hailstorm of graft scandals, Brazilian scholar Markus Fraundorfer warned of the curse of velha política; 'white, old men, with mindsets stuck in the past, desperately clinging to their privileges [and] responsible for Brazil's backwardness and irrelevance in international politics for the last few centuries'.[106]

Bolsonaro is not a weak and graft-tainted president like Temer, but he has not shown the acuity in foreign policy that comes from a keen understanding of Brazil's mojo, its geographical and historical import, and its relevance in a multipolar world. I concluded Chapter II with the thought that Turkey cannot realise its regional and global power potential unless the perpetually incumbent Erdogan departs and a new generation takes over. Bolsonaro entered Palácio do Planalto in January 2019 for a first four-year term and should be given time in office before being judged. But his populist infatuation with Trump and blissful ignorance about the progress of the post-American world are not propitious signs. Trump's America will undoubtedly be friendly to Bolsonaro's Brazil but fickly so. Like Trump, Bolsonaro's atavistic bid to make Brazil great by restoring its white Western identity is an anomaly that can only hold back his country from claiming its deserved status as a separate pole in the Western Hemisphere, distinct from the US and unchained from China.

Brazil should not have to wait until Bolsonaro falls or muddles through his tenure before getting back into its internationalist groove. It is too sophisticated and evolved a nation to atrophy forever. Course correction can happen if critical voices come together and pressure Bolsonaro to abjure his more reactionary impulses. The instances where factions within the Bolsonaro administration neutralised some of his zany foreign policy ideas suggest that there are silver linings. Brazil's famed social movements, citizen activists, corporate houses and intellectual class—all have to advocate and mobilise to ensure that the 'Brazilian way',[107] which brought balance, creativity and variety to international politics, is not irredeemably lost.

Endnotes

1. Silas Marti, 'Trump Serves as an Example, Says Congressman Bolsonaro While in the United States,' *Folha De S.Paulo*, 10 October 2017, https://www1.folha.uol.com.br/internacional/en/brazil/2017/10/1925870-trump-serves-as-an-example-says-congressman-bolsonaro-while-in-the-united-states.shtml.
2. 'Remarks by President Trump and President Bolsonaro of the Federative Republic of Brazil in Joint Press Conference,' 19 March 2019, Rose Garden, White House, https://www.whitehouse.gov/briefings-statements/remarks-president-trump-president-bolsonaro-federative-republic-brazil-joint-press-conference/.
3. Kevin Liptak, '"Trump of the Tropics" Fawns Over US President, Decries "Fake News",' CNN, 19 March 2019, https://edition.cnn.com/2019/03/19/politics/donald-trump-jair-bolsonaro-brazil-white-house/.
4. Brian Winter, 'System Failure: Behind the Rise of Jair Bolsonaro,' *Americas Quarterly*, Vol. 11, Issue 1 (2018).
5. Ricardo Senra, 'Steve Bannon Declares Support for Bolsonaro But Denies Link to Campaign: "He is Brilliant",' BBC, 26 October 2018, https://www.bbc.com/portuguese/brasil-45989131.
6. Brad Brooks, 'A Trump-Bolsonaro Bromance Could Be Brewing After Brazilian's Big Win,' Reuters, 29 October 2018, https://www.reuters.com/article/us-brazil-election-trump/a-trump-bolsonaro-bromance-could-be-brewing-after-brazilians-big-win-idUSKCN1N31BZ.
7. Rodrigo Delfim, 'The Tropical Trump? Bolsonaro Follows Closely the US President's Style,' *Folha De S.Paulo*, 18 December 2018, https://www1.folha.uol.com.br/internacional/en/world/2018/12/the-tropical-trump-bolsonaro-follows-closely-the-us-presidents-style.shtml.
8. Dom Phillips, '"Same Rhetoric": Bolsonaro's US Visit to Showcase Populist Alliance with Trump,' *The Guardian*, 18 March 2019, https://www.theguardian.com/world/2019/mar/18/jair-bolsonaro-us-visit-alliance-trump.
9. AFP, 'Son of Brazil's President Bolsonaro Joins Steve Bannon's Nationalist Group,' *The Times of Israel*, 2 February 2019, https://www.timesofisrael.com/son-of-brazils-bolsonaro-joins-steve-bannons-nationalist-group/.
10. Ben Schreckinger, 'Right-wing Movements Merge as Bolsonaro Visits Trump,' *Politico*, 19 March 2019, https://www.politico.com/story/2019/03/19/bolsonaro-brazil-trump-visit-1227573.

11. Simone Iglesias, 'Bolsonaro Sees Himself Ending "Dirty Ideology of the Left" in Brazil,' *Bloomberg*, 18 March 2019, https://www.bloomberg.com/news/articles/2019-03-18/bolsonaro-calls-for-an-end-to-communism-on-visit-to-washington.
12. Jill Colvin and Peter Prengaman, 'President Trump Praises "Trump of the Tropics" in Meeting with Brazilian Leader,' *Time*, 19 March 2019.
13. Oliver Stuenkel, 'What to Expect When Bolsonaro Meets Trump,' *Americas Quarterly*, 14 March 2019, https://www.americasquarterly.org/content/inside-bolsonaros-foreign-policy-bet-trump.
14. Dom Phillips, 'Fox News, Nepotism and Bigotry: Bolsonaro Brings His Trump Act to DC,' *The Guardian*, 20 March 2019, https://www.theguardian.com/world/2019/mar/20/bolsonaro-trump-visit-fox-news-interview-white-house.
15. Jose Sarney, 'Brazil: A President's Story,' *Foreign Affairs*, Vol. 65, Issue 1 (Fall 1986): 115.
16. Sarney, 'Brazil,' 117.
17. Tullo Vigevani and Marcela Oliveira, 'Brazilian Foreign Policy in the Cardoso Era: The Search for Autonomy Through Integration,' *Latin American Perspectives*, Vol. 34, Issue 5 (September 2007): 68.
18. Fernando Cardoso and Enzo Faletto, *Dependency and Development in Latin America* (Berkeley: University of California Press, 1979).
19. Carlos Teixeira, 'Brazil and the Institutionalisation of South America: From Hemispheric Estrangement to Cooperative Hegemony,' *Revista Brasileira de Política Internacional*, Vol. 54, Issue 2 (2011): 192.
20. Bruno Binetti, 'South America's PROSUR: The Answer to a Question Nobody Asked,' *Americas Quarterly*, 26 February 2019, https://www.americasquarterly.org/content/south-americas-PROSUR-answer-question-nobody-asked.
21. Jose Briceno-Ruiz and Andrea Hoffmann, 'Post-Hegemonic Regionalism, UNASUR, and the Reconfiguration of Regional Cooperation in South America,' *Canadian Journal of Latin American and Caribbean Studies*, Vol. 40, Issue 1 (January 2015): 48.
22. Jorge Battaglino, 'Defence in a Post-Hegemonic Regional Agenda: The Case of the South American Defence Council,' in *The Rise of Post-Hegemonic Regionalism: The Case of Latin America*, eds. Pia Riggirozzi and Diana Tussie (London: Springer, 2012), 92.
23. Henry Kissinger, *Does America Need a Foreign Policy? Toward a Diplomacy for the 21st Century* (New York: Simon & Schuster, 2001), 97–98.
24. Khatchik Ghougassian, 'The Post-Washington Consensus Regional Integration in South America: Convergence and Divergence in ALBA and UNASUR: A Comparative Perspective,' in *Decline of US Hegemony? A Challenge of ALBA and a New Latin American Integration of the Twenty-First Century*, eds. Bruce Bagley and Magdalena Defort (Lanham: Lexington Books, 2015), 178.
25. David Luhnow, 'The Two Latin Americas,' *The Wall Street Journal*, 3 January 2014, https://www.wsj.com/articles/the-two-latin-americas-1388709050.
26. Sean Burges, 'Consensual Hegemony: Theorizing Brazilian Foreign Policy After the Cold War,' *International Relations*, Vol. 22, Issue 1 (March 2008): 75.
27. Gian Gardini, 'Brazil: What Rise of What Power?' *Bulletin of Latin American Research*, Vol. 35, Issue 1 (January 2016): 15.
28. 'Interview Transcript: President Luiz Inacio Lula da Silva,' *Financial Times*, 8 November 2009.
29. Kwang Chun, *The BRICs Superpower Challenge: Foreign and Security Policy Analysis* (Farnham: Ashgate, 2013), 51.

30. 'IBSA—Introduction,' India Brazil South Africa Forum, accessed 2 June 2019, http://www.ibsa-trilateral.org/about_ibsa.html.
31. Sandeep Dikshit, 'In the World Economy, There Must be Freedom for People and Ideas to Move,' *The Hindu*, 26 October 2007.
32. Mario Osava, 'Interview with Celso Amorim: "IBSA is a Beacon for Political Strategising and South-South Cooperation",' Inter Press Service, 27 June 2011, http://www.ipsnews.net/2011/06/interview-with-celso-amorim-quotibsa-is-a-beacon-for-political-strategising-and-south-south-cooperationquot/.
33. Oliver Stuenkel, *India-Brazil-South Africa Dialogue Forum (IBSA): The Rise of the Global South* (Abingdon: Routledge, 2015), 109.
34. Celso Amorim, 'The BRICS and the Reorganization of the World,' *Folha De S.Paulo*, 8 June 2008.
35. Oliver Stuenkel, 'Why Brazil Benefits from BRICS Membership,' Post-Western World, 5 July 2014, https://www.postwesternworld.com/2014/07/05/brazil-benefits-membership/.
36. Celso Amorim, *Acting Globally: Memoirs of Brazil's Assertive Foreign Policy* (Lanham: Hamilton Books, 2017), 158.
37. Ian Taylor, *Africa Rising? BRICS—Diversifying Dependency* (Woodbridge: Boydell & Brewer, 2014), 52.
38. Marco Vieira and Henrique Menezes, 'Brazil is Breaking with its South-South Focus. What it Means for BRICS,' The Conversation, 20 November 2016, https://theconversation.com/brazil-is-breaking-with-its-south-south-focus-what-it-means-for-brics-69008.
39. Danilo Marcondes and Emma Mawdsley, 'South-South in Retreat? The Transitions from Lula to Rousseff to Temer and Brazilian Development Cooperation,' *International Affairs*, Vol. 93, Issue 3 (May 2017): 695.
40. AFP, 'Trump hosts "Trump of the Tropics" Bolsonaro at White House,' France24, 19 March 2019. https://www.france24.com/en/20190319-trump-hosts-trump-tropics-bolsonaro-white-house.
41. Daniel Flemes, 'Brazil in the BRIC Initiative: Soft Balancing in the Shifting World Order?' *Revista Brasileira de Política Internacional*, Vol. 53, Issue 1 (January/July 2010): 141–56.
42. Jair M. Bolsonaro (@jairbolsonaro), Twitter post, 17 March 2019, https://twitter.com/jairbolsonaro/status/1107414783362564108.
43. Vincent Bevins, 'Jair Bolsonaro, Brazil's Would-be Dictator,' *The New York Review of Books*, 12 October 2018, https://www.nybooks.com/daily/2018/10/12/jair-bolsonaro-brazils-would-be-dictator/.
44. 'Remarks by President Trump and President Bolsonaro.'
45. Gianpaolo Baiocchi and Marcelo Silva, 'Who Supports Brazil's New Strongman?' *Boston Review*, 12 October 2018, http://bostonreview.net/world/gianpaolo-baiocchi-marcelo-k-silva-who-supports-brazils-new-strongman.
46. Tom Phillips, 'Brazil Census Shows African-Brazilians in the Majority for the First Time,' *The Guardian*, 17 November 2011, https://www.theguardian.com/world/2011/nov/17/brazil-census-african-brazilians-majority.
47. Iara Leite et al., 'Brazilian South-South Development Cooperation: The Case of the Ministry of Social Development in Africa,' *Journal of International Development*, Vol. 27, Issue 8 (November 2015): 1452.
48. Andre Cicalo, 'From Racial Mixture to Black Nation: Racialising Discourses in Brazil's African Affairs,' *Bulletin of Latin American Research*, Vol. 33, Issue 1 (January 2014): 25.

49. Felipe Seligman, 'Brazil, India and South Africa Optimistic About Future Ties,' Inter Press Service, 13 September 2006, http://www.ipsnews.net/2006/09/trade-brazil-india-and-south-africa-optimistic-about-future-ties/.
50. Paulo Pacha, 'Why the Brazilian Far Right Loves the European Middle Ages,' *Pacific Standard*, 18 February 2019, https://psmag.com/ideas/why-the-brazilian-far-right-is-obsessed-with-the-crusades.
51. Michael Waller, 'Brazil's New Foreign Minister Gives Profound Philosophical Base to Trumpian Populism,' Center for Security Policy, 7 January 2019, https://www.centerforsecuritypolicy.org/2019/01/07/brazils-new-foreign-minister-gives-profound-philosophical-base-to-trumpian-populism/.
52. 'Remarks by Secretary Pompeo and Brazilian Foreign Minister Araujo at Press Availability,' 2 January 2019, Brasilia, https://br.usembassy.gov/remarks-by-secretary-pompeo-and-brazilian-foreign-minister-arauja-at-press-availability/.
53. Marcela Ayres, 'Appeal to Trump Could Clinch Brazil OECD Membership: Ministry,' Reuters, 6 December 2018, https://www.reuters.com/article/us-brazil-usa-oecd/appeal-to-trump-could-clinch-brazil-oecd-membership-ministry-idUSKBN1O42KX.
54. '"Brazil Loves the USA," says Guedes by Offering Unilateral Opening to the Trump Government,' Sputnik, 18 March 2019.
55. Danielle Brant and Arthur Cagliari, 'Trump Says Brazil Is Unfair to American Companies,' *Folha De S.Paulo*, 2 October 2018, https://www1.folha.uol.com.br/internacional/en/business/2018/10/trump-says-brazil-is-unfair-to-american-companies.shtml.
56. Marcelo Rochabrun, 'Brazil President Says He Wants Free Trade with "The Entire World",' Reuters, 13 January 2019, https://www.reuters.com/article/us-brazil-politics-trade/brazil-president-says-he-wants-free-trade-with-the-entire-world-idUSKCN1P60PK.
57. 'Remarks by President Trump and President Bolsonaro.'
58. 'Prosur: Seven Countries Launch Forum for Progress of South America in Chile,' *The Santiago Times*, 24 March 2019, https://santiagotimes.cl/2019/03/24/prosur-seven-countries-launch-forum-for-progress-of-south-america-in-chile/.
59. Anna Kaiser, '"Fascist, Violent, Dangerous": Protests Planned as Bolsonaro Arrives in Chile,' *The Guardian*, 22 March 2019, https://www.theguardian.com/world/2019/mar/22/fascist-violent-dangerous-protests-planned-as-bolsonaro-arrives-in-chile.
60. AFP, 'Brazilian President Bolsonaro visits CIA,' France24, 18 March 2019, https://www.france24.com/en/20190318-brazilian-president-bolsonaro-visits-cia.
61. Roberta Rampton, 'Trump Says He Intends to Designate Brazil as "Maybe a NATO Ally",' Reuters, 19 March 2019, https://www.reuters.com/article/us-usa-brazil-trump-nato/trump-says-he-intends-to-designate-brazil-as-maybe-a-nato-ally-idUSKCN1R02DK.
62. Ben Fox, 'Brazilian President Jair Bolsonaro Visited the CIA During His Trip to the US,' *Time*, 19 March 2019.
63. Ernesto Londono and Shasta Darlington, 'US and Brazil Chose Similar Leaders. It May Lead to Smoother Relations,' *The New York Times*, 20 November 2018, https://www.nytimes.com/2018/11/20/world/americas/bolsonaro-brazil-trump.html.
64. 'Remarks by President Trump to the Venezuelan American Community,' 18 February 2019, Florida International University Ocean Bank Convocation Center, Miami, https://www.whitehouse.gov/briefings-statements/remarks-president-trump-venezuelan-american-community/.
65. 'Remarks by National Security Advisor Ambassador John R. Bolton on the Administration's Policies in Latin America,' 2 November 2018, Miami Dade

College, Miami, https://www.whitehouse.gov/briefings-statements/remarks-national-security-advisor-ambassador-john-r-bolton-administrations-policies-latin-america/.
66. 'Remarks by President Trump and President Bolsonaro.'
67. Brian Ellsworth, 'Trump Says US Military Intervention in Venezuela "An Option"; Russia Objects,' Reuters, 3 February 2019, https://www.reuters.com/article/us-venezuela-politics/trump-says-u-s-military-intervention-in-venezuela-an-option-russia-objects-idUSKCN1PS0DK.
68. Annie Karni and Patricia Mazzei, 'Trump, in Miami, Attacks Maduro, and Some See Bid for Florida Votes,' *The New York Times*, 18 February 2019, https://www.nytimes.com/2019/02/18/world/americas/trump-maduro-miami-speech.html.
69. Lauren Gurley, 'Marco Rubio, Trump's Shadow Secretary of State,' *The New Republic*, 14 February 2019, https://newrepublic.com/article/153115/marco-rubio-trumps-shadow-secretary-state.
70. Alex Ward, 'Trump is Exploiting the Venezuela Crisis in Order to Win the 2020 Presidential Election,' Vox, 19 February 2019, https://www.vox.com/2019/2/19/18231438/trump-venezuela-socialism-sanders.
71. Tom Phillips and Dom Phillips, 'The New Venezuela? Brazil Populist Bolsonaro's Scare Tactic Gains Traction,' *The Guardian*, 11 October 2018, https://www.theguardian.com/world/2018/oct/11/brazil-venezuela-jair-bolsonaro-workers-party.
72. Matthew Bristow, 'Colombia Says it Doesn't Understand Bolton's "5,000 Troops" Note,' *Bloomberg*, 29 January 2019, https://www.bloomberg.com/news/articles/2019-01-29/colombia-says-it-doesn-t-understand-bolton-s-5-000-troops-note.
73. 'Remarks of Secretary of State Rex Tillerson on US Engagement in the Western Hemisphere,' 1 February 2018, University of Texas at Austin, https://br.usembassy.gov/remarks-secretary-state-rex-tillerson-u-s-engagement-western-hemisphere/.
74. Keith Johnson, 'Kerry Makes It Official: "Era of Monroe Doctrine Is Over",' *The Wall Street Journal*, 18 November 2013, https://blogs.wsj.com/washwire/2013/11/18/kerry-makes-it-official-era-of-monroe-doctrine-is-over/.
75. 'Remarks of Secretary of State Rex Tillerson.'
76. Londono and Darlington, 'US and Brazil Chose Similar Leaders.'
77. Nathalia Passarinho, 'Crisis in Venezuela: What are the Risks to Brazil of a Military Action in the Neighbouring Country?' BBC, 26 February 2019, https://www.bbc.com/portuguese/internacional-47365133.
78. Igor Gielow, 'Brazilian General Assigned to the US Southern Command,' *Folha De S.Paulo*, 14 February 2019, https://www1.folha.uol.com.br/internacional/en/world/2019/02/brazilian-general-assigned-to-the-us-southern-command.shtml.
79. Por Camarotti, '"No Adventures," Says Mourao Anticipating the Brazilian Position Against Intervention in Venezuela,' Globo, 25 February 2019, https://g1.globo.com/politica/blog/gerson-camarotti/post/2019/02/25/sem-aventuras-diz-mourao-antecipando-a-posicao-brasileira-contra-intervencao-na-venezuela.ghtml.
80. Anthony Boadle, 'Brazilian Offer of US Base in Doubt, Opposed by Military,' Reuters, 8 January 2019, https://www.reuters.com/article/us-brazil-usa-base/brazilian-offer-of-u-s-base-in-doubt-opposed-by-military-idUSKCN1P214H.
81. Natasha Madov, 'Bolsonaro Displeases Military Officers for Giving Juan Guaido a Chief of State Reception in Brasília,' *Folha De S.Paulo*, 1 March 2019, https://www1.folha.uol.com.br/internacional/en/world/2019/03/bolsonaro-displeases-military-officers-for-giving-juan-guaido-a-chief-of-state-reception-in-brasilia.shtml.

82. Christopher Beddor, 'Brazil's Bolsonaro Gives China Electric Shock,' Reuters, 5 November 2018, https://www.reuters.com/article/us-brazil-election-breakingviews/breakingviews-brazils-bolsonaro-gives-china-electric-shock-idUSKCN1NA07W.
83. AFP, 'Brazil Lawmakers' Trip to China Stirs Anger,' *Daily Mail*, 18 January 2019, https://www.dailymail.co.uk/wires/afp/article-6608275/Brazil-lawmakers-trip-China-stirs-anger.html.
84. John Rathbone, 'The Mask of Bolsonaro's Guru, Olavo de Carvalho, Slips,' *Financial Times*, 22 March 2019.
85. Euan Marshall, 'Brazil More Dependent on China than Ever,' The Brazilian Report, 14 November 2018, https://brazilian.report/money/2018/11/14/brazil-trade-china-commodities/.
86. Liu Jianxi, 'Bolsonaro Cannot Afford to Upset Ties with China,' China Global Television Network, 29 October 2018. https://news.cgtn.com/news/3d3d414d316b544d30457a6333566d54/share_p.html.
87. 'Brazil Will Not Enter the War between China and the United States, Says Paulo Guedes,' Barra News, 19 March 2019, http://barranews.com.br/brasil-nao-vai-entrar-na-guerra-entre-china-e-eua-garante-paulo-guedes/.
88. Wellton Maximo, 'Brazil to Diversify Sales to China,' Agencia Brasil, 18 January 2019, http://agenciabrasil.ebc.com.br/en/economia/noticia/2019-01/brazil-diversify-sales-china.
89. Kevin Gallagher and Roberto Porzecanski, *The Dragon in the Room: China and the Future of Latin American Industrialization* (Palo Alto: Stanford University Press, 2010).
90. Manuela Andreoni, 'China Made Brazil a Global Agricultural Powerhouse. But Who Benefits?' Dialogo Chino, 7 January 2019, https://dialogochino.net/19746-china-made-brazil-a-global-agricultural-powerhouse-but-who-benefits/.
91. 'Remarks by President Trump and President Bolsonaro.'
92. John Lyons and Paul Kiernan, 'How Brazil's China-Driven Commodities Boom Went Bust,' *The Wall Street Journal*, 27 August 2015, https://www.wsj.com/articles/how-brazils-china-driven-commodities-boom-went-bust-1440728049.
93. Tullo Vigevani and Gabriel Cepaluni, 'Lula's Foreign Policy and the Quest for Autonomy Through Diversification,' *Third World Quarterly*, Vol. 28, Issue 7 (2007): 1321, 1324.
94. Michael Reid, *The Troubled Rise of a Global Power* (New Haven: Yale University Press, 2015), 259.
95. '2019 Military Strength Ranking,' GlobalFirepower, accessed 2 June 2019, https://www.globalfirepower.com/countries-listing.asp.
96. Matias Spektor and Guilherme Fasolin, 'Brazil and the United States: Will President Bolsonaro Bandwagon?' E-International Relations, 15 November 2018, https://www.e-ir.info/2018/11/15/brazil-and-the-united-states-will-president-bolsonaro-bandwagon/.
97. Dan Williams, 'Brazil Opens Trade Mission in Jerusalem, Short of Full Embassy Move,' Reuters, 31 March 2019, https://www.reuters.com/article/us-israel-brazil/brazil-opens-israel-trade-mission-in-jerusalem-short-of-full-embassy-move-idUSKCN1RC097.
98. Gustavo Ribeiro, 'How to Undermine 40 years of Middle-East Diplomacy in Two Days,' *The Brazilian Report*, 2 April 2019, https://brazilian.report/newsletters/daily-briefing/2019/04/02/tbr-daily-briefing-april-2-2019-newsletter-about-brazil/.
99. Andrew Fishman and Rafael Martins, 'Brazil's Jair Bolsonaro Meets with Donald Trump to Consolidate their Far-Right Alliance,' The Intercept, 19 March 2019, https://theintercept.com/2019/03/18/bolsonaro-trump-meeting/.

100. AFP, 'Bolsonaro's Brazil Clouding EU–Mercosur Deal: Macron,' *France 24*, 29 November 2018, https://www.france24.com/en/20181129-bolsonaros-brazil-clouding-eu-mercosur-deal-macron.
101. Tullo Vigevani and Haroldo Ramanzini, 'The Changing Nature of Multilateralism and Brazilian Foreign Policy,' *The International Spectator*, Vol. 45, Issue 4 (2010): 63.
102. Shannon O'Neill, 'Latin America's Right Turn Could Draw its Economies Closer,' *Bloomberg*, 25 February 2019, https://www.bloomberg.com/opinion/articles/2019-02-25/latin-america-s-right-turn-could-bring-its-economies-closer.
103. Andres Malamud, 'A Leader Without Followers? The Growing Divergence Between the Regional and Global Performance of Brazilian Foreign Policy,' *Latin American Politics and Society*, Vol. 53, Issue 3 (Fall 2011): 1–24.
104. Laura Mahrenbach, *The Trade Policy of Emerging Powers: Strategic Choices of Brazil and India* (New York: Palgrave Macmillan, 2013).
105. Harold Trinkunas, 'Brazil's New President: Strongman at Home, Weak Man Abroad?' Brookings, 31 October 2018, https://www.brookings.edu/blog/order-from-chaos/2018/10/31/brazils-new-president-strongman-at-home-weak-man-abroad/.
106. Markus Fraundorfer, 'Brazil's Rise and Decline in Global Governance. Glory and Pain in the Tropics,' World Government Research Network, 11 April 2018, http://wgresearch.org/brazils-rise-and-decline-in-global-governance-glory-and-pain-in-the-tropics/.
107. Charles Call and Adriana Abdenur, 'A "Brazilian Way"? Brazil's Approach to Peacebuilding,' Brookings, February 2017, https://www.brookings.edu/research/a-brazilian-way-brazils-approach-to-peacebuilding/.

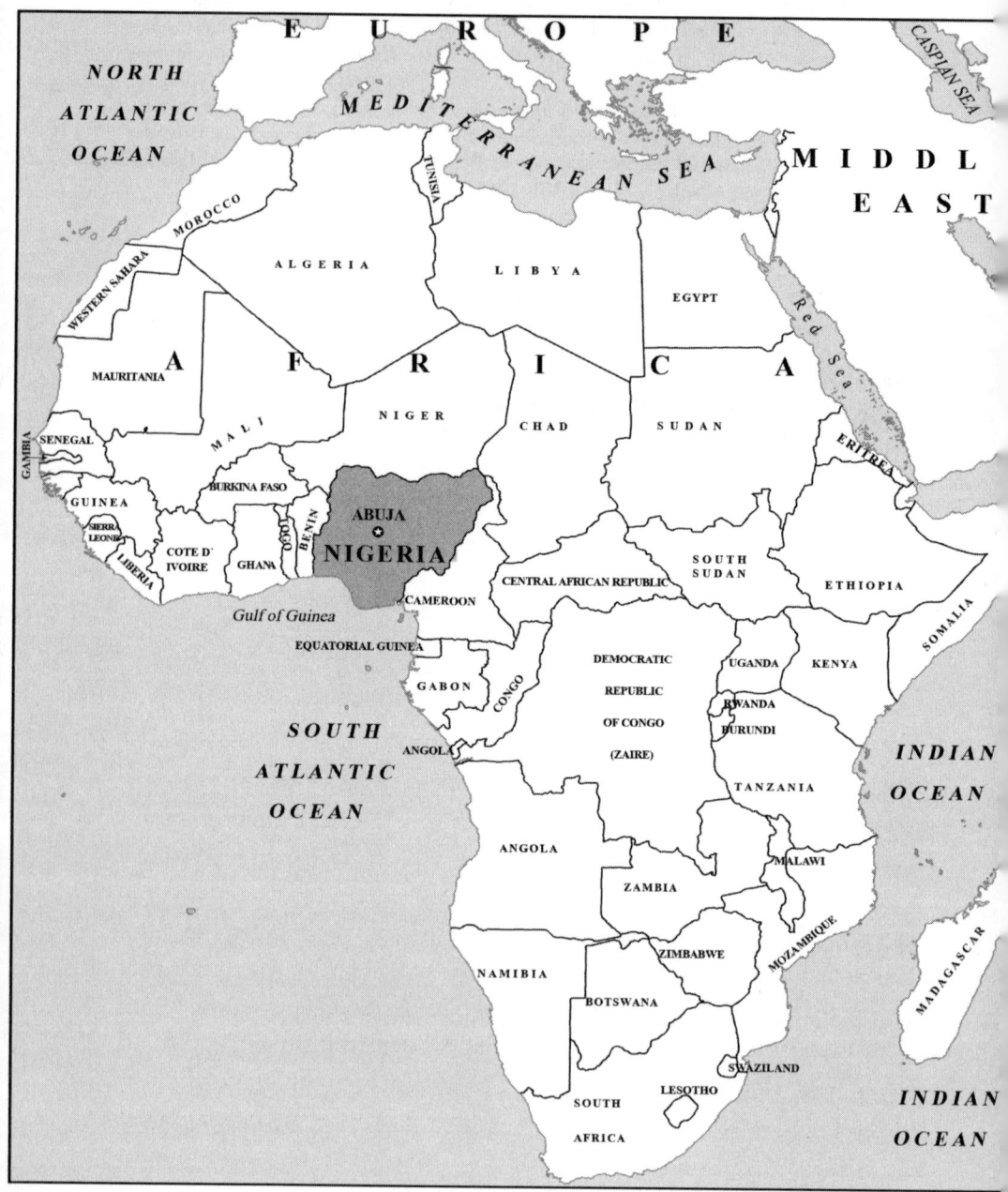

Map not to scale.

IV
Nigeria: Counter-Hegemony to Pax Africana

We are very grateful to the United States for agreeing to give us the aircraft we asked for—the spare parts. We are even more grateful for the physical presence of the United States military that are going to our institutions in Nigeria, and train them and go to the front, in the northeast, to see how they are performing, as an example of the training given to them. So the commitment of the United States to get rid of terrorism across the world, we have first-hand experience of that, and we are very grateful for it.

—President Muhammadu Buhari, 30 April 2018[1]

… we more and more are not wanting to be the policeman of the world. And we're spending tremendous amounts of money for decades on policing the world, and that shouldn't be our priority. We want to police ourselves, and we want to rebuild our country. And the President (of Nigeria) understands that. And they've come a long way. They're doing a great job. We're contributing to that job, but they have done a great job.

—President Donald Trump, 30 April 2018[2]

The Retrencher and 'Baba Go Slow'

As two septuagenarians walked gingerly to the rostrums on a spring morning in the Rose Garden of the White House, the differences in their personalities and expectations could not have been starker. Nigeria's veteran politician and former military strongman Muhammadu Buhari was the epitome of caution and propriety in public office and pursuing a decades-long foreign policy goal of trying to establish his country's regional leadership in Africa and enlisting the US for that cause. America's brash, populist president Trump was looking to exit from substantial US commitments to Africa and upending the liberal internationalist structure under which all his predecessors had sought to engage prominent African powers like Nigeria. If Buhari arrived in Washington for the summit meeting as 'a supplicant with important security challenges that he needs American help to confront',[3] he got some from Trump in terms of counter-terrorism materiel for sale, but was also reminded that the preachy and deeply regionally embedded US, which Nigeria had dealt with since the end of the Cold War, had retreated.

To Trump, the value of Nigeria was not what it used to be for past globalist American presidents—a vector for democracy in an authoritarian neighbourhood, a keeper of the balance of power in volatile West Africa, and a major supplier of oil to the US. Instead, Nigeria got redefined as a customer of American weapons and a large market of 190 million consumers that had to be prised open to American goods and services. Trump's transactional America cares for revenues and profits for US companies and jobs for US workers above broad liberal or geopolitical objectives. Its reductionist rendering of Nigeria, Africa's most populous country, is a double-edged sword. As Buhari realised while meeting Trump, appealing to the latter's populist mercantilist instincts and presenting Nigeria as eager to buy American civilian and military wares can overcome past hurdles and address some of Nigeria's pressing national security challenges. The liberal Obama administration's refusal to sell lethal attack aircraft to Nigeria owing to concerns in the White House and Congress about human rights abuses and massacres of civilians by the Nigerian military had drawn a furore in Abuja. Soon after entering office in 2015, Buhari bitterly blamed the US for having 'unwittingly and unintentionally… aided and abetted the Boko Haram terrorists' by denying Abuja the weapons it sorely wanted.[4] When the illiberal Trump overrode human rights lobbies and decided to deliver A-29 Super Tucano light fighter jets costing $345 million to Nigeria, he took credit for the change.

> We're getting them approved. Part of the problem is you weren't allowed to buy helicopters in our country and now you are; I worked

that out. We make the best military equipment in the world. And our friends can now buy that equipment.⁵

In early 2018, Trump tasked US State Department diplomats around the world with a new 'Buy American' mandate of 'drumming up arms sales for (US) defence contractors'. Investigative journalist Ronan Farrow noted, 'A spate of new deals under the Trump administration suggested a widening gulf between such sales and any diplomacy that might provide context and direction for them.'⁶ Throughout this book, we've seen how Trump was so eager to expand American arms sales to India and Turkey, he was willing to countenance their purchases of other weapons systems from NATO foes like Russia. In Chapter II, I explained how Trump refused valid human rights justifications to act tough on Saudi Arabia since it was a valuable customer for American military equipment sales. The same happened with Nigeria. The neo-mercantilist Trump not only forsook liberal human rights considerations but also took a dig at them.

> They (Nigeria) weren't allowed to buy the helicopters for various reasons, which frankly weren't good reasons. Now they get them, and they get them very quickly, and they are the best helicopters in the world.⁷

Apart from the business of arms sales, Trump's self-conception as a scourge of 'radical Islamic terrorism' and his contextualisation of Nigerians as victims of the anti-Christian and anti-Western Boko Haram jihadist group were also helpful in pushing through the Tucano sales to Abuja. When Nigerian Foreign Affairs Minister Geoffrey Onyeama was asked what kind of human rights concerns Trump raised during his meeting with Buhari, his response was telling.

> There were some letters written to the US government… some Christian religious groups felt they were being persecuted (in Nigeria). We have a secular government and that was not at all the case. This is often localised, easy to put a religious twist on conflicts born out of economic issues, land squabbles… so there is no religious agenda on the part of the government… the US Embassy in Nigeria has conveyed that to Washington.⁸

In other words, Trump's primary focus was on alleged religiously motivated attacks on Christian civilians by Muslim civilians in Nigeria that were being highlighted by Christian advocacy lobbies. The evangelical pressure groups in the US, who are part of Trump's voting base, fan such incidents that occur abroad. In fact, the violence which Trump assumed to be anti-Christian was occurring in a complex environment of land conflict between cattle herders and farmers in Nigeria's Middle Belt states. The bigger human rights problem stemming from impunity of the Nigerian military against Muslim and Christian civilians alike, which Obama emoted with, fell below the radar in Trump's worldview.

What is more ironic is that the Nigerian army cited Trump to justify its fatal shootings of dozens of rock-throwing protesters belonging to a Shiite sect in November 2018. A Twitter post by the army carried a video clip of Trump vowing to act tough on immigrant stone-pelters at the Mexico–US border. The American president menacingly vowed in it, 'We're not going to put up with that. They want to throw rocks at our military, our military fights back.' An army spokesman said, 'We released that video to say if President Trump can say that rocks are as good as a rifle, who is Amnesty International?'[9] Needless to mention, there was no condemnation from Trump of the shootings or the Nigerian state's usage of his analogy. From the angle of a habitually abusive Nigerian state apparatus, Trump is a blessing because any military engaged in warfare with jihadists, no matter how crude and brutal its tactics, can secure his thumbs up.

But the other side of the coin is that Trump's casual racism against people of colour, his general disinterest in Africa and dislike for liberal internationalist creeds of intervening in the continent for nation-building, democratisation and economic development mean that Nigeria cannot count on American backing to enhance its capacities to supply public goods to its surroundings. In January 2018, it was alleged that Trump vented spleen against Africans in front of legislators and cabinet officials, asking why he should accept 'all these people from shithole countries' as immigrants rather than from places like Norway. He is also said to have complained about admitting Haitians into the US as 'they all had AIDS', and passed derogatory remarks at Nigerians who 'would never go back to their huts' once they see the US.[10] Although the White House disowned these comments, Trump went public in July 2018 with his prejudice by remarking at NATO headquarters that Africa had 'things going on there that nobody could believe in this room. If you saw some of the things that I see through intelligence, what's going on in Africa, it is so sad and so vicious and violent.'[11] On another occasion, Trump tweeted that the 'South African Government is now seizing land from white farmers' and that he had instructed 'Secretary of State @SecPompeo to closely study the expropriations and the large scale killing of farmers'.[12] It was a factually fabricated claim but incendiary because white minorities still dominate farming and business and continue to profess white supremacist ideology in post-apartheid South Africa. As a far-right politician, Trump has a jaundiced and condescending view of black Africans, which informs his foreign policy of turning his back and stepping away from the continent. Annual budgets proposed by the Trump administration since 2017 have involved steep cuts in health, development, humanitarian, democratisation and peacekeeping contributions to Africa as ways to offset higher American defence spending.[13] Trump's withdrawal from the Paris Climate Change accord and repudiation of America's $3-billion contribution to the Green Climate Fund also adversely impacted Africa, where several foreign-funded environmental protection projects were jeopardised. On trade, although the volumes of two-way exchanges between the US and sub-Saharan Africa are low, Trump aggressively arm-twisted African countries to grant more market share for American exports[14] and clouded the future of the African Growth and Opportunity Act (AGOA), which allows duty-free access to the US for exports by several African countries, including Nigeria. The USTR has mooted a new 'free trade agreement that could serve as a model for developing countries',[15] that is, one based on strict reciprocity rather than magnanimity, dealing a further blow to African economies. The Trump administration's refrain that its vision for Africa 'is one of independence, self-reliance, and growth—not dependency, domination, and debt',[16] rhetorically sounds as a welcome departure from the liberal internationalist charitable model of the past, but Trump is also being punitive in his own way by harming African economic competitiveness through neo-mercantilist and bilateral one-on-one trade negotiations with vulnerable countries.

On security, notwithstanding Trump's verbal sympathies for countries like Nigeria that are battling jihadists, his policy inclination is to cut and run from Africa's troubled spots. In November 2018, after four American troops were killed by jihadists in Niger, the Pentagon announced it would pull out 10 per cent of its 7,200-plus troops from Africa, mostly based in Nigeria's neighbouring countries like Chad, Niger and Mali with a brief for countering Islamist terrorist movements and building capacity of local African militaries. The force reductions in West Africa occurred as part of a broader shift of the NSS under the Trump administration to 'focus on large global competitors, particularly China and Russia'[17] and replace American boots on the ground with drones. Trump opted to retrench from Africa despite an uptick in violent attacks by jihadists linked to Al Qaeda and ISIS across the Sahel region, the northern desert stretch abutting Nigeria. Former CIA analyst Michael Shurkin summed up the Trump mindset as 'scepticism towards things like security-forces training [and] scepticism about doing anything in Africa'.[18]

In Chapters I and II, I showed how Trump pulled back American forces from Afghanistan and Syria with an explicit expectation that the resulting security vacuums would be filled by local actors, even if they are illiberal or authoritarian, in Asia and the Middle East. As part of the same burden-shifting doctrine in Africa, he has placed the onus on regional governments to pick up the slack. Most intriguing is his willingness to concede strategic space to France, which has historical colonial stakes and neocolonial presence in West Africa and has for a long time been a thorn in the flesh to Nigeria's bid to unify the subregion behind it. With around 10 West African states grouped together as part of La Francophonie, that is, a French sphere of financial and military influence, Paris has for decades frustrated Nigeria (a so-called Anglophone nation due to its background as a former British colony) from achieving effective leadership in its neighbourhood. Under globalist American presidents, the US competed with France and deployed troops and cultivated allies parallel to French initiatives.

Trump wants to abandon that neocolonial competition game and cede West Africa to France. According to Alexandra Scheffer and Martin Quencez of the German Marshall Fund, '[Trump] expects French troops in West Africa to backfill US troop withdrawal [and] sees great utility in having a deputy sheriff in Africa, as French "leadership from the front" has saved the United States from having to assume another major military mission.'[19] In response to liberal criticism that America is exiting West Africa when terrorism is proliferating there, the Trump administration has claimed that it is not disappearing but transferring more responsibilities to the combined defence forces of the G5 Sahel group of countries—Burkina Faso, Mali, Niger, Chad and Mauritania— which are receiving $242 million in military aid from the US.[20] The G5 is a creation of France and an integral component of La Francophonie. It has drawn suspicion in Nigeria as yet another French tool to keep the subregion divided and on the boil. I will return later in this chapter to the permanent French presence and interference in West Africa and its negative connotations for Nigeria's leadership. Here, it suffices to note that the populist Trump has complicated what the former Nigerian Foreign Minister Ibrahim Gambari called his country's two core 'concentric circles'; first, its territorial integrity and relations with immediate neighbours, and second, its ties with members of the broader Economic Community of West African States (ECOWAS).[21] Presumably, if Nigeria had the will and the means to substitute for the US departing the region, Trump would have no problem letting that happen. But if Nigeria's bugbear France were to be the deputy sheriff and Nigeria prevaricated, Washington would yield to Paris.

The proverbial glass Trump is offering is thus half full but also half empty and it is up to Nigeria to intelligently comprehend this mixed blessing and recalibrate its strategy for growing into Africa's leading power. Whether it can grasp the historic shift that Trump is undertaking in American foreign policy in Africa and adjust its diplomacy depends on the frequently ailing Buhari, who has earned the moniker 'Baba Go Slow' for his sluggish and gradualist governance style since winning the landmark 2015 Nigerian presidential election, and breathing fresh life into his nation's faltering Fourth Republic which commenced in 1999 with great hopes of genuine democratisation and accountability of rulers. Buhari's squeaky clean image as a personally non-corrupt and stern taskmaster improved Nigeria's international reputation after it took a beating under military dictatorships and military-guided civilian authoritarian regimes. His relatively credible re-election in 2019 in spite of not succeeding in accomplishing his first-term promise of sweeping away all corruption with a broom, the symbol of his All Progressives Congress (APC) party, proved that Nigerians still approved of his personal integrity and moral compass amid a sea of venal and compromised political elites.[22]

In foreign policy, Buhari has to show alacrity and shrewdness for tiding over Trump's disruptive changes to the international system and crafting a revised blueprint for Nigeria's rise. Buhari has somewhat managed to overcome what the Ethiopian scholar Belachew Gebrewold critiqued as Nigeria's 'considerable gap between aspirations and ability to act as regional stabilizer, mainly due to a lack of legitimacy'.[23] But the double whammy of economic recession from 2016 due to the collapse of global oil prices and the continued threat of the Boko Haram Islamist insurgency in northeast Nigeria has tied down the Buhari administration in domestic crisis management at the cost of making a bigger regional and international impact. Internal weaknesses such as governance failure and ethnic fratricide have frequently frustrated Nigeria's ambitions to mould the West African subregion and take the lead on wider continental issues. Nigerian academic Gubak Daniel has questioned the 'credibility of the country… in terms of our weight to intervene successfully to resolve African conflicts when Nigeria is not able to resolve its own internal conflicts'.[24] As with many previous governments, the Buhari regime has not succeeded in convincing Nigerian citizens to shed their traditional reluctance and apathy towards activist and interventionist foreign policies across Africa, which are seen as expensive, elitist and distracting from addressing core domestic security and developmental needs of common folk. For example, in April 2019, when Buhari was in Jordan to attend a World Economic Forum regional meeting, his political rivals accused him of callously neglecting violent outbreaks in Nigeria's northern Zamfara state while jet-setting internationally.[25] Buhari retorted on Twitter that it was

> ridiculous and unfair to suggest that I am not concerned about the situation in Zamfara, or doing anything about it. Ensuring the protection of the people of Nigeria is one of my primary responsibilities and functions. No other issue dominates my attention as much.[26]

The lack of social consensus at home to endorse costly peacekeeping missions and building of collective security institutions in Africa goes back to the era of military dictatorships of the later twentieth century, when average Nigerians 'believed that the country had little to show for the generosity and sacrifices it had made in regional and continental diplomacy'.[27] In response to lasting public doubts about concrete economic returns from Nigeria's Afrocentric foreign policy of providing regional public goods and sustaining what the Kenyan political scientist Ali Mazrui termed 'Pax Nigeriana [of] keeping the peace in West Africa under Nigeria's auspices',[28] the Fourth Republic under President Olusegun Obasanjo began moving in a more pragmatic direction after 1999. Foreign policy was made to better serve and project domestic Nigerian interests. Nonetheless, Obasanjo was derided at home as a 'travelling president' who was too close for comfort to the US and embarked on regional peacekeeping and mediation initiatives at the behest of the Americans without much gain for Nigeria. Steve Itugbu, a presidential aide, recalled how Nigeria's peacekeeping missions in Liberia and Sierra Leone under Obasanjo cost more than $1 million a day and triggered 'domestic pressures' and 'intense opposition'.[29] The George W. Bush administration's assessment, 'Obasanjo may be disliked at home, but he is good for Africa',[30] confirmed that the gap between Nigeria's internationalism and internal struggles persisted under civilian rule.

Regular bouts of internal security crises and economic underperformance have at times hampered Nigerian leaders' balanced pursuit of narrower national interests and altruistic ventures in West Africa and beyond. The Nigerian public's perception of a zero-sum-game between foreign entanglements such as peacekeeping operations and funding of less privileged neighbouring nations of ECOWAS on one hand, and the welfare and security needs of Nigeria's own impoverished and volatile society on the other, have put brakes on Abuja from assuming additional foreign responsibilities and chasing a continental leadership role. John Campbell, the American ambassador to Nigeria from 2004 to 2007 and a prominent Western caricaturist of Nigeria, has written about the drag effect of domestic public opinion on Abuja's proactive role in Africa.

> I frequently heard complaints that Obasanjo's diplomatic activism, like that of (former presidents) Abacha and Babangida, has as its goal the enhancement of his own personal, international prestige, rather than the interests of Nigeria. Other, perhaps kinder, critics ascribed Obasanjo's emphasis on his international role as a compensation for his inability to deal with Nigeria's intractable domestic problems.[31]

The verdict by one group of Nigerian academics, that 'foreign policy from Abubakar Tafawa Balewa (the nation's first post-independence Prime Minister) to Obasanjo's second coming has sacrificed the true national interest of Nigeria on the altar of African-centredness',[32] is a sobering one, although such admonitions have not deterred Nigerian elites from trying to live up to the tag 'giant of Africa'. To his credit, Buhari engineered a decisive intervention to ensure a democratic transition in tiny Gambia in 2017 by rallying ECOWAS and deploying military force. His ultimatum to Gambia's dictator Yahya Jammeh to step down with the words, 'If he wanted to challenge the subregion, he was welcome,' was a show of Nigeria's institutional power and will to lead its neighbourhood.[33] As the ECOWAS Chairperson in 2018, Buhari reported having 'acted proactively to neutralize some potential conflicts through preventive diplomacy before they exploded', and being 'able to douse tension and restore confidence in some potentially disruptive political situations, particularly in Guinea Bissau, Togo and Mali'.[34] Despite Nigeria entering an economic recession in 2016, Buhari assured ECOWAS members it would continue to pay the lion's share of the regional institution's budget 'since we don't want to be big for nothing'.[35] Buhari has also urged ECOWAS to move forward the long-stalled negotiation process for adopting a West African single currency, pledging that 'as the largest economy in the region, a lot of responsibility rested on Nigeria for the establishment and sustainability of the monetary union'.[36] At the broader level of the African Union (AU), Buhari has assumed a high-profile moral leadership as the designated 'Champion on Anti-Corruption' and cited his personal rectitude and Nigeria's consolidation of democracy as signals for cleaning up the continent's governance culture.[37]

'New France' and New America

Resource constraints are not the primary obstacles to Nigeria expanding its leadership role in Africa. France was and is the main geopolitical adversary that Nigeria has had to contend with. From the 1967–70 Nigeria-Biafra War, when a southeastern region of Nigeria waged an armed insurgency for secession with French connivance, to contemporary Boko Haram terrorism in northeast Nigeria—which many Nigerians believe to be benefiting France[38]—Paris has been a pain in the neck for Abuja. During the Cold War, France's goal was to 'dismantle the Nigerian state, which was considered as a pole of attraction (and thus a potential threat) to the preservation of French influence in the neighbouring Francophone states'.[39] The French version of the Monroe Doctrine treated its former colonies of West Africa as its exclusive *chasse gardée* or private hunting ground where no other Western or African power like Nigeria should meddle. Since the US was preoccupied with destabilising Southern Africa where Soviet-backed or native socialist regimes arose, it tacitly endorsed La Francophonie as a bulwark against communism in West Africa. French academics depicted France as 'Washington's de facto *gendarme* (policeman) in francophone Africa', in what became a 'complementary Cold War regime' with no scramble for power between Washington and Paris.[40] There was no discernible American policy in the Cold War era to bolster Nigeria as an Anglophone counterbalance to La Francophonie, and Abuja's civilian and military regimes professed neutrality between Eastern and Western Blocs and assisted liberation struggles of Africa's people against extra-regional imperialism. Nigeria's 'frontline state' tag for confronting the apartheid regime and other Western-allied minority stooges in Southern Africa often pitted it diplomatically against the US, even though Nigeria became a top supplier of oil to the US and American oil companies built huge stakes in Nigeria. Abuja's complex mix of 'political non-alignment and economic alignment' with the West[41] meant that Washington was neither an ally nor a foe.

After the Cold War, Washington discovered a new zeal for trade and corporate access to Francophone countries, with Bill Clinton's administration officials reminding France that 'the African market is open to everyone'.[42] French and American oil companies waged political turf wars in Francophone areas to grab oil concessions and successive American post-Cold War administrations used the stick of selective support for democratisation to check despotic client states of Paris, which privileged French corporate interests over American ones in Africa. Nigeria's value as an asset for the US in confronting La Francophonie grew in this period, especially after civilian rule returned with Obasanjo in 1999.

The Bush administration, which designated African oil as a 'strategic national interest' of the US, trumpeted Obasanjo as the democratic hope of Africa with the motive of strengthening American companies like ExxonMobil and ChevronTexaco in Nigeria, which, at that time, accounted for 10 per cent of total US oil imports. Weaponry, training and funds for regional peacekeeping operations and mediation efforts flowed from Washington to Abuja in the Bush–Obasanjo partnership years. It was no coincidence then that 'the principal target of US military assistance programs is Nigeria, the country that is America's most important source of oil imports from sub-Saharan Africa'.[43] Bush also helped Obasanjo write off $18 billion of debt from the Paris Club of creditors in 2006, freeing Nigeria from a crushing burden.

According to the US Ambassador to Nigeria during the Bush presidency, Obasanjo was prized by America as a 'proxy in various regional crises where Washington will not or cannot be involved… the Bush administration appeared beholden to President Obasanjo because, at US urging, he agreed to the deployment of Nigerian peacekeepers,'[44] and coordinated with the US in Liberia, Sierra Leone, Guinea Bissau, Togo, Côte d'Ivoire and Sudan.[45] Obasanjo's keenness to be a core participant in Bush's global war on terror (GWOT) in Africa was also striking, with the US Congressional Research Service commending the Nigerian leader for 'a critical role in building consensus on the continent for cooperation in US counter-terrorism efforts'.[46] Nigeria was not bandwagoning to the US during the GWOT, but the fact that America was increasing its military and economic footprint in Africa as France was retrenching under budgetary duress redressed Abuja's strategic dilemmas to an extent.

America's abusive invasions and occupations of Afghanistan and Iraq under the GWOT pretext aroused intense resentment in Nigeria's Muslim North. Domestic opposition in Nigeria to the US military's demand for its new Africa Command (AFRICOM) to be based in the oil-rich Gulf of Guinea, off Nigeria's southern coast, deterred Obasanjo's successor, President Umaru Yar'adua (2007–10). As a nationalistic and Afrocentric powerhouse, Nigeria never legitimated AFRICOM, but its security and economic cooperation with the US remained a cornerstone of Nigerian foreign policy under President Goodluck Jonathan (2010–15).

Jonathan shed past inhibitions about directly hosting US soldiers on Nigerian soil and requested Obama to send American combat troops to battle Boko Haram. He reasoned that Boko Haram was linked to ISIS and maintained, 'Look, they (Americans) are our friends. If Nigeria has a problem, then I expect the US to come and assist us.'[47] Jonathan kept Nigeria in America's Trans-Sahara Counterterrorism Partnership and also joined Obama's Security Governance Initiative, tying Nigerian national security and regional leadership closely to the American mast.[48]

Yet, as I mentioned earlier in this chapter, the liberal internationalist Obama and the US Congress were perturbed by human rights violations by the Nigerian military and withheld weapons sales, pushing Abuja to approach Moscow for hardware.[49] The Obama administration also grew dismayed by Jonathan's domestic authoritarianism and attempts to rig the 2015 Nigerian presidential election. After Jonathan lost to Buhari, the former president lashed out at Obama and his Secretary of State John Kerry for 'prodding the electorate to vote for the opposition to form a new government', behaving in a condescending manner and applying 'foreign pressure' to ensure his downfall.[50] While Jonathan was exaggerating and proffering an alibi for his failure, his episode exposed the tension between America's geopolitical goals in Africa and its selective advocacy for democratisation. The Clinton administration had also suspended military assistance and sales to Nigeria in the 1990s as punishment for abusive military dictatorships under Generals Ibrahim Babangida and Sani Abacha. Unlike France, which has been steadily dedicated to its puppet dictators in Africa, US presidents until Trump walked on two legs of realpolitik and liberal values, fluctuating with changing political winds in the continent.

Still, France's overall decline in monopolising West Africa was evident during the presidency of Nikolas Sarkozy (2007–12). Unable to financially sustain La Francophonie, he moved France 'not only to burden-share by "Europeanizing" its security policy in Africa, but to "Americanize" it as well, by welcoming AFRICOM's increased role on the continent and cutting back its own'.[51] The disastrous NATO attack on Libya in 2011 to dethrone Colonel Muammar Qaddafi was Sarkozy's baby but it was parented by Obama who was 'leading from behind' with the liberal internationalist humanitarian mantra of saving Libyan civilians from massacres by an evil dictator. France and Britain's 'massive dependence on US military assets' in the Libyan intervention[52] proved that the baton had passed from Paris to Washington. Years later, Obama regretted the Libyan misadventure as he realised it had unleashed chaos and terrorism across northern and western Africa, and he blamed France and Britain for not doing the 'follow-up' after overthrowing Qaddafi.[53] Enfeebled by the global financial crisis, France let Libya fall apart into mayhem and then had to contend with the blowback in La Francophonie.

The Islamist rebellion in Mali from 2012 was a direct consequence of the NATO campaign in Libya, which empowered jihadist forces across the region. Fearing complete unravelling of its Francophone vassal state system, Paris scampered and deployed more than 5,000 French troops in Mali in a desperate attempt to pre-empt Nigeria, which had put together an African peacekeeping force (AFISMA) under the ECOWAS banner to roll back the Malian Islamists. This conflict replayed the France-Nigeria rivalry in broad daylight, with Paris erecting a parallel military infrastructure outside the ambit of ECOWAS and the AU so that France could have skin in the game. But as the Malian war dragged on and the French military got bogged down without eradicating the jihadist menace, Paris yet again turned to lean on the US to finance its interventions in West Africa. French President Francois Hollande (2012–17) talked up a 'renewed alliance' with Obama and highlighted that 'nowhere is our new partnership on more vivid display than in Africa'.[54]

Like Hollande and Sarkozy, President Emmanuel Macron (2017–present) spread the rhetoric of a 'new' French policy in Africa that 'would not tell Africans what to do, no longer invest solely in government-to-government operations', and desist from abetting 'organised corruption operations' by Francophone African despots.[55] But like his predecessors, his heart remained imperialistic. He could not afford costly military presence and aid programmes in West Africa but still wanted to rule the roost there. In 2017, he launched the G5 Sahel force to pool militaries of Francophone countries and combat multiple Islamist terrorist outfits across the region. It was a typical French neocolonial initiative to compete with a prior 'crowded security field' with overlapping memberships, wherein Nigeria had already established a Multinational Joint Task Force (MNJTF) comprising Cameroon, Niger and Chad to counter

Boko Haram in the nearby Lake Chad Basin, and a larger UN mission for stabilising Mali (MINUSMA) was also present on the ground.[56] Beninese activist scholar Gilles Yabi observed correctly, '[By] setting up a new autonomous force with mostly external financing, [France would] distract from the absolute necessity of consolidating the states in all their dimensions.'[57]

France is today less of a hegemonic colossus in Africa and more a spoiler and nuisance that wants to impede Nigeria's leadership. Beset by class unrest and mass protests at home, France lacks the economic might to project power in Nigeria's surroundings, hence Macron's repeated attempts to find multilateral funding for G5 Sahel through the auspices of the EU and the US. He reached out to Germany for 'reinforced cooperation' in Mali[58] and lobbied the Trump administration in vain to get G5 equipped with a UN mandate so that its private army in West Africa can be sustained through American largesse.[59]

The fact that Trump reversed his earlier reluctance to shell out money to G5 and succour France a little in late 2018 is a saving grace for Macron. Throughout this book, I have demonstrated the 'two-track presidency' complex, which has engendered incoherent and mercurial foreign policies under Trump. The same phenomenon affected the debate on US policy towards Africa. Liberal internationalist Defence Secretary Jim Mattis insisted on continuing Obama's strategy of building military capacity of African partner countries and increasing funding for multilateral peacekeeping operations on the continent. But once Mattis quit, National Security Adviser John Bolton went about implementing Trump's populist platform of slashing spending on Africa by rebuking 'unproductive, unsuccessful and unaccountable' UN peacekeeping missions and singling out G5 Sahel as an alternative model and a 'great example of the enormous potential for African joint security cooperation'.[60] From a budget-trimming perspective, the US opted for a cheaper deal by financing the smaller French-guided G5 Sahel than the larger MINUSMA and other AU-blessed large-group multilateral security and humanitarian missions.

But given Trump's habitual uncertainty and miserliness, Paris cannot count on retaining its 'deputy sheriff' status in Africa by riding on American coat-tails. Spiels of a 'new France' that wants to relinquish its old domineering role in Africa are routine, but there is a new America under Trump that makes Washington a wild card for Paris. Moreover, French companies are losing ground to another great power that is fast gaining influence in La Francophonie through loans, grants and mega construction projects—China.[61] Macron's wooing of non-Francophone African countries for trade and investment with the promise of 'respectful partnership' as a foil to China's method of racking up 'excessive, unsustainable debts'[62] indicates that Beijing has already beaten Paris in its historic *chasse gardée*. From a Nigerian perspective, if the US since the Bush administration had offset or smothered French hegemony in West Africa, China's advent could have a similar knock-on effect and atrophy La Francophonie.

Enter the Dragon

Unlike the fierce controversy around China's debt trap, predatory lending and resource-grabbing in smaller African countries like Zambia, Angola, Sudan, Kenya, Cameroon and Djibouti,[63] Nigeria has been mostly positive and self-assured about China's entry into a variety of sectors in its own economy, ranging from energy and transportation to agriculture. Buhari has defended his government's racking up of Chinese loans worth $6 billion by listing the infrastructural improvements Nigeria has accrued from them. Refuting notions that Nigeria was also falling into a debt trap, he asserted,

> These vital infrastructure projects synchronize perfectly with our Economic Recovery and Growth Plan. Some of the debts incurred are self-liquidating. Our country is able to repay loans as and when due in keeping with our policy of fiscal prudence and sound housekeeping.[64]

Indeed, China has not been able to monopolise Nigeria's most precious and abundant resource—oil—for itself. Chinese oil companies like Sinopec and China National Offshore Oil Corporation (CNOOC) have bagged lucrative permits for energy exploration and extraction in Nigeria, but their stakes are smaller than those of their French, British and American competitors. Chinese investors in Nigeria's massive offshore energy sector have preferred to buy 'equity shares in oil blocs, not sole control', and relied on Western oil firms to jointly extract and produce to minimise risk and share costs.⁶⁵ Because Nigeria has a diversified set of foreign investors, significant economic clout (its GDP is the largest in Africa and 14 times bigger than the most notorious Chinese debt-trapped African country, Zambia), and majority stakes in the oil industry for the state-owned Nigerian National Petroleum Corporation (NNPC), it has levers to forge an even-handed relationship with China compared to weaker African countries. As we saw in earlier chapters, rising powers do not bandwagon with existing great powers but can opportunistically partner with them to improve their own hard power or geopolitical positions.

In Abuja, there is less fear of Chinese enslavement and more of a pragmatic openness to Beijing. Jonathan Coker, the Nigerian Ambassador to China under Obasanjo, summed up the economic benefits aptly: 'China has helped rebuild rail lines, roads and bridges that Nigeria could not do itself. The cost came out so much cheaper for us than going to the traditional friends such as France, the UK, Canada.'⁶⁶ Chinese companies' bribery of Nigerian state officials and working practices that are degrading Nigeria's environmental conditions are surely harmful, but they pale before the terrible predatory record of Western companies abetting gigantic corruption and abuse in Nigeria through illegal bunkering of oil and money laundering via a network of overseas offshore havens. The Buhari administration's demand in 2019 that Western oil majors pay $20 billion in back taxes for outstanding royalties revealed how the local venality for which Nigeria is infamous has unaccountable international collaborators.⁶⁷ In recent years, Nigerian private capitalists have acquired major onshore and offshore oil and gas blocs from Western companies, which divested some stakes in Nigeria. By 2017, native Nigerian entrepreneurs controlled 18.9 per cent of oil production and 18.2 per cent of gas output, rendering Nigeria 'unprecedented' among 'cash-poor, resource-rich economies' where foreign companies predominate and crowd out local competitors.⁶⁸ Although the process by which Nigerian businesspersons took greater ownership over oil and gas was corrupt, their strategic impact is to lessen Nigeria's economic dependence on the West. Chinese firms as well as local entrepreneurs are counterbalancing biggies like Exxon, Norway's

Statoil, France's Total and the Anglo-Dutch Shell, and boosting Abuja's autonomy to handle these countries.

Geopolitically, if China's rapid strides in La Francophonie have alarmed France,[69] then Beijing's rise to pole position throughout Africa has spooked globalists and liberal internationalists in the US. In December 2018, the Trump administration announced a new Africa policy with a heavy Cold War ring to it. Bolton declared that America's chief priority was to counter 'serious threats' posed by 'great power competitors, namely China and Russia', whose 'predatory practices' were stunting Africa and shifting the balance of power in vital subregions like the Horn of Africa against the US. He bemoaned that 'billions upon billions of US taxpayer dollars' in the form of aid to Africa had gone down the drain and not stopped China and Russia 'from taking advantage of African states to increase their own power and influence'. Henceforward, he vowed, America's Africa policy would be based on 'a new foreign assistance strategy [to] address the pressing challenge of great power competition, [and on] new economic initiatives [to] support American jobs and expand market access for US exports'.[70]

Beijing quickly issued a riposte that Washington, 'apart from talking about the United States' own needs, wasn't thinking about Africa, but about China and Russia'.[71] Obasanjo reacted, saying, 'The history of superpower rivalry in Africa is messy, destructive and occasionally bloody. The continent should do everything to avoid this happening again.' In his reckoning, 'The United States is unlikely to beat China at its African game of delivering low-cost infrastructure in exchange for resources and contracts,' and should instead focus on promoting democracy, good governance and accountability on the continent.[72] But such analyses presuppose that Trump will start all-out military and economic counterbalancing of China in Africa the way liberal internationalist American presidents did against the Soviet Union during the Cold War by ravaging Africa via proxy wars.

Trump is not at all committed to any such costly and penetrative campaign in Africa to push back Chinese influence. In late 2018, he and the Congress did create a new $60 billion US International Development Finance Corporation (USIDFC) to 'better incentivize private sector investment in emerging economies and provide strong alternatives to state-directed initiatives that come with hidden strings attached',[73] that is, to challenge China. As per Riva Levinson, an American lobbyist in Africa, USIDFC is meant to 'direct private capital flows towards developing countries [and] to counter China's debt diplomacy'. It would 'provide additive US government resources' through loans, loan guarantees and risk insurance to private American investors 'to enter markets where commercial investment terms would otherwise make such investments uncompetitive'. She adds, though, 'China spends $40 billion per year through its DFIs [development finance institutions], and USIDFC can hardly be viewed as a counterweight to these large flows of capital, which often come with an ease of execution and few strings attached outside of debt financing.'[74] As a populist, Trump wants more American private sector investment inside the US and less of it in the developing world. He has also been a fervent critic of 'corporate welfare', where US taxpayers' dollars are spent to subsidise American companies investing abroad. USIDFC is a half-hearted ploy to satisfy globalists in Trump's 'two-track presidency' who are itching to roll back China in Africa, but it cannot match Chinese statist development aid in the continent. In the words of conservative American scholar Derek Scissors, with USIDFC, 'We've finessed the public relations problem. But we aren't really competing with the Chinese.'[75] As American trade and aid flows to Africa declined, the prognosis by the Economist Intelligence Unit in 2018 was quite realistic.

> In the absence of appetite in the US to strengthen relations, we think it unlikely that these trends will reverse anytime soon… the president's (Trump's) disinterest in the continent makes it unlikely that US–Africa economic relations will be revived anytime soon. Hence, as the US's economic footprint in Africa fades, so too will influence, and the previous efforts of US administrations to encourage compliance with the so-called Washington Consensus—of liberalism, deregulation and privatisation—look set to grow increasingly silent.[76]

American diplomats posted in Lagos have argued that 'Nigeria could benefit so much from the recently created USIDFC if it is able to attract American investors, as the corporation seeks to support businesses investing in emerging markets like Nigeria.'[77] But with American oil companies divesting from Nigeria and concentrating more on domestic American shale production[78] while Chinese oil majors are doubling down and committing larger sums there,[79] the fact is that China needs

Nigeria for its energy security far more than the energy self-sufficient US. Buhari has appealed to American businesses to invest in Nigeria's non-petro-carbon sectors like agriculture, manufacturing, mining and infrastructure by dangling carrots like the country's huge labour pool and domestic consumption base, 'speed and efficiency of land titling and business registration [and] radical departure from a past characterized by large-scale state-sponsored corruption'.[80] But by 2018, the US was significantly behind the UK in importing capital into Nigeria and the bulk of inward flows were in the form of portfolio investments into Nigeria's banking and finance stocks rather than as foreign direct investment (FDI) in agriculture or manufacturing.[81] Trump's America is neither an antidote to China's expansion in Nigeria and Africa as a whole nor a panacea for Nigeria's GDP growth or infrastructural and developmental uplift.

Back to the Centrepiece

Ultimately, it is not by latching on to the US or China that Nigeria can find prosperity for its teeming masses or enhance its leadership and power in the world. The inexorable pathway for Nigeria to realise its true potential lies in integrating itself deeper into its own West African subregion and the wider AU framework. Nigeria's foreign policy compass had, for decades, been informed by the pan-Africanist scholar Adebayo Adedeji's maxim of 'Africa as centrepiece' and Gambari's concentric circles formulation, wherein the first three circles for maximum prioritisation were all within Africa and only the fourth and outermost circle touched countries and institutions beyond Africa.[82] But as we noted earlier, Afrocentrism in Nigeria's external relations has had to contend with a narrower domestic conception of national interests since the Fourth Republic in 1999.

To Nigerian realists like the economist and politician Obadiah Mailafia, Afrocentrism has been a mistaken top-down foreign policy by Nigerian elites to waste precious national resources throughout the continent without gaining influence or reciprocal benefits. Recounting that 'Nigeria spent over US$10 billion and lost 5,000 of its soldiers to restore peace in Sierra Leone and Liberia, [and] over US$60 billion in financial assistance to various African and Caribbean countries,'

Mailafia contends, 'It is foolish to spread largesse everywhere and not demand something in return.' His slogan, 'We have to put Nigeria first,'[83] is populist and echoes Trump's own cutback of US foreign assistance globally in the name of America First. Although such Nigerian populism has been rejected at the ballot, its tenets have affected continent-wide foreign policy freedom of many presidents.

For instance, in 2013, Jonathan withdrew most of Nigeria's 1,200-strong peacekeepers from multinational missions in Mali and Sudan citing Boko Haram's insurgency at home and the need to 'tackle the country's own insurgency'.[84] In 2016, oil price-induced economic recession forced Buhari to adopt a protectionist policy of banning imports and sowed misgivings about joining the historic African Continental Free Trade Area (AfCFTA) treaty, which aims to create a $3-trillion single market for all 55 nations of the AU and its 1.2 billion people. Nigerian labour and manufacturers' associations petitioned the government to protect local producers and Buhari went against his Afrocentric instinct to strike a defiant nationalistic tone. He tweeted in March 2018, 'We will not agree to anything that will undermine local manufacturers and entrepreneurs, or that may lead to Nigeria becoming a dumping ground for finished goods.'[85] By June 2019, 52 of the 55 AU members signed AfCFTA, but the irony was that Nigeria, the largest economy of the continent, whose GDP is 17 per cent of Africa, had not yet done so and sought more time for domestic consultations. It finally signed in July 2019.

One of the fears about AfCFTA expressed by Nigerian businesses and unions was its potential to be abused by China to dump its products in Nigeria's large domestic market by disguising them as exports from other African countries. Nigeria's Vice-President Yemi Osinbajo sought 'safeguards to ensure that third parties to the AfCFTA shall be prevented from the abuse of origin rules to trans-ship and dump',[86] an obvious reference to China. Nigeria also watched Trump's trade war against China with trepidation because of the fear that China, being denied free access to the US market, will redirect its exports to populous nations like Nigeria. Nigerian economist Akpan Ekpo cautioned, 'We import almost everything from China. So, if Chinese had to pay more to trade with the US, they will pass it on to us. So, Chinese goods in Nigeria may also go up and may result into what we partly call imported inflation.'[87]

Aliko Dangote, the prominent Nigerian cement tycoon and Africa's richest man, used Trump's America First rationale to propose protectionist policies to shield Nigeria from China's predatory exports.

> If you look at what president Trump is doing right now—not that I agree with what he is doing because they are in a totally different economy to what we are—but if you look at where we are today, where there's no protection, then you are not going to have any industries.[88]

Another Nigerian billionaire, Abdul Samad Rabiu, argued that Nigeria must first remove obstacles to freer trade within the ECOWAS subregion before heading to continental market integration. He listed problems of Nigerian cement exports being blocked by Benin and Burkina Faso even though these countries are part of ECOWAS' Trade Liberalisation Scheme.

> We cannot sell either cement or clinker to Burkina Faso, yet they import clinker from China, Turkey, from other parts of the world. If this treaty, which is smaller than what we are talking about (AfCFTA), if this is not working, how are we sure that a bigger arrangement is going to work?[89]

In Chapter III, we saw how Brazil had been protectionist towards its neighbours in Latin America and hence lost the chance to unify and lead the region by granting access to its vast consumer market. Nigeria is in a similar quandary. Like Brazil, it is the largest economy in its continent with the biggest population, but by not ratifying AfCFTA, it will forfeit its prestige as the leader of Africa. The protectionist line in Nigeria—that its manufacturing sector is still in its infancy and must be shielded from a surge of imports from more industrialised African nations like South Africa or the giant third party, China—is a dangerous self-fulfilling prophecy that keeps Nigerian industrialisation forever in infancy and leaves the rest of Africa perennially disappointed at not being able to access Nigeria's 190 million consumers. Nigerian trade lawyer Olu Fasan has shown how successive Nigerian governments since the early 1980s resorted to trade protectionism as temporary moves to boost domestic manufacturing, but the resultant pattern of import restrictions benefited 'powerful interest groups' linked to Nigerian politicians instead of paving the way for industrialisation.[90]

As of 2018, services made up 53.97 per cent of Nigeria's GDP, agriculture contributed 22.86 per cent and industries accounted for only 23.18 per cent. Oil had declined to just 8.55 per cent of GDP. Yet, nearly 90 per cent of all Nigerian exports were still of petroleum products (oil and gas),[91] skewing Nigeria's trade to remain oriented to countries outside Africa. The top destinations of Nigerian exports in 2018 were India (15.9 per cent), the Netherlands (10.7 per cent), Spain (10.1 per cent), France (7.9 per cent) and South Africa (6.4 per cent), while fellow ECOWAS members Côte d'Ivoire (2.2 per cent) and Togo (1.8 per cent) came way down as marginal partners. Only 9.2 per cent of Nigeria's total exports went into Africa, in contrast to 27.7 per cent to Asia and 43.9 per cent to Europe.[92] From these statistics, it is clear that as long as Nigeria's exports are predicated on oil, Africa would not matter much to it in concrete economic weightage.

Nigerian and international economists have warned that the only way Nigeria can avoid economic stagnation is 'if it does something dramatic about increasing non-oil exports' in sectors like agriculture, airline and shipping services.[93] When the non-oil sectors flourish in Nigeria's product mix, the rest of Africa with its youthful demography and rising GDP growth rates would beckon as Nigeria's most attractive trading destination. AfCFTA should be a no-brainer for Abuja if it plans strategically for the future and diversifies its trade profile. Already, Nollywood movies and Afrobeats music are wildly popular cultural exports circulating in Africa, earning foreign exchange for Nigeria and counteracting negative stereotypes about Nigerians.[94] Nigerian scholar Prince Oguguo noted, 'About 40% of Nigerians aged 18-64 are entrepreneurs, almost three times the global average,' most of whom work in the retail sector. The closer Nigeria integrates with Africa via AfCFTA, the more it will provide self-reliant Nigerians 'options for sourcing and consequently drive their costs down'.[95] Agriculture employs 70 per cent of Nigeria's labour force and surveys have found that 'exporters of agricultural commodities view Nigeria as competitive within the continent and believe that AfCFTA will give them access to do business in African countries that are otherwise not easily accessible'.[96]

In June 2018, Nigeria achieved the dubious distinction of overtaking India as the country with the largest absolute number of people living in extreme poverty. About 87 million Nigerians were living in penury compared to 73 million Indians, figures that are all the more disquieting for Nigeria if measured in terms of percentages of total populations. India has 1.2 billion people while Nigeria has 190 million. One of the authors of this depressing finding observed, 'Nigeria is a rich country but because much of its wealth comes from the production and sale of oil, it doesn't directly go to the pockets of ordinary people.'[97] So, seen from the interests of Nigeria's poor, diversification towards non-oil sectors accompanied by full economic integration with Africa is the only salvation. The 190-million Nigerians need to merge with the remaining 1 billion Africans into a single self-reliant mega entity to shake off the vestiges of centuries of colonial exploitation by extra-regional powers.

To understand how revitalised endogenous integration with the rest of Africa holds the key to Nigeria's future, one must examine the environmental movement to save and replenish Lake Chad, a shrinking water body on which 40 million people of Chad, Cameroon, Niger and Nigeria depend for agriculture, fishing, livestock and trade. To restore Lake Chad from years of drought- and climate change-induced drying, the Nigerian government convened an international conference in Abuja in February 2018, where it was agreed that inter-basin water transfer from the Congo river of Central Africa via a 2,400-kilometre-long canal and water transfer system up to Lake Chad was 'no longer an option but a necessity'. The prominence of Nigerian water engineers, hydrologists and climate scientists in leading this initiative and Buhari's forceful statement, 'The time to act is now. The time to bail out the region is now. The time to show our humanity is now,' revealed the seriousness with which Abuja was approaching a life-and-death question for its Boko Haram-infested northeast from a continental perspective. Yet, coordinating with multiple African countries through which the canal would transit is a mammoth task. Pan-Africanist scholar Horace Campbell argues, 'Saving Lake Chad cannot be undertaken within the context of the organisation of the present international economic and social system, [and] progressive forces in all parts of the Pan-African world will have to work hard for climate change and system change.'[98] In other words, if 'Nigeria first' and other such narrow nationalistic and statist doctrines were to prevail, Lake

Chad would disappear and exacerbate socioeconomic pressures fuelling Boko Haram-like phenomena.

The urgency of an Africa First policy to uplift and strengthen Nigeria as an emerging power is equally felt in the realm of security. While Nigeria has led subregional peacekeeping missions in West Africa under the ECOWAS and Lake Chad Basin Commission banners, it has also been a champion of the African Peace and Security Architecture (APSA) concept since its inception in 2002. APSA is an AU-level idea to develop indigenous capacities for managing and resolving conflicts on the continent through early warning, preventive diplomacy, peacemaking and peace-building. Within APSA, African countries pledged to form a 25,000-strong African Standby Force (ASF) with subregional components that would deploy rapidly around the continent's trouble zones and keep the peace under the AU's direction without dependence on non-African powers. But APSA has not weaned itself from reliance on extra-regional funding, with donors from the EU contributing most of its operational budget. Nigerian Foreign Affairs Minister Onyeama has urged fellow AU members to pay more for an African Security Fund so that the AU has the material capability to train ASF troops and intervene in crisis spots without waiting for the conditional benevolence of non-African donors.

> As we are seeing now, the UN is not willing to intervene in a number of the conflicts on the continent. And, we now see that other non-African countries that are supporting us are now reducing the funding. So we have to find our own solution… the African Union has to devise innovative strategies in raising the funding to address some of the security challenges on the continent especially ones that are terrorism-related.[99]

Onyeama's point is that the old liberal international interventionist itch of the West has vanished and banking on it to build the AU's capacities is no longer an option. Starting with Trump, the right-wing populist wave sweeping the West has threatened whatever meagre multilateral funding mechanisms were in place for peace and stability in Africa. European populists favour funding individual African countries to stem the flow of migrants up north through the Mediterranean Sea, but not systemic transformative projects like the APSA or even UN-mandated multinational peacekeeping missions on the continent. Nigerian scholar Adekeye Adebajo observed,

> The fact that the budget of the African Union, over 90 per cent of the budget in the security field is funded by external actors, largely the EU, that means that interventions often occur in areas where the EU has an interest as opposed to where the needs may be.[100]

The AU's decision in 2016 to levy a 0.2 per cent duty on imports from non-member states to finance its peace and security functions is a step in the right direction, but financial independence for Africans to manage African crises is work in progress.

As Africa's largest economies, the onus is on Nigeria and South Africa to collaborate closely and make the ASF dream an operational reality. Frustrated by coordination delays and funding shortages in getting ASF off the ground, and citing the ignominy of France muscling its way into Mali and the Central African Republic in 2013 in the absence of a potent AU army, South Africa proposed launching a stopgap African Capacity for Immediate Response to Crises (ACIRC) force, comprising a smaller coalition of the willing with a dozen or more African countries. Nigeria pulled the plug on ACIRC, presumably as it hurt its ego to admit the South African military on its doorstep and also as 'Nigeria was unwilling to cede operational command and control to anyone but its own army' in the fight against Boko Haram in the Lake Chad area.[101] Ghanaian analyst Linda Darkwa noted, 'Against the historical background of geopolitical rivalries between Nigeria and South Africa… it will be challenging to have a deployment of the Southern African Development Community's (SADC) Standby Force in West Africa, and vice versa.' Her prediction is that since Africa's subregional security structures like those under ECOWAS in West Africa, SADC in Southern Africa and the Intergovernmental Authority on Development (IGAD) in the Horn and East Africa are entrenched and vested in their respective domains, a pan-African ASF will never materialise.[102]

But it is precisely this parcelling of African problems into subregions that prevents Nigeria's rise as a big continental power. Nigerian elites must rethink a fundamental question: Are they maximising their country's potential as a provider of public goods by being primus inter pares in West Africa alone or as one among few leaders of all Africa? Nigerian politicians often boast that one out of every five black people in the world is a Nigerian and express pride in their country's illustrious participation in the anti-colonial liberation struggles across different African subregions. But their praxis has often been restricted to countering the hegemony of France in West Africa and upholding Pax Nigeriana in the ECOWAS sphere. Arguably, the narrow mandate of Pax Nigeriana itself is unaccomplished. Despite Buhari's exhortations to expedite a single currency for ECOWAS, Côte d'Ivoire, one of its prominent members, has sworn allegiance to the France-guaranteed CFA franc currency and proposed 'a new political union in West Africa' exclusively of the Francophone subgroup.[103] I explained earlier how Nigeria's subregional unification and stabilisation designs had been hamstrung by France and abandoned by Trump's isolationist America. The only viable strategy for Nigeria to break out of its so-called 'illusory hegemony' in West Africa[104] is to eschew exclusive nationalistic insecurities and pool its capabilities into a larger pan-African stream that can project combined power of the continent's leading lights.

Writing at the turn of the millennium, Adebajo had argued that Nigeria could replace France as the *gendarme* of Africa if it built 'strategic alliances' with key states like Côte d'Ivoire, South Africa and even France. While the proposition of France becoming an ally of Nigeria is illogical due to the fundamental conflict of interest between Paris and Abuja, Adebajo's recommendation that Nigeria must focus on bilateral coordination with its neighbour Côte d'Ivoire to 'bridge the Anglophone/Francophone dichotomy' and pair up with South Africa to 'together provide a beacon of democracy and an engine of economic growth for Africa',[105] makes eminent sense. I would add Ethiopia and Kenya to this roster because they have clout in the Horn, East and Central Africa, which often suffer bouts of political instability and violence. Emerging powers must identify pivotal actors in their broader region and form plurilateral coalitions to advance not only their individual self-interest but secure the collective interests of smaller nations lying between and around them.

In Chapter II, I proposed that Turkey prioritise construction of a broad coalition of Persian and Arab forces to terminate the cycles of war and terrorism in the Middle East. Likewise, in Chapter I, India was posited as the ideal candidate for 'minilateral' intra-Asian stabilising coalitions. In Africa, it is incumbent upon Nigeria to convene a select group of countries with their own subregional leadership ambitions and weld them into a pan-African collective security mechanism. In 2007, the AU established a 'Panel of the Wise' consisting of five highly respected African public personalities like retired heads of state from the continent's five subregions, who could draw upon their diplomatic experience and persuasion to prevent conflicts, mediate and promote peace across Africa. Martin Ewi, who served in the AU headquarters in Ethiopia, described the panel as 'the most versatile tool for responding to complex emergencies [and] an embodiment of African solutions to African problems' or what Mazrui termed 'Pax Africana'.[106] While the panel's elders have made a substantial contribution to tackling the continent's ills through their moral fibre and elite connections, there is no substitute to powerful states of Africa welding into a small group and fielding joint missions against terrorists and illegitimate despots.

A timely and coercive show of military force and economic sanctions required in certain crises can only materialise if Nigeria acts in concert with other notables under the aegis of APSA. Alone and bereft of strategic planning with fellow African leading powers, Nigeria is akin to what Nigerian scholar Ebere Adigbuo calls a 'crippled giant', whose positions on the continent are 'challenged and in many cases overturned by other African states'. His argument that 'leadership is a relational phenomenon' rather than mere possession of superior material capabilities, and that Nigeria's aspiration is hamstrung by 'how she is perceived by other African states'[107] places the onus on Nigeria to rebrand itself as a different sort of power that can gain acceptability in every corner of the continent by being a smarter team player. This would involve conceding market access and political prominence to smaller countries and appearing in tandem with Africa's other biggies.

In April 2019, I interacted with Major General Chris Eze, Nigeria's High Commissioner to India and a close political associate of President Buhari. I asked him what Buhari's vision was to counter the remnants of French neocolonialism and realise Nigeria's potential as the natural leader of Africa. Eze replied that Buhari wants Nigeria to always be 'our brothers' keeper' in West Africa but faced the roadblock of La Francophonie and the 'unfortunate truth that the apron strings of some neighbours are still tied to France'. According to Eze, Buhari wanted to overcome internal resistance to Nigeria's prominence within Africa through a 'combination of soft power and hard power'. Abuja, he said, was consciously 'trying to subsume Nigeria's initiatives under the umbrella of AU processes' and following the maxim of 'talk softly and carry a big stick' so as not to rake up the insecurities of smaller African countries. He predicted that if Buhari's domestic reforms succeeded, then Nigeria would be 'unrecognisable in five years [and possess] a sufficient internal economy to sustain a powerful foreign policy throughout Africa'. As to the fourth concentric circle outside Africa, Eze emphatically said Buhari wanted to 'look East to India and China instead of the US and the EU for economic and military partnerships', including by welcoming the Indian Navy to undertake force projection up to the Gulf of Guinea to keep it safe.

Taken as a whole, this independent and South-South cooperation line has merits, particularly in light of Trump's populist cost-cutting meanness and his far-right racist and religious biases against Africa and Africans. Nigerian scholar Olaiyiwola Abegunrin noted in 2018, '[With] the irrational behaviour, and erratic and isolationist approach of President Trump and his destruction of US foreign policy not only to African States, but also to friends and allies of the United States, Nigeria-US relations has reached its lowest ebb.'[108] Trump's indifference at best and contempt at worst for Nigeria is also buttressed by the big shift of the US becoming a net exporter of oil after the shale revolution. Nigerian petroleum exports to America fell from 36.4 million barrels in 2010 to just 5.6 million barrels by early 2019, and Europe also balked from higher priced Nigerian oil as it was 'flooded by a sea of cheap US oil'.[109] The sea change in the political economy of US-Nigeria relations from what used to be a buyer-seller symbiosis to fierce competition for market share in third countries is bound to exacerbate the Trump effect. Exxon and Chevron still profit from Nigeria, but as we noted earlier, they are divesting and heading homewards. Petro-carbons will not be the locus of US-Nigeria ties in the future.

The liberal West, as it once existed in the pre-populist era, is so fractured that searching for convergence between Nigeria as a democracy and the US, which props up democratic Nigeria as a role model for the rest of Africa, is a wild goose chase. In spite of routine invocations by career diplomats from the 'steady state' in the US that they are cheering Nigeria to play 'a larger role' in peacekeeping and advancing democracy in Africa and reassurances that the US has 'an unwavering commitment to Africa',[110] statistics do not lie. Total US bilateral foreign assistance to Nigeria, covering a panoply of sectors and projects, has progressively declined from $469 million in Obama's final year in office to $351 million by 2019.[111] In July 2015, just after Trump formally entered the presidential election contest, he tweeted, 'Obama is in Africa pledging 1 billion dollars to help them. How about that money to help America. Trump for POTUS.'[112] After he won the presidential election in November 2016, the Trump transition team was also said to have echoed this populist attitude by reviewing the fundamentals of American policy and asking, 'With so much corruption in Africa, how much of our funding is stolen? Why should we spend these funds on Africa when we are suffering here in the US?'[113]

As I elaborated in the Introduction of this book, after entering the White House, Trump doubled down on the America First ideology and consistently adhered to it. At a group luncheon for African presidents including Buhari in September 2017 in New York, Trump clearly spelt out what he wanted from Africa. 'We hope to extend our economic partnerships with countries who are committed to self-reliance and to fostering opportunities for job creation in both Africa and the United States.'[114] In the far-right populist imagination, America's liberal internationalist establishment had been feeding Africans generously and getting nothing in return. Trump the hard taskmaster wants to correct what he sees as historical errors of his liberal predecessors.

The Western populist narrative is, of course, phony because American and European companies have been extracting oil and other strategic minerals in Africa for decades and reaping exorbitant profits. Development aid from the US and European donors has been a sop and cover for systematic plunder of Africa's natural wealth. In 2014, London-based NGO Health Poverty Action estimated,

> While western countries send about $30bn in development aid to Africa every year, more than six times that amount leaves the continent, mainly to the same countries providing that aid. The perverse reality [is that] wealthy governments celebrate their generosity whilst simultaneously assisting their companies to drain Africa's resources.[115]

From the beginning of his presidential tenure, Buhari flagged the gargantuan problem of 'stolen assets' of billions of dollars stashed abroad by corrupt Nigerian elites and their foreign corporate accomplices. He had moderate success with Switzerland and the UK in repatriating some illegally laundered Nigerian money. In May 2018, Buhari announced a collaboration with the US government for 'ensuring the return to Nigeria of over $500m looted funds stashed away in banks around the world'.[116] But Trump's decision to withdraw the US as an implementing country from the Extractive Industries Transparency Initiative (EITI), a multilateral effort to fight corruption in oil, gas and mineral extraction, was a fundamental blow to Nigeria and several other oil-rich African countries. American legislators attributed Trump's exit from EITI to 'the result of "Big Oil and Gas" money and influence' and lamented the 'painful abdication of American leadership on transparency and good governance'.[117]

Counting on Trump for enabling Nigeria's rise in any issue area is a fool's errand. The type of special equation between Bush and Obasanjo, which seemed to augur extremely privileged relations and ramp up Nigeria's international stature, is nowhere on the horizon today in the context of a transformed post-liberal America. Nigerians should not be mourning the loss of attention from Washington or taking offence at Trump's blatant racism and bigotry. At least he has cleared the facade of ambiguity and complexity behind which the liberal international system was ravaging Africa. I concur with John Stremlau, a scholar at a South African think tank.

> For African countries long accustomed to receiving help from the US, sometimes to the point of dependency, there is now another big incentive to achieve greater self-reliance, individually and collectively, as well as new and more balanced partnerships with non-African actors. This may eventually turn out to be at least one 'silver lining' to the damaging Trump era.[118]

When the isolationist US president is withdrawing and himself plumping for 'self-reliance' of Africa, it is high time for Nigeria to drop any remnants of dependence on the US, pick up the gauntlet and lead a collective endogenous drive for Pax Africana.

Endnotes

1. 'Remarks by President Trump and President Buhari of the Federal Republic of Nigeria Before Bilateral Meeting,' 30 April 2018, Oval Office, White House, https://www.whitehouse.gov/briefings-statements/remarks-president-trump-president-buhari-federal-republic-nigeria-bilateral-meeting/.
2. 'Remarks by President Trump and President Buhari of the Federal Republic of Nigeria in Joint Press Conference,' 30 April 2018, Rose Garden, White House, https://www.whitehouse.gov/briefings-statements/remarks-president-trump-president-buhari-federal-republic-nigeria-joint-press-conference/.
3. Julie Davis, 'What Vulgar Remarks? Trump and Buhari, Nigeria's Leader, Avoid Clash,' *The New York Times*, 30 April 2018, https://www.nytimes.com/2018/04/30/us/politics/trump-muhammadu-buhari-visit-nigeria.html.
4. Adam Nossiter, 'Boko Haram Helped by US Policies, Nigerian President Says,' *The New York Times*, 23 July 2015, https://www.nytimes.com/2015/07/24/world/africa/muhammadu-buhari-says-us-should-arm-nigeria-against-boko-haram.html.
5. Isiaka Wakili, 'Trump to Buhari—We'll Release Fighter Jets to Nigeria Soon,' *Daily Trust*, 1 May 2018, https://www.dailytrust.com.ng/well-release-fighter-jets-to-nigeria-soon-says-trump.html.
6. Ronan Farrow, *War on Peace: The End of Diplomacy and the Decline of American Influence* (New York: W.W. Norton, 2018), 157.
7. Isiaka Wakili, 'Trump to Buhari',' *Daily Trust*.
8. 'Press Briefing by Geoffrey Onyeama, Minister for Foreign Affairs of the Federal Republic of Nigeria,' 21 September 2018, UN Headquarters, New York, video, http://webtv.un.org/watch/press-briefing-by-h.e.-mr.-geoffrey-onyeama-minister-for-foreign-affairs-of-the-federal-republic-of-nigeria-press-conference-21-september-2018/5838322225001/.
9. Dionne Searcey and Emmanuel Akinwotu, 'Nigerian Army Uses Trump's Words to Justify Fatal Shooting of Rock-Throwing Protesters,' *The New York Times*, 2 November 2018, https://www.nytimes.com/2018/11/02/world/africa/nigeria-trump-rocks.html.
10. Julie Davis et al., 'Trump Alarms Lawmakers with Disparaging Words for Haiti and Africa,' *The New York Times*, 11 January 2018, https://www.nytimes.com/2018/01/11/us/politics/trump-shithole-countries.html.
11. 'Remarks by President Trump at Press Conference After NATO Summit,' 12 July 2018, NATO Headquarters, Brussels, Belgium, https://www.whitehouse.gov/briefings-statements/remarks-president-trump-press-conference-nato-summit-brussels-belgium/.
12. Kimon De Greef and Palko Karasz, 'Trump Cites False Claims of Widespread Attacks on White Farmers in South Africa,' *The New York Times*, 23 August 2018, https://www.nytimes.com/2018/08/23/world/africa/trump-south-africa-white-farmers.html.
13. Ty McCormick, 'Trump's America First Budget Puts Africa Last,' *Foreign Policy*, 22 March 2017, https://foreignpolicy.com/2017/03/22/trumps-america-first-budget-puts-africa-last/; Gulistan Elidemir, 'Trump's Budget Cuts Aid to Africa to Boost Spending on Military,' *Morning Star*, 14 March 2019, https://morningstaronline.co.uk/article/w/trumps-budget-cuts-aid-to-africa-to-boost-spending-on-military.
14. Garth Frazer, 'America's Petty Policy on Used Clothes for Africa,' The Conversation, 18 April 2018, https://theconversation.com/americas-petty-policy-on-used-clothes-for-africa-95132.

15. 'Trump Administration Looks Toward the Future US-African Trade and Investment Relationship,' 29 June 2018, Office of the USTR, Washington, https://ustr.gov/about-us/policy-offices/press-office/press-releases/2018/june/trump-administration-looks-toward-0.
16. 'Remarks by National Security Advisor Ambassador John R. Bolton on the Trump Administration's New Africa Strategy,' December 13, 2018, Heritage Foundation, Washington DC, https://www.whitehouse.gov/briefings-statements/remarks-national-security-advisor-ambassador-john-r-bolton-trump-administrations-new-africa-strategy/.
17. Gordon Lubold, 'Pentagon to Scale Back Number of Forces in Africa,' *The Wall Street Journal*, 15 November 2018, https://www.wsj.com/articles/pentagon-to-scale-back-number-of-forces-in-africa-1542323356.
18. Michael Phillips and Joe Parkinson, 'In West Africa, Violent Extremism Spreads as US Trims Military Footprint,' *The Wall Street Journal*, 24 February 2019, https://www.wsj.com/articles/in-west-africa-violent-extremism-spreads-as-u-s-trims-military-footprint-11551013201.
19. Alexandra Scheffer and Martin Quencez, 'US "Burden-Shifting" Strategy in Africa Validates France's Ambition for Greater European Strategic Autonomy,' German Marshall Fund, 23 January 2019, http://www.gmfus.org/blog/2019/01/23/us-burden-shifting-strategy-africa-validates-frances-ambition-greater-european.
20. Eric Schmitt, 'Where Terrorism is Rising in Africa and the US is Leaving,' *The New York Times*, 1 March 2019, https://www.nytimes.com/2019/03/01/world/africa/africa-terror-attacks.html.
21. Ibrahim Gambari, *Theory and Reality in Foreign Policy Making: Nigeria After the Second Republic* (Amherst: Prometheus Books, 1992).
22. Matt Mossman, 'Nigeria's Anti-Corruption Vote,' *Foreign Policy*, 28 February 2019, https://foreignpolicy.com/2019/02/28/nigerias-anti-corruption-vote/.
23. Belachew Gebrewold, 'Legitimate Regional Powers? A Failed Test for Ethiopia, Nigeria and South Africa,' *African Security*, Vol. 7, Issue 1 (March 2014): 18.
24. Gubak H. Daniel, 'Impact of State Weakness on Nigerian Foreign Policy Reputation: A Critical Analysis,' *International Journal of Scientific and Research Publications*, Vol. 5, Issue 12 (December 2015): 640.
25. Reno Omokri, 'Zamfara Voted for Next Level, New Zealand and Jordan Did Not,' *This Day*, 7 April 2019, https://www.thisdaylive.com/index.php/2019/04/07/zamfara-voted-for-next-level-new-zealand-and-jordan-did-not/.
26. Wale Odunsi, 'Zamfara Killings: Buhari Reacts to Outrage Against Him,' *Daily Post*, 7 April 2019, https://dailypost.ng/2019/04/07/zamfara-killings-buhari-reacts-outrage/.
27. Abiodun Alao, 'Nigeria and the Global Powers: Continuity and Change in Policy and Perceptions,' South African Foreign Policy and African Drivers Programme, SAIIA, Occasional Paper Number 96 (October 2011): 7.
28. Ali Mazrui, 'The Path to Nigeria's Greatness: Between Exceptionalism and Typicality,' *The Guardian*, 1 November 2004.
29. Steve Itugbu, *Foreign Policy and Leadership in Nigeria: Obasanjo and the Challenge of African Diplomacy* (London: I.B. Tauris, 2017), 28.
30. John Campbell, *Nigeria: Dancing on the Brink* (Lanham: Rowman & Littlefield, 2011), 128.
31. Campbell, *Nigeria*, 154.
32. Kia Bariledum et al., 'Foreign Policy Strategy of the Federal Republic of Nigeria 1960–2012: The Missing Link,' *Journal of International Relations and Foreign Policy*, Vol. 4, Issue 1 (June 2016): 36.

33. NAN, 'Buhari Played Game-Changing Role in Gambian Politics—Barrow,' *Punch*, 16 January 2018, https://punchng.com/buhari-played-game-changing-role-in-gambian-politics-barrow/.
34. Fikayo Olowolagba, 'What Buhari Said at ECOWAS Summit,' *Daily Post*, 22 December 2018, http://dailypost.ng/2018/12/22/buhari-said-ecowas-summit-full-speech/.
35. Olalekan Adetayo, 'Nigeria Will Not Stop Funding ECOWAS, Says Buhari,' *Punch*, 28 September 2018, https://punchng.com/nigeria-will-always-look-for-money-to-give-ecowas-says-buhari/.
36. Ifeanyi Onuba, 'Intensify Efforts on a Single Currency, Buhari Tells ECOWAS Countries,' *Punch*, 15 September 2018, https://punchng.com/intensify-efforts-on-single-currency-buhari-tells-ecowas-countries/.
37. Muhammadu Buhari, 'African Anti-Corruption Day is a Call to Action,' *The Guardian*, 14 July 2018, https://www.theguardian.com/commentisfree/2018/jul/14/african-anti-corruption-day-call-to-action-muhammadu-buhari.
38. John Nwachukwu, 'France Speaks on Foreigners' "Involvement" in Boko Haram, Herdsmen Killings,' *Daily Post*, 15 July 2018, https://dailypost.ng/2018/07/15/france-speaks-foreigners-involvement-boko-haram-herdsmen-killings/.
39. Michael Anda, *International Relations in Contemporary Africa* (Lanham: University Press of America, 2000), 201.
40. Peter Schraeder, 'Cold War to Cold Peace: Explaining US–French Competition in Francophone Africa,' *Political Science Quarterly*, Vol. 115, Issue 3 (Autumn 2000): 399.
41. Douglas Anglin, 'Nigeria: Political Non-alignment and Economic Alignment,' *The Journal of Modern African Studies*, Vol. 2, Issue 2 (July 1964): 247–63.
42. Anglin, 'Nigeria: Political Non-alignment,' 404.
43. Daniel Volman, 'The Bush Administration and African Oil: The Security Implications of US Energy Policy,' *Review of African Political Economy*, Vol. 30, Issue 98 (December 2003): 577.
44. Campbell, *Nigeria*, 144.
45. Vanguard, 'Obasanjo Briefs Bush on Peacekeeping Efforts in Togo, Sudan,' *Sudan Tribune*, 7 May 2005, http://www.sudantribune.com/spip.php?article9436.
46. Lauren Ploch, 'Nigeria: Current Issues,' Congressional Research Service (December 2007): 21.
47. Neanda Salvaterra and Drew Hinshaw, 'Nigerian President Goodluck Jonathan Wants US Troops to Fight Boko Haram,' *The Wall Street Journal*, 13 February 2015, https://www.wsj.com/articles/nigerian-president-wants-u-s-troops-to-fight-boko-haram-1423850893.
48. 'US Efforts to Assist the Nigerian Government in Its Fight Against Boko Haram,' 14 October 2014, White House, https://obamawhitehouse.archives.gov/the-press-office/2014/10/14/fact-sheet-us-efforts-assist-nigerian-government-its-fight-against-boko-.
49. Ronald Mutum, 'Trump's Rhetoric Disturbing—Foreign Ministry,' *Daily Trust*, 13 January 2017, https://www.dailytrust.com.ng/trumps-rhetoric-disturbing-foreign-ministry.html.
50. Samuel Ogundipe, 'How Obama Plotted My Defeat in 2015—Goodluck Jonathan,' *Premium Times*, 20 November 2018, https://www.premiumtimesng.com/news/headlines/296675-how-obama-plotted-my-defeat-in-2015-goodluck-jonathan.html.

51. David Brown, 'AFRICOM at 5 Years: The Maturation of a New US Combatant Command,' *The Letort Papers*, Strategic Study Institute, US Army War College (August 2013): 76.
52. Fabrizio Coticchia, 'The "Enemy" at the Gates? Assessing the European Military Contribution to the Libyan War,' *Perspectives on Federalism*, Vol. 3, Issue 3 (2011): 49.
53. Jeffrey Goldberg, 'The Obama Doctrine,' *The Atlantic*, April 2016, https://www.theatlantic.com/magazine/archive/2016/04/the-obama-doctrine/471525/.
54. Francois Hollande and Barack Obama, 'France and the US Enjoyed a Renewed Alliance,' *The Washington Post*, 10 February 2014, https://www.washingtonpost.com/opinions/obama-and-hollande-france-and-the-us-enjoy-a-renewed-alliance/2014/02/09/039ffd34-91af-11e3-b46a-5a3d0d2130da_story.html.
55. Alex Smith, 'France's Macron Outlines New Approach to African Policy,' BBC News, 28 November 2017, https://www.bbc.com/news/world-africa-42151353.
56. 'Finding the Right Role for the G5 Sahel Joint Force,' International Crisis Group, Report Number 258, 12 December 2017.
57. John Irish and Emma Farge, 'Heading to Sahel, France's Macron Scrambles for Exit Strategy,' Reuters, 30 June 2017, https://www.reuters.com/article/us-france-sahel-idUSKBN19L0FM.
58. Marine Pennetier, 'Macron Vows to Step Up French Fight Against Islamists in Africa,' Reuters, 19 May 2017, https://www.reuters.com/article/us-france-mali/macron-vows-to-step-up-french-fight-against-islamists-in-africa-idUSKCN18F0DV.
59. Michelle Nichols, 'US Wants Sahel Force Strategy Before Giving Money: Officials,' Reuters, 28 October 2017, https://www.reuters.com/article/us-africa-security-usa/u-s-wants-sahel-force-strategy-before-giving-money-officials-idUSKBN1CX06Z.
60. Matthieu Fernandez, 'Bolton's Risky Bet in the Sahel,' Atlantic Council Blog, 5 February 2019, https://www.atlanticcouncil.org/blogs/africasource/bolton-s-risky-bet-in-the-sahel.
61. Pauline Bax and Olivier Monnier, 'China Battles France for Business in Former African Colonies,' *Bloomberg*, 18 July 2018, https://www.bloomberg.com/news/articles/2018-07-17/china-battles-france-for-business-in-its-former-african-colonies.
62. Chanel Monteine, 'Macron's Africa Visit Reveals Determination to Weaken China's Grip on the Continent,' CNBC, 16 March 2019, https://www.cnbc.com/2019/03/16/macrons-africa-visit-reveals-determination-to-weaken-chinas-grip-on-the-continent.html.
63. Jonathan Rosen, '"China Must be Stopped": Zambia Debates the Threat of "Debt-Trap" Diplomacy,' *World Politics Review*, 18 December 2018, https://www.worldpoliticsreview.com/insights/27027/china-must-be-stopped-zambia-debates-the-threat-of-debt-trap-diplomacy.
64. Chijioke Jannah, 'What Nigeria Did with $5b Chinese Loan Under My Govt—Buhari', *Daily Post*, 5 September 2018, https://dailypost.ng/2018/09/05/nigeria-5b-chinese-loan-govt-buhari/.
65. Gold Kafilah Lola and Evelyn Devadason, 'The Engagement of China in Nigeria's Oil Sector: Is the Transformation Positive?' *Contemporary Chinese Political Economy and Strategic Relations: An International Journal*, Vol. 4, Issue 3 (December 2018): 1035.
66. Emily Feng, 'Chinese Investment Extends its Influence in Nigeria,' *Financial Times*, 21 November 2018.

67. Ron Bousso, 'Nigeria Hits Oil Majors with Billions in Back Taxes,' Reuters, 21 February 2019, https://www.reuters.com/article/us-nigeria-oil-debt-exclusive/exclusive-nigeria-hits-oil-majors-with-billions-in-back-taxes-idUSKCN1QA1EK.
68. Matt Mossman, 'How Nigeria's Oil Industry Went Local,' *Foreign Affairs*, 29 November 2017, https://www.foreignaffairs.com/articles/nigeria/2017-11-29/how-nigerias-oil-industry-went-local.
69. John Irish, 'Macron Warns of Chinese Risk to African Sovereignty,' Reuters, 12 March 2019, https://www.reuters.com/article/us-djibouti-france/macron-warns-of-chinese-risk-to-african-sovereignty-idUSKBN1QS2QP.
70. 'Remarks by National Security Advisor.'
71. Steve Holland and Lesley Wroughton, 'US to Counter China, Russia Influence in Africa: Bolton,' Reuters, 13 December 2018, https://uk.reuters.com/article/uk-usa-trump-africa/u-s-to-counter-china-russia-influence-in-africa-bolton-idUKKBN1OC1XZ.
72. Olusegun Obasanjo and Greg Mills, 'The US Should Focus on Soft Power and China Cooperation in Africa—Not Rivalry,' Quartz, 19 December 2018, https://qz.com/africa/1501023/president-obasanjo-says-trumps-africa-strategy-cant-rival-china/.
73. 'Statement from the Press Secretary,' 3 October 2018, https://www.whitehouse.gov/briefings-statements/statement-press-secretary-35/.
74. Mercy Kuo, 'The US International Development Finance Corporation and China,' *The Diplomat*, 25 October 2018, https://thediplomat.com/2018/10/the-us-international-development-finance-corporation-and-china/.
75. Glenn Thrush, 'Trump Embraces Foreign Aid to Counter China's Global Influence,' *The New York Times*, 14 October 2018, https://www.nytimes.com/2018/10/14/world/asia/donald-trump-foreign-aid-bill.html.
76. 'The US Retreat from Africa,' *The Economist* Intelligence Unit, 15 March 2018, http://country.eiu.com/article.aspx?articleid=1046522488&Country=Kenya&topic=Politics.
77. Femi Adekoya, 'Nigeria: Sustainability, Policy Predictability Key Concerns for Foreign Investors,' *The Guardian*, 2 November 2018, https://guardian.ng/business-services/sustainability-policy-predictability-key-concerns-for-foreign-investors/.
78. Ron Bousso and Julia Payne, 'Exxon Weighs Sale of Nigerian Oil and Gas Fields for up to $3 Billion,' Reuters, 2 April 2019, https://in.reuters.com/article/us-exxon-mobil-nigeria-exclusive/exclusive-exxon-weighs-sale-of-nigerian-oil-and-gas-fields-for-up-to-3-billion-idINKCN1RE0ZB.
79. Zheng Xin, 'CNOOC to Increase Investment in Nigeria,' *China Daily*, 4 September 2018, http://www.chinadaily.com.cn/a/201809/04/WS5b8ddb22a310add14f389672.html.
80. 'Buhari Addresses US–Africa Business Forum,' Sahara Reporters, 21 September 2016, http://saharareporters.com/2016/09/21/buhari-addresses-us-africa-business-forum.
81. 'Nigerian Capital Importation (Q1 2018),' National Bureau of Statistics, Nigeria, May 2018.
82. Ibrahim Gambari, 'Concepts and Conceptualization in Nigeria's Foreign Policy-Making Since Independence,' *Nigerian Journal of Policy and Strategy*, Vol. 1, Issue 1 (1987): 75.
83. Obadiah Mailafia, 'Putting Nigeria First,' *Business Day*, 10 February 2014, https://businessday.ng/columnist/article/putting-nigeria-first-2/.

84. Tim Cocks et al., 'Nigeria to Pull Many Peacekeepers from Mali, Darfur,' Reuters, 19 July 2013, https://www.reuters.com/article/us-nigeria-un-mali/nigeria-to-pull-many-peacekeepers-from-mali-darfur-idUSBRE96I0PA20130719.
85. Clement Uwiringiyimana, 'Nigeria Keen to Ensure Africa Trade Bloc Good for Itself: President,' Reuters, 21 March 2018, https://www.reuters.com/article/us-africa-trade/nigeria-keen-to-ensure-africa-trade-bloc-good-for-itself-president-idUSKBN1GX29V.
86. 'VP Osinbajo at The African Trade Forum (Full Remarks),' 2 November 2018, Lagos, Nigeria, video, https://www.yemiosinbajo.ng/vp-osinbajo-at-the-african-trade-forum-full-remarks-on-02-11-2018/.
87. Obinna Chima, 'How U.S.-China Trade "War" Will Affect Nigeria,' *This Day*, 23 April 2018, https://www.thisdaylive.com/index.php/2018/04/23/how-us-china-trade-war-will-affect-nigeria/.
88. Lynsey Chutel, 'Africa's Richest Man Thinks Donald Trump is on to Something with Higher Tariffs,' Quartz, 20 July 2018, https://qz.com/africa/1332932/dangote-says-africa-needs-donald-trump-style-china-tariffs/.
89. Fakoyejo Olalekan, 'BUA Group's Chairman Reveals Why Nigeria is Stalling AfCFTA One Year After,' Nairametrics, 1 April 2019, https://nairametrics.com/2019/04/01/one-year-after-afcfta-treaty-bua-chairman-reveals-why-nigeria-is-stalling/.
90. Olu Fasan, 'Nigeria's Import Restrictions: A Bad Policy That Harms Trade Relations,' Africa at LSE Blog, 17 August 2015, https://blogs.lse.ac.uk/africaatlse/2015/08/17/nigerias-import-restrictions-a-bad-policy-that-harms-trade-relations/.
91. Abdulwahab Isa, 'Awolowo: Nigeria Should Broaden,' *New Telegraph*, 13 August 2018.
92. Daniel Workman, 'Nigeria's Top Trading Partners,' WTEx, 28 March 2019, http://www.worldstopexports.com/nigerias-top-trading-partners/.
93. Adedeji Adeniran et al., 'Why Nigeria Urgently Needs to Grow Non-Oil Exports,' The Conversation, 11 September 2018, https://theconversation.com/why-nigeria-urgently-needs-to-grow-non-oil-exports-99304.
94. Oluwaseun Tella, 'Is Nigeria a Soft Power State?' *Social Dynamics*, Vol. 44, Issue 2 (2018): 376–94.
95. Prince Oguguo, 'Nigeria Isn't Buying into Africa's Free-Trade Area—But Should,' The Conversation, 8 February 2019, https://theconversation.com/debate-nigeria-isnt-buying-into-africas-free-trade-area-but-should-106108.
96. Bell Ihua et al., 'An Independent Study on the Potential Benefits of the African Continental Free Trade Area (AfCFTA) on Nigeria,' Study Report for Nigerian Office for Trade Negotiations (May 2018): 6.
97. Peter Beaumont and Isaac Abrak, 'Oil-Rich Nigeria Outstrips India as Country with Most People in Poverty,' *The Guardian*, 16 July 2018, https://www.theguardian.com/global-development/2018/jul/16/oil-rich-nigeria-outstrips-india-most-people-in-poverty.
98. Horace Campbell, 'Saving Lake Chad: A Pan-African Project,' Pambazuka News, 16 March 2018, https://www.pambazuka.org/human-security/saving-lake-chad-pan-african-project.
99. 'Nigeria Advocates African Standby Force, Security Fund,' *P.M. News*, 25 September 2018, https://www.pmnewsnigeria.com/2018/09/25/nigeria-advocates-african-standby-force-security-fund/.
100. 'Dr. Adekeye Adebajo on Nigeria and South Africa,' International Peace Institute, 29 March 2019, https://www.ipinst.org/2019/03/nigeria-south-africa-regional-dynamics-in-changing-world#1.

101. Gustavo De Carvalho and Annette Leijenaar, 'Streamlining the AU's Rapid Response Capabilities,' Institute for Security Studies, 11 March 2019, https://issafrica.org/iss-today/streamlining-the-aus-rapid-response-capabilities.
102. Linda Darkwa, 'The African Standby Force: The African Union's Tool for the Maintenance of Peace and Security,' *Contemporary Security Policy*, Vol. 38, Issue 3 (July 2017): 471, 478.
103. Isaac Kaledzi, 'Ouattara Pushes for New African Political Union,' Africa Feeds, 12 January 2019, https://africafeeds.com/2019/01/11/ouattara-pushes-for-new-african-political-union/.
104. Jason Warner, 'Nigeria and "Illusory Hegemony" in Foreign and Security Policymaking: Pax-Nigeriana and the Challenges of Boko Haram,' *Foreign Policy Analysis*, Vol. 13, Issue 3 (July 2017): 638–61.
105. Adekeye Adebajo, 'Nigeria: Africa's New Gendarme?' *Security Dialogue*, Vol. 31, Issue 2 (June 2000): 193–94.
106. Martin Ewi, 'The African Union Panel of the Wise: An Assessment of Its Role and Significance as a Mechanism for Conflict Resolution and Mediation in Africa,' Swedish Defence Research Agency, Division of Defence Analysis (January 2009): 2–3.
107. Ebere Adigbuo, 'Nigeria's Leadership Role Quests: The Race of the Crippled,' *Journal of Global Analysis*, Vol. 7, Issue 2 (Summer 2017): 157, 166.
108. Olaiyowla Abegunrin, *Nigeria–United States Relations, 1960–2016* (Lanham: Lexington Books, 2018), XXIX.
109. Noah Browning, 'Squeezed by US Shale, Nigerian Oil Propped up by Asian Demand,' Reuters, 8 April 2019, https://af.reuters.com/article/nigeriaNews/idAFL8N21M564.
110. Tibor P. Nagy, Jr., 'The Enduring Partnership Between the United States and Nigeria,' 9 November 2018, Baze University, Abuja, https://www.state.gov/bureau-of-african-affairs-releases/the-enduring-partnership-between-the-united-states-and-nigeria/.
111. Lauren Ploch Blanchard and Tomas Husted, 'Nigeria: Current Issues and US Policy,' Congressional Research Service (February 2019): 21–22.
112. Donald J. Trump (@realDonaldTrump), Twitter post, 26 July 2015, https://twitter.com/realdonaldtrump/status/625478235804073984?lang=en.
113. Helene Cooper, 'Trump Team's Queries About Africa Point to Skepticism About Aid,' *The New York Times*, 13 January 2017, https://www.nytimes.com/2017/01/13/world/africa/africa-donald-trump.html.
114. 'Remarks by President Trump at Working Lunch with African Leaders,' 20 September 2017, Lotte New York Palace Hotel, New York, https://www.whitehouse.gov/briefings-statements/remarks-president-trump-working-lunch-african-leaders/.
115. Mark Anderson, 'Aid to Africa: Donations from West Mask "$60bn Looting" of Continent,' *The Guardian*, 15 July 2014, https://www.theguardian.com/global-development/2014/jul/15/aid-africa-west-looting-continent.
116. 'Nigeria, US to Repatriate $500m Looted Fund—Buhari,' *Punch*, 1 May 2018, https://punchng.com/nigeria-us-to-repatriate-500m-looted-fund-buhari/.
117. Julia Simon, 'US Withdraws from Extractive Industries Anti-Corruption Effort,' Reuters, 2 November 2017, https://www.reuters.com/article/us-usa-eiti/u-s-withdraws-from-extractive-industries-anti-corruption-effort-idUSKBN1D2290.
118. John Stremlau, 'An Early Diagnosis of Trump's Impact on US-Africa Relations and on Sustainable Democracy in the US and Africa,' SAIIA Special Report Series (October 2017): 23.

Epilogue

Globalism, Nationalism and Regionalism

In July 2017, Trump reportedly confided in John Kelly, the newly appointed White House Chief of Staff, about how his economic nationalism was being undermined by insiders in his administration.

> John, you haven't been in a trade discussion before, so I want to share with you my views. For the last six months, this same group of geniuses comes in here all the time and I tell them, 'Tariffs. I want tariffs.' No tariffs came, however. John, let me tell you why they didn't bring me any tariffs… I know there are some people in the room right now that are upset. I know there are some globalists in the room right now. And they don't want them, John, they don't want the tariffs. But I'm telling you, I want tariffs.[1]

The president's utter frustration on being blocked at different levels on a variety of populist policy choices brought to relief the fundamental division between his inward 'patriotism', and liberal 'globalism' on the basis of which Pax Americana had been built since 1945. Throughout this book, I have offered vignettes about America's 'two-track presidency' and the tussle between Trump's narrow nationalism and the broad internationalism ingrained in different branches of the US government. It was evident right from the time that Trump was vying for the Republican Party's nomination for the 2016 presidential election that his foreign policy prescriptions were a recipe for the implosion of the liberal international order. Two American scholars sympathetic to Trump's populist ideology, Daniel Mills and Steven Rosefielde, wrote in

September 2016, about the dichotomy at the core of Trump's militant approach to foreign policy.

> Nationalism as we conceive it is inclusive and democratic. It is contrasted with cosmopolitanism which is basically elitist and insider-dominated. The basic issue is who rules the country—an establishment or its people? Trump proposes what might be considered a government policy that preserves core American political culture… and serves ordinary Americans. We use 'cosmopolitan' to mean an attitude that wants to rule globally and obliterate Western core culture in favour of approved forms of multiculturalism.[2]

This book has sufficiently demonstrated that ruling globally and stomping around as the world's sheriff is not at all Trump's agenda. His reluctance to keep up an American-built world order is widely agreeable to large proportions of the US public. The paring down of US troops from multiple war theatres, downsizing America's civilian and diplomatic engagement in crisis zones, stemming of foreign aid flows to poor areas of the world, diminution of democracy and human rights promotion in international relations, the absence of the US in rule-making international institutions for global governance, and the replacement of complex multilateralism entailing distributed benefits with a simple bilateral transactional approach that seeks concentrated gains for the US—all these traits bear testimony to the non-imperialistic nature of Trump's foreign policy. Marxists like John Bellamy Foster have mischaracterised Trump as a 'neo-fascist' who armed America to the teeth and allegedly acted belligerently and militaristically around the world. Claims that Trump is part of the 'mainstream of US foreign policy' and that he is out to establish 'a new unipolar world empire, supported by the entire US ruling class'[3] are gross concoctions. Trump did indeed increase US defence spending from $611 billion in 2016 to $716 billion in 2019, and the Pentagon justified the massive outlays as necessary to 'strongly position the US military for great power competition for decades to come'.[4] But conversely, Trump continued the transition started by Obama of curtailing America's overseas military involvements. The geopolitical competition with China and Russia the 'steady state' in the Trump administration touted was not matched by any viable military and diplomatic containment strategy of illiberal great powers in crucial regions around the world.

In Chapter I, we noted that Trump believes in air power and avoidance of costly land wars. The requirements for world empire are permanent power projection on land, sea and air, browbeating opponents through demonstration of superior military force and compelling violence, and colonising various regions through occupation and economic dominance. Trump has consciously done none of these. His concept of national security is literally national, defensive and homeland-centric, that is, a fortress America that is closed to immigrants and militarily impregnable. Barring occasional flashes of clinical missile strikes on Syria to deter Syrian President Bashar al-Assad's alleged use of chemical weapons or aerial pounding of ISIS and Al Qaeda targets in Libya, Yemen and Somalia, Trump has been a reserved commander-in-chief of the US military. His tightening of economic sanctions on North Korea and 'fire and fury' threats to obliterate it did not induce a surrender from Supreme Leader Kim Jong-un or deter him from clandestinely advancing missile development,[5] thus drawing a clear line under the limitations of America's hegemonic enforcement of order.

Moreover, an empire must exert political influence on its vast array of vassal states and principalities. Trump has knowingly forfeited a variety of soft levers through which his liberal internationalist predecessors used to manipulate policies and decision-making processes in different countries as well as regional and international organisations. Pax Americana was never solely or primarily a project resting on brute force. It was a liberal hegemonic arrangement where Washington defended the primacy of the US dollar, controlled global financial flows, expanded markets and stakes abroad for American companies, disbursed development aid through NGOs, and patronised friendly client regimes. Notwithstanding pressures from globalists within his administration and the American foreign policy establishment to carry on with these time-tested ways, Trump the populist has sought to abandon involvement in internal affairs of most countries and attempted to rein in American corporations from investing outside the US.

The needs of American capitalism are so vast and spread-out that Trump cannot force US private corporations to wholly pack their bags from far-flung outposts and come home. But right-wing populists want nationalistic capitalism rather than transnational capitalism. Trump and European populists' concentration on domestic problems and interests makes them anything but foreign conquest-loving fascists. I have maintained in this book that the wave of populism in the West is a product of a crisis of capitalism and democracy, just as fascism once was. But the offspring of crises are different in different eras. Right-wing populist leaders do fan racism and religious bigotry, as Trump's meteoric political career proves, but they are not wired to physically eliminate non-white and non-Christian people through military extermination campaigns or territorial aggrandisement.

Rather than the far-fetched comparisons Marxists have drawn to Mussolini and Hitler, the Introduction of this book drew a logical parallel between Trump and the isolationist Republican presidents of the 1920s. To reiterate, unless the US homeland faces another 9/11-like devastating attack, there is little possibility that Trump or his successors will return to a globalist path. Trump is a bellwether for America's exhaustion and relative decline in world politics, a trend that will continue under whoever follows him into the White House. American presidential historian Ron Chernow has characterised the Trump administration as a 'topsy-turvy moment' and a 'surreal interlude in American life',[6] implying that Trump's impact is transient in that he represents a temporary freakish deviation from the norm. But Chernow has failed to read the tectonic structural shifts of which Trump is just a manifestation. I am more convinced by American political scientist Daniel Drezner, who has predicted that Trump's foreign policy revolution will have a lasting effect because constraints on the US government's executive branch's foreign policymaking have progressively eroded while social polarisation in America could produce more populist presidents of the right or left after Trump.

> The public is still checked out on world politics. The combination of worn-down guardrails and presidents emerging from the ends of the political spectrum may well whipsaw US foreign policy between 'America first' and a new Second International. The very concept of a consistent, durable grand strategy will not be sustainable.[7]

If the globalism versus nationalism contest continues to stunt American foreign policy, emerging powers are at a different stage of history with a different mindscape. This book has illustrated how Trump generated unexpected openings for rising powers to move towards great power status by harnessing a middle point between the two extremes of globalism and nationalism, that is, regionalism. Every emerging power worth its salt is, of course, guided by nationalism and its own sense of self-importance. All four case studies I've analysed—India, Turkey, Brazil and Nigeria—have national identities based on exceptional narratives and self-conceptions of special or chosen nations that have to play a grand leadership role in their regions and the wider world. But these upcoming powers cannot afford to be narrowly nationalistic at this juncture in their evolution. In Chapter I, we noted that Narendra Modi's India First ideology is quite distinct from Trump's America First. In New Delhi, putting one's national interests first means standing up to extra-regional great powers like China or the US when they act to repress India's rise, and unifying South Asia and the Indo-Pacific through provision of regional public goods and endogenous collective security.

Regional and broader South-South cooperation are the building blocks for emerging powers to escape the fate of bandwagoning with one or the other great powers. With Trump's US in retreat, Western liberals have sounded alarms of a clear and present danger of China filling in America's shoes and taking over whole regions under its vassalage. But this transfer of hegemony from Washington to Beijing can be averted by emerging powers if they consolidate their respective regions under their leadership and form wider networks with other emerging powers. In Chapter III, I laid out the erroneous path taken by far-right populist President Jair Bolsonaro's Brazil to ingratiate itself with the US and turn its back on South-South cooperation. Bandwagoning with an unreliable and uncommitted great power like Trump's US and extricating Brazil from its former role as a star of South-South integration amount to Brazil hacking at its own feet.

One of the lessons of this book is that emerging powers must be accommodative and magnanimous in asserting their leadership within their regions. Taking one's backyard for granted is a strategic blunder.

Chapter II on Turkey demonstrated how President Recep Tayyip Erdogan overplayed his hegemonic hand with Arabs and Persians in the Middle East through military misadventures and paid the price by losing the legitimacy and acceptability to have a say in shaping the region's economy and security. If emerging powers behaved the way great powers do, that is, throwing their weight around and using military and economic coercion to divide their region, they will fail to appeal to smaller neighbours who may have no choice but to bandwagon to outsiders like Russia or China.

Emerging powers who want to carve out their own spheres of influence and ward off China or the US should have plenty of cooperative DNA in their regional diplomacy. They must actively strengthen regional and inter-regional institutions and also participate with gusto in global forums. British academic Andrew Hurrell identified 'institutional enmeshment' as one of the key strategies for would-be great powers because institutionalism helps them to counterbalance and 'tie down Gulliver' (great powers) and 'build new coalitions… congruent with their interests'.[8] Trump's de facto exit from multilateral institutions like the UN, G20, WTO and other issue-specific global governance regimes is all the more reason emerging powers must redouble their initiatives in these institutions. Without the constant and heavy pressure of the liberal hegemonic US, these multilateral institutions can be restructured to increase the bargaining leverage of emerging powers.

Indian-Canadian scholar Amitav Acharya argued in 2007 for an 'agency-oriented perspective' on the 'endogenous construction of regions', wherein local actors within different areas of the world have the means to organise themselves without having to rely on great powers. His keynote observation, 'Regions are constructed more from within than from without,'[9] is more valid in today's 'Trumped' environment than in earlier periods when the US immersed itself in shaping regions to serve the grand American strategy of counterbalancing illiberal rival states. With the isolationist and populist US practically stepping out of the way, Asia, the Middle East, Latin America and Africa have a historic opportunity to determine their own fates. However, even if extra-regional powers are kept at bay, power politics and asymmetry are inescapable realities within these regions. Emerging powers are best positioned to condition their respective surroundings because they have greater material resources than their weaker neighbours. For example, Chapter IV demonstrated that Nigeria has infinitely greater capabilities than any other West African state and has only South Africa as a peer on the African continental level. Pax Africana cannot be brought about by a Ghana, Kenya or Ethiopia—weaker states with lesser endowments than Nigeria or South Africa.

Emerging powers have the best chance in contemporary history to rise up as great powers because Trump is pulling the US back from its habitual internationalist and interventionist role. But a central message of this book is that rising nations can only seize this moment if they have the apt political leadership at home. Politicians like Erdogan and Bolsonaro do not bode well for Turkey and Brazil to fulfil their manifest destinies. Modi and Buhari, on the other hand, are safer bets because they appear to understand the historical moment we are in and have the foresight to sagaciously chart their countries' ships to glorious shores. But Modi is pushing 70 in age and Buhari is in his late seventies. They are heading countries where the average ages are 29 and 18 years. Nations endure while leaders come and go. The will to lead and the urge to serve region and world have to be institutionalised in the youthful societies of emerging powers. They have long voyages ahead with many ups and downs. But the good news is that Trump has set the platform nicely for a multipolar world.

Endnotes

1. Ivo Daalder and James Lindsay, *The Empty Throne: America's Abdication of Global Leadership* (New York: PublicAffairs, 2018): 146.
2. Daniel Mills and Steven Rosefielde, *The Trump Phenomenon and the Future of US Foreign Policy* (Singapore: World Scientific, 2016), 6.
3. John Foster, *Trump in the White House: Tragedy and France* (New York: Monthly Review Press, 2017), 76.
4. Jeff Stein and Aaron Gregg, 'US Military Spending Set to Increase for Fifth Consecutive Year, Nearing Levels During Height of Iraq War,' *The Washington Post*, 18 April 2019, https://www.washingtonpost.com/us-policy/2019/04/18/us-military-spending-set-increase-fifth-consecutive-year-nearing-levels-during-height-iraq-war/.
5. Lena Sun, 'Report Identifies Another Secret North Korea Missile Site, One of 20,' *The Washington Post*, 21 January 2019, https://www.washingtonpost.com/politics/report-identifies-another-secret-north-korea-missile-site-one-of-20/2019/01/21/4066aeec-1db0-11e9-9145-3f74070bbdb9_story.html.

6. Gillian Brockell, 'Ron Chernow Delivers a History of Presidents and the Press,' *The Washington Post*, 28 April 2019, https://www.washingtonpost.com/history/2019/04/28/museum-presidential-decorum-chernow-touts-presidents-respect-press-correspondents-dinner/.
7. Daniel Drezner, 'This Time is Different: Why US Foreign Policy Will Never Recover,' *Foreign Affairs*, Vol. 98, Issue 3 (May/June 2019): 16.
8. Andrew Hurrell, 'Hegemony, Liberalism and Global Order: What Space for Would-Be Great Powers?' *International Affairs*, Vol. 82, Issue 1 (January 2006): 11.
9. Amitav Acharya, 'The Emerging Regional Architecture of World Politics,' *World Politics*, Vol. 59, Issue 4 (July 2007): 630.

Index

A

Abacha, Sani 196, 199
Abe, Shinzo 90
Acharya, Amitav ii, xvi, 230
Africa Command (AFRICOM) 198, 199
African Continental Free Trade Area (AfCFTA) 207-209
African Peace and Security Architecture (APSA) 211, 214
African Union (AU) 196, 200, 207, 211, 212, 214
Afrocentrism 195, 198, 206, 207, 211
Al Qaeda 18, 87, 114, 121, 192, 227
al-Assad, Bashar 121-122, 124, 227
America First 6, 14-15, 20, 21, 32, 37, 43, 62-63, 68, 72, 75, 79, 83, 86, 89, 120, 130-131, 207, 208, 216, 228-229
Amorim, Celso 25, 156, 158, 161, 164
anti-globalisation politics 9-13, 22, 25-26, 30, 35, 38, 59, 63, 71, 135
anti-immigration politics 10, 13, 18, 20, 21, 65, 149, 162, 168, 190, 227
Araujo, Ernesto 162
Ashoka 34

Asia–Africa Growth Corridor (AAGC) 95
Axis of Evil 166, 168

B

Babangida, Ibrahim 196, 199
Balewa, Abubakar 196
bandwagoning 45-46, 79, 88, 89, 137, 156, 171, 175, 176, 198, 203, 229, 230
Bannon, Steve 8, 30, 148-150, 171
Beijing Consensus 42, 135, 157
Belt and Road Initiative (BRI) 41, 80, 91, 95
Boko Haram 188, 189, 194, 197, 199, 201, 207, 210, 211, 212
Bolsonaro, Eduardo 149, 164, 165
Bolsonaro, Jair xiii, xiv, 147-179, 229, 231
Bolton, John 108, 116, 148, 165-166, 168, 201, 204
BRICS countries xii, 10, 133, 156-158, 177
Brunson, Andrew 119-120, 133
Bryan, William 13-14, 22
Buchanan, Pat 19-20

Buhari, Muhammadu 187-217, 231
Bush, George W. 4, 6, 7, 16, 25, 28-30, 47, 60-61, 69, 71, 74-75, 107, 112, 114, 131, 153, 166, 168, 195, 198, 202, 217
Buy American 65, 189

C

Cardoso, Fernando 152, 155, 172
Carvalho, Olavo de 149-150, 171
Cavusoglu, Mevlut 110
Chavez, Hugo 154, 167
Cheney, Dick 29
climate change 59, 94-95, 149, 191, 210
Clinton, Bill 7, 20, 60, 61, 75, 114, 152, 197, 199
Clinton, Hillary xv, 2, 13, 24, 30, 36, 37, 88
Coolidge, Calvin 20

D

Dangote, Aliko 208
Davutoglu, Ahmet 112, 127, 128
deep state 32, 78, 107-108, 124, 126, 136, 174
Dom Pedro II 34

E

Economic Community of West African States (ECOWAS) 193, 195-196, 200, 208, 209, 211-213
economic nationalism 9, 12, 14, 21, 36, 38, 63, 66-67, 89, 125, 173, 225

emerging market economies (EMEs) 10-11, 67, 133, 173
endogenous coalitions i, 26, 45, 88, 90, 137, 153, 210, 217, 229, 230
Erdogan, Recep xiii, xiv, 105-138, 178, 230, 231
European Union (EU) xi, xiv, 4, 9, 30, 67, 68, 111, 128, 133, 135, 153, 171, 173, 176, 201, 211, 212, 215
evangelical Christians 109, 117-120, 127, 160, 168, 175, 190

F

far-right politics xiii, 12-13, 30, 41, 48, 87, 106, 147, 149, 151, 159-161, 164, 167, 171, 174-176, 191, 215, 216, 229
Flynn, Michael 109
Francophonie 192-193, 197, 199-200, 202, 204, 214
frontline state 121, 197
Fukuyama, Francis 25, 42

G

Gambari, Ibrahim 193, 206
global war on terrorism (GWOT) 4, 16, 71, 112, 114, 198
Gorbachev, Mikhail 35
Goulart, Joao 151
Guaido, Juan 170
Guedes, Paulo 150, 163, 172
Gulen, Fethullah 109-110, 119, 136

H

H1B visas 65

Harding, Warren 20, 22
Hollande, Francois 200
Hoover, Herbert 20-21
Hussein, Saddam 111

I

IBSA countries 156-158, 161, 171, 173, 177
India First 74, 86, 229
Indo-Pacific 8, 37-40, 46, 74-75, 77, 88, 90, 95, 229
Ing-wen, Tsai 37
Islamic State (ISIS) 18-19, 31, 87, 114-117, 121, 192, 199, 227
Islamist extremism 4, 15, 16, 18, 81, 87, 108-109, 135, 192, 194, 200
isolationism xiii, 12-15, 17, 19-22, 36, 40, 48, 59, 70, 77, 82, 84, 91, 96, 108, 115, 117, 120, 137, 138, 165, 166, 168, 169, 213, 215, 217, 228

J

Jae-in, Moon 46, 89
Jammeh, Yahya 196
jihadist terrorism 18-19, 31, 82, 85-87, 114, 121-122, 135, 189, 190, 192, 200
Jinping, Xi xiii, 39, 40-43, 78-79, 90
Jonathan, Goodluck 198-199, 207
Jong-un, Kim 32, 227

K

Kashmir conflict 81, 87
Kelly, John 225
Keohane, Robert 27
Kerry, John 169, 199
Khashoggi, Jamal 129-131
Kissinger, Henry 31, 154
Kurdish separatism 111, 113-116, 123, 127-128, 133

L

Lake Chad Basin 201, 211
liberal international order i, ii, xi, 5, 22-23, 25-28, 36, 48, 60, 106, 110, 131, 136, 149, 157-158, 225
Lighthizer, Robert 64
Lima Group 177, 178
Lindbergh, Charles 15
Long, Huey 13-14

M

Macron, Emmanuel 132, 200-202
Made in China 2025 38, 66
Maduro, Nicolas 166-170, 177
Make America Great Again 64, 75, 148
Make in India 64, 66, 72
Mattis, Jim 33, 73, 74, 78-79, 83, 116, 201
Mazrui, Ali 195, 214
McCain, John 62
McMaster, H.R. 74, 78, 79, 108
Mearsheimer, John 24, 33
Merkel, Angela 132
minilateralism 91, 213
Modi, Narendra xiii, 59-96, 107, 132, 175, 229, 231
Monroe Doctrine 22, 153, 168-169, 197

Mourao, Hamilton 150, 169-170, 175
multilateralism 19, 40, 155, 156, 157, 176, 226
multipolar world order 2, 5, 10, 25, 27, 37, 43, 75, 82, 92-93, 156, 158, 178, 231

N

neoconservatism 16, 112, 166, 168
neo-mercantilism 9, 38, 62, 72, 89, 125, 131, 188, 189, 191
neo-Ottomanism 117, 120, 134-137
Netanyahu, Benjamin 118
Nigeria First 207, 210
North American Free Trade Agreement (NAFTA) 20, 67, 152, 154
North Atlantic Treaty Organization (NATO) xi, 9, 30, 75, 83, 109-110, 120-126, 129, 132, 136, 137, 164, 189, 191, 199-200

O

Obama, Barack xi, 5-7, 16, 25, 29, 31, 36, 39-41, 42, 46, 47, 59-62, 69, 74-75, 77, 84, 86, 87, 88, 91, 92, 95, 96, 107, 109, 114, 118, 119, 122, 125, 127, 131, 137, 165, 168, 169, 174, 188, 190, 199-201, 216, 226
Obasanjo, Olusegun 195-198, 203, 204, 217
offshore balancing 61, 88,
Onyeama, Geoffrey 189, 211
Osinbajo, Yemi 207

P

pan-Africanism xvi, 206, 210, 212-214
Pax Africana xiv, 187, 214, 217, 231
Pax Americana xv, 9, 26, 27, 29, 36, 42, 225
Pax Nigeriana 195, 213
Pax Sinica 45
Pence, Mike 39, 117, 128
pivot to Asia 6, 61, 75, 96
Pompeo, Mike 73, 108-109, 116, 117, 123, 127, 162, 191
populism xi, xiii, 7, 11-15, 17, 19-22, 28, 30, 32, 33, 35-36, 38, 48, 65, 67, 69, 74-75, 80, 83, 85, 87, 88, 105-108, 110, 115-117, 120, 125-127, 129-131, 136, 138, 147-150, 159, 160, 165-169, 171-174, 176, 178, 188, 193, 201, 205, 207, 211, 215-216, 225, 227-230
Puri, Hardeep 25
Putin, Vladimir 29-32, 106, 107, 123-125, 127, 136-137

Q

Qaddafi, Muammar 199-200
Quad countries 95-96

R

Rabiu, Abdul 208
racism 21, 148, 160, 190, 191, 215, 217, 228
Reagan, Ronald 7, 12, 70, 111

Roosevelt, Franklin 1, 6, 13–14, 15, 21, 23, 36
Rouhani, Hassan 123
Rubio, Marco 167
Russia investigation 31, 32, 73, 81, 109

S

S-400 missile system 72–74, 78, 86, 124–126, 128
Salman, Mohammed bin 129–130
Sanders, Bernie 12
Sarkozy, Nicolas 199–200
Sarney, Jose 151–152
Silva, Lula da 147–148, 153–158, 161, 165, 173, 176, 177
Simms, Brendan i, xvi, 70
South China Sea 39–40, 79, 93
Southern Common Market (Mercosur) 27, 152–154, 164, 176, 178
South-South Cooperation 25, 136, 151, 155–156, 158–161, 171, 173, 215, 229
Soylu, Suleyman 135
steady state 32, 78, 169, 215, 226
strategic depth 85, 112
Swaraj, Sushma 88, 96
swing state 82, 175

T

Temer, Michel 159, 162, 178
Tillerson, Rex 79, 168, 169
trade protectionism 10, 13, 21, 63–64, 67, 80, 96, 153–154, 163, 171, 207–208

trade war 38–40, 42, 66–67, 69, 79, 129, 207
transactionalism xi, xiii, 28, 38, 40, 44, 62, 66, 89, 128, 131, 159, 169, 175, 188, 226
Trans-Pacific Partnership (TPP) xi, 6, 12, 41, 90
Truman, Harry 36, 111
two-track presidency 32, 33, 108

U

unilateralism 4, 28, 29, 70, 82, 83, 105, 176
Union of South American Nations (UNASUR) 153–154, 164
United Nations Security Council xii, 60, 157

V

Vision 2023 132

W

Washington Consensus 135, 154, 157, 205
Wilson, Woodrow 23
Wolfowitz, Paul 16
World Trade Organization (WTO) xi, 64, 66–68, 157, 163, 177, 230

Y

Yar'adua, Umaru 198

Z

Zakaria, Fareed xii, 4

About the Author

Sreeram Chaulia is Professor and Dean at the Jindal School of International Affairs, O.P. Jindal Global University, Sonipat, India. He is an eclectic political scientist specialising in both international security and international political economy.

He received a BA Honours in History from St. Stephen's College, University of Delhi; a second BA in History from University College, Oxford University; an MSc in History of International Relations from The London School of Economics and Political Science, University of London; and an MA and Ph.D in International Relations from the Maxwell School of Citizenship and Public Affairs, Syracuse University. He is a contributing editor of *People Who Influenced the World Over the Past 100 Years* (2005) and the sole author of *International Organizations and Civilian Protection: Power, Ideas and Humanitarian Aid in Conflict Zones* (2011) and *Politics of the Global Economic Crisis: Regulation, Responsibility and Radicalism* (2013). His last book, *Modi Doctrine: The Foreign Policy of India's Prime Minister* (2016), was a bestseller from Bloomsbury. He is a leading opinion columnist for Indian newspapers—*The Economic Times* and *The Asian Age*—on world affairs and a commentator on international current issues on radio and television in India and abroad. He has worked as an international civilian peacekeeper in the warzones of Sri Lanka and the Philippines.